CAPTAIN MARRYAT

CAPTAIN MARRYAT

Seaman, Writer and Adventurer

Tom Pocock

STACKPOLE
BOOKS

By the same author

Nelson and His World
Chelsea Reach
Fighting General
Remember Nelson
The Young Nelson in the Americas
1945: The Dawn Came Up Like Thunder
East and West of Suez
Horatio Nelson
Alan Moorehead
Sailor King
Rider Haggard and the Lost Empire
Norfolk
A Thirst for Glory
Travels of a London Schoolboy, 1826–30 (ed)
Battle for Empire
Nelson's Women

Travel

London Walks
Essential Venice

Copyright © Tom Pocock 2000

First published in Great Britain in 2000 by
Chatham Publishing,
61 Frith Street, London W1V 5TA

Chatham Publishing is an imprint of
Gerald Duckworth & Co Ltd

Published in North America by
STACKPOLE BOOKS
5067 Ritter Road
Mechanicsburg, PA 17055
www.stackpolebooks.com

Designed and typeset by Dorwyn Ltd, Rowlands Castle, Hants

Printed and bound in the United Kingdom by The Cromwell
Press, Trowbridge, Wilts

10 9 8 7 6 5 4 3 2 1

FIRST EDITION

Contents

List of Plates

The Duke of Sussex, Engraving after R Cruikshank (National Portrait Gallery).

George Cruikshank, (Private Collection).

Charles Dickens, by Samuel Laurence (National Portrait Gallery).

Captain Frederick Marryat, by William Behnes (Private Collection).

Marryat the Farmer, by Frank Marryat (National Maritime Museum).

Captain George Thomas of the Coastguard, by Frank Marryat (National Maritime Museum).

Augusta Marryat in her Chaise, by Frank Marryat (National Maritime Museum).

The Divided Family, by Frank Marryat (National Maritime Museum).

Langham Manor Cottage, by W Browne (Norfolk Record Office).

Norfolk in Winter, by Frank Marryat (National Maritime Museum).

For Adam Key

Introduction

Captain who? That is the most likely response at the beginning of the twenty-first century when the name of Captain Frederick Marryat arises. This was not always the case. Certainly, during the first half of the last century, anybody with the slightest grounding in English literature would know the name, and probably have read the books, of the most celebrated English novelist between Jane Austen and Charles Dickens. Even more recently, the late Handasyde Buchanan, of Heywood Hill's bookshop in London, once recommended Marryat's *Peter Simple* to an elderly earl as a suitable birthday present for a god-daughter; both Buchanan and his customer forgot this, the same advice was again asked and given and the girl received the book on her birthday three years running. Today Marryat is mostly remembered as the author of a television production of *The Children of the New Forest*.

So why write about Captain Marryat? The answer has to be personal. Some years ago, I bought a first edition of his first novel, *The Naval Officer, or Scenes and Adventures in the Life of Frank Mildmay*, at a second-hand bookshop in Paris and was surprised by what I read. It was not only that his descriptions of sea and war and people were so vivid but the character of the hero was so unexpected. In 1829, when it was written, most such stories were of ordeals survived, problems solved and virtues rewarded. In this case the hero was an unpleasant young man, selfish and ruthless, yet he still triumphed in the end. I then read studies of Marryat by two historians I knew and admired. Christopher Lloyd wrote in his *Captain Marryat and the Old Navy*, just before the Second World War, that the author of *Frank Mildmay* had confirmed that the descriptive passages were, in

9

fact, accounts of his own experiences but that the hero was certainly not a self-portrait. And yet, reading Oliver Warner's *Captain Marryat: A Rediscovery*, written just after the war, it seemed that there was, indeed, a streak of ruthlessness – occasionally almost amounting to savagery and recalling Mildmay – running through Marryat's celebrated wit and charm.

Oliver Warner said that he had enjoyed working on this book as much as anything he had ever done and I noted that Marryat's life covered several areas that appealed to me. He was a Londoner, like myself; he had served in the sailing Navy; he had toured America (he was half-American); he had been a member of Charles Dickens's circle of bohemian friends, as had my own great-grandfather; and he had lived in rural Norfolk, where I have roots. Like Lord Nelson, who had lived near Marryat's home in Norfolk, both were complex characters presenting a challenge to the biographer.

Yet there were problems. Most of Marryat's private papers were destroyed on his own instructions and he told his daughter Florence that he wanted no memoirs written; an order which, happily, she disobeyed. Her charming two-volume biography, published in 1867, seemed a true reflection of the man. It was supported by surviving letters to and from friends, memoirs of contemporary naval officers and the Dickens circle, and those passages in his books and journalism, which Christopher Lloyd had identified as having been, in effect, reportage.

There seemed several approaches to Marryat. One was the literary biography, which would mean reading the three million words he wrote; but that had been done – albeit in French and never translated into English – by Maurice-Paul Gautier in 1972. Or there were the six volumes of his marvellous American journal, never published in full since 1839, although short extracts describing American cities were published in New York in 1960.

But the more I discovered about Marryat, the more I was convinced that his life should be treated as a yarn, as stuffed with action, contrast and piquancy as any he might have written but, of course, none of it fiction. So here we follow him to sea, through storm and battle – into the melodramatic fleet action off

Rochefort and up the dangerous rivers of Burma; into Fleet Street and the literary salons of London; to the United States and then to fight in another war, this time in the snow and ice of a Canadian winter; finally to the Norfolk countryside for a life in total contrast to all that had gone before.

Was Marryat unique? I think not, as a flotilla of literary and artistic naval officers of the past two centuries come to mind. Perhaps the closest to him in character, if not in fame, was the late Captain Jackie Broome, a great fighting seaman of the Second World War and also an author, humorist and caricaturist; like Marryat, he was a member of the Garrick Club.

In preparing this book, I am grateful for advice and help in a variety of ways to Admiral Sir Peter Abbott, Capitaine de Vaisseau Jean-Claude Bertault and Madame Bertault, Mrs Lily McCarthy, Pieter van der Merwe, Michael Nash, Dr Gordon Ostlere (Richard Gordon), Geoffrey Pocock, Michael Pocock, John and Maxine Samuels and John Saumarez Smith; in Norfolk, to Mrs Blanche Allen, Philip Athill, Ronald Fiske, Mrs Scilla Landale, Rear-Admiral Rodney Lees, Bernard and Carla Phillips, Michael Tapper, and the Prioress and Sisters of the Carmel of Our Lady of Walsingham, who live on the site of Marryat's house in Langham; Clive Powell and Alan Giddings of the Manuscripts Department of the National Maritime Museum were exceptionally helpful as were the librarians, archivists and staff of the Royal Naval Museum, the National Army Museum, the Norfolk Record Office, the London Library, the Guildhall Library and the National Portrait Gallery. I am also grateful to my wife, Penny, for compiling the index and to Robert Gardiner of Chatham Publishing for his faith in this book and enthusiasm for its subject.

TOM POCOCK
Chelsea, 2000

CHAPTER ONE

The Hard World of Men

Smoke curled from the chimneys of London into the clear, cold air. On the morning of 9 January 1806, the dark plumes against the blue, frosty sky found reflection below in the street, where black was predominant. Buildings were swagged with funereal crepe and the crowds, who had thronged Whitehall, the Strand, Fleet Street and Ludgate Hill since before dawn, wore black, even if just a hat, cravat, or arm-band as a sign of mourning.

There were bright colours, too, beneath the blue winter sky that completed the reflection of conflicting emotions with which the capital was charged that day. The people of London were still triumphant over the victory at sea off Cape Trafalgar less than three months before; but they were also stricken with grief for the death of their hero, Superman and Everyman, dead at forty-seven; killed in the act of winning them global supremacy at sea. They were gathering along the processional way to watch the body of Vice-Admiral Viscount Nelson carried to his tomb in St Paul's Cathedral.

Hours before dawn, drums had beaten in the darkness, summoning the soldiers and militia to parade. In Hyde Park, cavalcades of mourning coaches were marshalled to collect their passengers in St James's Park, where scores of courtiers and ambassadors, peers and politicians, admirals and generals jostled in search of their transport to the cathedral. The great bell of St Paul's began to toll at half-past eight but it was not until early afternoon that the head of the procession entered the long canyon of the Strand and Fleet Street. As the silent crowds heard the first, distant strains of the *Dead March in Saul*, a rustle was heard as of sea on sand; it was the sound of hats being removed, heads bared in homage.

From the windows of the flat-fronted houses lining the gentle curve of Ludgate Hill, a tide of red, white, blue and black seemed to be flowing towards the vast portico, bell towers and dome of the cathedral. The procession was more military than naval with six battalions of infantry, six squadrons of cavalry and eleven horse-drawn guns behind the bands.

Amongst those with the influence to command such a window on Ludgate Hill were the worthies of the City of London, the merchants and administrators, whose commerce had now been secured by the dead man being borne towards them. One such, Joseph Marryat – a handsome, commanding man of fifty with a face that would look well in marble – was there with his son. Aged thirteen, Frederick was well-built with a square jaw, snub nose, curly hair and bright, alert eyes fixed upon the spectacle below.

To the sounds of the booming bell and the mournful music were now added the tramp of soldiers' boots, the clatter of cavalry and guns and the rumble of carriages. Then the red coats, white cross-belts and black shakos of the infantry gave way to something remarkable. After those drilled ranks came nearly fifty stocky, agile men in round hats, blue jackets and wide, white canvas trousers, each holding the edge of a huge, tattered flag. They were sailors from Lord Nelson's flagship, the *Victory*, bearing the shot-torn ensign she had flown at the Battle of Trafalgar. There followed the most extraordinary sight of all: a black juggernaut of a funeral car, drawn by sable horses, with the figurehead and poop of a ship, emblazoned with heraldic emblems and crowned with nodding black plumes above a canopy sheltering the coffin of the dead admiral. All knew that the coffin had been made from the main mast of the French flagship, *l'Orient*, which had exploded at the height of the Battle of the Nile, when Nelson had won the first decisive victory over the French. Just then was heard the unearthly sound of what seemed heavenly choirs from within the doors of the cathedral, open to receive the dead hero.

Frederick Marryat had never seen anything like it and knew he never would again. Of this, he was as aware then as he was when he remembered with a touch of self-mockery, 'As the triumphal car disappeared from my aching eye, I felt that death could have no terrors if followed by such a funeral; and I determined that I would be buried in the same manner.'[1]

The theatricality of the spectacle, as much as the melodramatic life it celebrated, had found an echo in the boy's imagination. All his life he had been aware of the dichotomy of the world of maritime trade, upon which the prosperity of both his family and his country relied. Born on Tower Hill, above the Pool of London, where merchant ships discharged their cargoes, he knew that his father was so busy with his ledgers, letter-writing and meetings that he had never even had time to visit the Tower of London nearby, the most celebrated building in the country. His father's work was involved with the shipping he could see discharging cargoes into lighters for unloading at docks farther upstream to be distributed by canal barge, or wagon. He was also aware that those ships relied upon the power of the Royal Navy, which he could not see in the Thames but whose press-gangs roamed the riverside streets and raided the dockside taverns in search of able-bodied men to work and fight its ships at sea. Taking such brutality for granted, a boy saw rather the excitement of storm, battle and far horizons. If it was to be a choice between the counting-house and the quarterdeck, Frederick knew which he would choose.

Like all mercantile families, the Marryats were intimately involved with seaborne trade and travel. Believing themselves to be of Norman, or Huguenot, descent, they had bred merchants, clergymen and at least one doctor – the eighteenth century Dr Joseph Marryat, the author of *Therapeutics, or the Art of Healing*. They also, like many middle class families of the time, fostered romantic legends of remote royal ancestry. Less appealing was the tradition that other Marryats had belonged to a religious sect that had practised the Ancient Egyptian custom of preserving the internal organs of their dead.

The Joseph Marryat who watched Nelson's funeral with his son enjoyed global connections that now seemed secure. When young he had crossed the Atlantic to trade in America and the Caribbean. On Grenada, he had acquired property – he was to become the island's commercial agent in London – and had moved to the United States in 1788. In Boston he met a loyalist of German descent, Frederick von Geyer, who had remained in the United States despite his affiliation; indeed, his mother had once opened an Independence Day ball, dancing with President George Washington. Joseph then met their youngest daughter, Charlotte, a celebrated beauty, and he married her a few months later. The couple returned to Grenada for a year, where their first child, also named Joseph, was born, and to England later that year. On 10 July 1792, while living at 4 Catherine Court in the City of London, they had a second son, Frederick.

Joseph Marryat was a versatile financier and, moving from trade to insurance, became an underwriter at Lloyd's and was more interested in the Bank of England and the Royal Exchange than the neighbouring maritime institutions of Trinity House and the Navy Office. It was the fruits of sea power that occupied his mind, just as its excitement enchanted his son.

A man of Joseph Marryat's substance could have been expected to have his sons educated at Westminster, or, perhaps, Eton, but he chose to send them to a boarding-school, Holmwood School at Ponder's End, near Enfield in Middlesex, kept by a flogging headmaster named Freeman. There, Frederick became a difficult child. With his quick intelligence, strong build and squared jaw, he did not seem a likely butt for bullying. But he was self-assertive, cheeky and suffered from a lisp, which invited teasing. Although 'learning with great facility, he forgot his tasks with equal readiness and, being of a genial temperament, he preferred play to lessons and was constantly flogged for idleness and inattention.'[2]

A natural rebel, he was disruptive as was recorded by a classmate, Charles Babbage*. He and another studious boy took to waking in the early hours of the morning, stealing down to the schoolroom to revise their work and returning to bed before dawn. Sensing adventure, Marryat begged to join them, was

---

* 1792–1871; mathematician; as inventor of a 'calculating engine' could be said to have been a father of the computer.

refused but made himself such a nuisance by setting traps that would wake him when the others crept downstairs, that Babbage eventually agreed. The outcome was as expected; Marryat brought friends with him but only for skylarking, exploding fireworks and eventual discovery by the headmaster. Even so, Marryat and Babbage became, and remained, friends.

Once, Freeman discovered Frederick balanced on his head, book in hand and apparently reading; 'dignified but graceful',[3] as he was to put it. Asked to explain, the boy replied, 'Well, I've been trying for three hours to learn it on my feet but I couldn't, so I thought I would try whether it would be easier to learn it on my head.'[4] Although his only recorded complaint was his resentment at having to wear his elder brother Joseph's cast-off, cut-down trousers, he felt stifled by a formal education in such a school. He ran away three times, saying that he wanted to go to sea, the ships moored to near his home having become symbolic of freedom.

On the last occasion, in 1804, he was caught and sent home, his father returning him to Ponder's End in the family's carriage with some money owing to the headmaster. But the carriage arrived empty and Frederick was finally discovered, using this to entertain a younger brother at the theatre. Realising he was out of control, his father allowed him to remain in London for a year under the eye of a tutor in mathematics. In 1805, the family moved to 5 The Crescent, near Ludgate Circus and between the seats of power in the City and Westminster. This was the year of Trafalgar.

Joseph Marryat tried to plan his sons' futures. There would be no problem over the eldest, Joseph; as his heir, he would inherit money and property and so could indulge his interest in art, notably porcelain. Frederick was different, but he had shown interest in a life at sea, which would not only keep the troublesome boy out of the way but, if he survived, could present the opportunities for making a fortune in prize-money, freelance cargo-carrying and the other means by which naval officers could supplement their pay. There were two paths to a commission in the Royal Navy: one by attending the Royal Naval Academy at Portsmouth, but Frederick was now aged fourteen, which was late to start such education; the other was to be taken to sea as a 'first-class volunteer', or 'captain's servant' by a friend commanding one of His Majesty's ships, where he would be initiated into seamanship and navigation, become a midshipman and eventually take the examination for a lieutenant's commission.

It would be a good time to go to sea. Lord Nelson might have ended the threat from the main enemy fleets but there was much activity at sea since the French were beginning to exclude British trade from Continental ports and trying to blockade those belonging to, or still used by, the British. On the Continent, the Emperor Napoleon reigned over all, having defeated the Austrians and Russians at Austerlitz and enlisted the Prussians against Britain. The death of William Pitt had followed Nelson's and the country seemed especially vulnerable without their leadership. The invasion of the British Isles might no longer be a danger but the protection of trade and the reduction of the enemy's would make ample demands upon the Royal Navy and a young man would have plenty of opportunities to prove his worth and, perhaps, make his fortune.

Lloyd's of London enjoyed close relations with senior naval officers, thanking them for protection of insured shipping and trade with presentation swords and engraved silver and raising funds to help wounded seamen and their dependants. Indeed, Joseph Marryat was chairman of the Lloyd's Patriotic Fund, which was helping to support children who had lost their fathers at Trafalgar. Through such connections he met the most famous fighting captain of all, Lord Cochrane.

Heir to the ninth Earl of Dundonald, but to no fortune, Thomas Cochrane had already made his own at sea. That same year, soon after Nelson's funeral, he had brought his frigate, the *Pallas*, into Plymouth Sound, after a successful cruise, with three golden candelabra lashed to her mastheads. He was even more famous for his capture of a Spanish frigate with a little sloop he had commanded, boarding the enemy and bringing her into Gibraltar with two hundred and sixty-three prisoners below deck. Fighting and fortune-hunting were not enough for Cochrane and he had just fought and won the Parliamentary seat of Honiton in Devon, his motive being the exposure of corrupt-ion and inefficiency in the administration of the Navy.

However, his first attacks on the Government cut so deep that the Admiralty found reason to get rid of him by appointing him to the command of another frigate. This was the *Impérieuse*, a former French prize, then fitting for sea at Plymouth. His ship's company from the *Pallas* wanted to transfer to his new ship but the 38-gun *Impérieuse* was bigger so, to recruit the extra seamen, all he needed was to post handbills at the dockyard gates an-nouncing: 'Wanted. Stout, able-bodied men who can run a quar-ter of a mile without stopping with a sackful of Spanish dollars on their backs.'[5]

A word from Joseph Marryat to Cochrane and the latter agreed to take the former's son to sea with him as a first class volunteer. First, the gear for shipboard life and a sea chest must be ordered, together with naval uniform, to the collar of which a midship-man's white patches could later be sewed when Frederick qualified and was promoted. 'The large chest, the sword, the cocked-hat, the half-boots, were all ordered in succession,' he was to write, 'and the arrival of each article, either of use or ornament, was anticipated by me with ... impatience. The cir-cumstances of my going to sea affected my father in no other way than as it interfered with his domestic comforts by the immode-rate grief of my poor mother ... my choice of a profession was a source of no regret to him. I had an elder brother, who was intended to have the family estates, and who was then at Oxford, receiving an education suitable to his rank in life and also to learn how to spend his money like a gentleman.'[6]

The final farewells took place outside the White Horse Cellars in Piccadilly, the coaching terminus for the West Country, as he boarded the coach to Exeter and thence to Plymouth. This 'com-pletely overthrew the small remains of fortitude which my dearest mother had reserved for our separation and she threw her arms around my neck in a frenzy of grief ... while she covered my stoic face with kisses and washed it with tears.' Already, the boy saw himself in the hard world of men, noting, 'I beheld her emotions with a countenance as unmoved as the figure-head of a ship.'[7]

CHAPTER TWO

The Lion's Whelp

L ord Cochrane was living ashore while his ship was being refitted and his cabin reeked of paint and tar, the decks strewn with wood shavings and oakum. So when Frederick Marryat, rigged in his new uniform, arrived at Plymouth on 22 September 1806, he followed instructions to call at the inn where his captain was staying.

Cochrane was a tall, muscular man of thirty-one, with red hair and an aggressive nose, 'like a ship's rudder'.[1] He eyed the boy and questioned him in his strong Scottish accent, then ordered him to report to the first lieutenant of the *Impérieuse*, lying at moorings in the Hamoaze river. Now formally appointed to his first ship, young Marryat's pride was boundless and he remembered it with amusement. Sending his baggage ahead, he strutted down the street towards the dockyard: 'my dirk was belted round my waist; a cocked hat of enormous size stuck on my head ... perfectly satisfied with my own appearance.'[2]

There was, of course, the etiquette of saluting, and being saluted, to be learned and this began when a group of men approached in a blaze of blue, white and gold.

A party of officers in full uniform were coming from a court-martial. 'Oh, ho!' said I, 'here come some of us.' I seized my dirk in my left hand, as I saw they held their swords, and I stuck my right hand into my bosom as some of them had done. I tried to imitate their erect and officer-like bearing; I put my cocked hat on fore and aft with the gold rosette dangling between my two eyes so that, looking at it, which I could not help doing, I must have squinted. And I held my head high, like a pig in a hurricane, fancying myself such an object of admiration to them as I was to myself.

We passed on opposite tacks and our respective velocities had separated us to a distance of twenty to thirty yards when one of them called in a voice evidently cracked in His Majesty's service, 'Hello, young gentleman, come back here'. I concluded that I was going to be complimented on the cut of my coat, to be asked the address of my tailor and to hear the rakish sit of the hat admired ... Judge then of my surprise and mortification when I was thus accosted in an angry and menacing tone by the oldest of the officers: 'Pray, sir, what ship do you belong to?'

'Sir,' said I, proud to be thus interrogated, 'I belong to His Majesty's ship the *Le* –' (having a French name, I clapped on both the French and English articles, as being more impressive).

'Oh, you do, do you?' said the veteran with an air of conscious superiority; 'then you will be so good as to turn round, go down to Mutton Cove, take a boat and have your person conveyed with all possible speed on board of His Majesty's ship the *Le* –' (imitating me) 'and tell the first lieutenant it is my order that you are not to be allowed any more leave while the ship is in port; and I shall tell your captain he must teach his officers better manners than to pass the port-admiral without touching their hats.'

The captains joined Admiral Sir William Young's laughter but the latter added in a more friendly voice, 'Well, young man, since you have never been at sea, it is some excuse for not knowing good manners; there is no necessity now for delivering my message to the first lieutenant but you may go on board your ship.'[3] Marryat, 'mortified and crestfallen', determined not to offend again and so 'conferred the honour of a salute on midshipmen, master's mates, sergeants of marines and two corporals'. A passing waterfront trollop asked him whether he was about to stand for election to Parliament, adding, 'I thought you might, seeing you are so d---d civil to everybody.'[4]

At last he found a boat plying for hire and was rowed by two women out to the frigate, lying in the river, winding beneath the steep, wooden Devonshire hills. Clambering up her side he saw 'what a sweet mess she was in ... the decks were covered with fresh pitch poured in the seams, the caulkers were sitting on their boxes, ready to renew their noisy labours once the dinner hour had expired.'[5] A midshipman met Marryat and presented him to the first lieutenant, who ordered him to be taken below and shown 'where to hang his hammock up'.[6]

Following his guide through a square hatch in the upper deck and down the scrubbed wooden steps of a companionway, Marryat entered a new world that was to become his own. At the foot of the steps 'sat a woman, selling bread and butter and red herrings to the sailors; she also had cherries and clotted cream and a cask of strong beer ... We passed her and descended another ladder, which brought us to the 'tween decks and into the steerage.'[7] This was 'crammed with casks and cases and chests and bags and hammocks; the noise of the caulkers was resumed over my head and all around me; the stench of bilge water, combining with the smoke of tobacco, the effluvia of gin and beer, the frying of beef-steaks and onions and red herrings – the pressure of a dark atmosphere and a heavy shower of rain all conspired to oppress my spirits.'[8]

In the steerage, abreast of the main mast, 'was my future residence – a small hole, which they called a berth; it was ten feet long by six and about five feet, four inches high; a small aperture, about nine inches square, admitted a very scant portion of that which we most needed, namely, fresh air and daylight. A deal table occupied a very considerable extent of this ... and on it stood a brass candlestick and a wick like a full-blown carnation.'[9] 'A dirty tablecloth, stained with wine and gravy, was spread, a sack of potatoes was propped in a corner' and 'the shelves all round ... were stuffed with plates, glasses, quadrants, knives and forks, loaves of sugar, dirty stockings and shirts and still fouler tablecloths, small tooth-combs and large clothes brushes.'[10] As Marryat's eyes became accustomed to the gloom, he saw that 'the black servant was preparing for dinner and I was shown the seat I was to occupy. "Good heavens!" thought I, as I squeezed myself between the ship's side and the mess-table, "and this is to be my future residence?" '[11]

Lord Cochrane did not join his ship for another three weeks. He could leave the fitting out to his first lieutenant as he had more pressing matters on his mind, which called for the attention of the House of Commons. That the captain of the *Impérieuse* seemed to spend more time criticising the Lords Commissioners of the Admiralty as a Member of Parliament than carrying out their orders displeased Admiral Young.

On the morning of 16 November, Captain Cochrane was at last piped aboard his command. He was in a black mood for he had come straight from a meeting with the admiral, who had ordered him to take his ship to sea immediately without any delay whatsoever. In vain, Cochrane had explained that the frigate was not ready for sea: she was not fully rigged, her provisions were not stowed in the holds and few of her guns were mounted on their carriages and those were not yet secured to their ringbolts; she was not seaworthy. It was to no avail. Admiral Young had explained that he had been told by the Admiralty that all ships at Plymouth that were ready for service should be sent to sea. That, he said, included ships that should be ready for service, such as the *Impérieuse*.

Cochrane gave no immediate order to cast off, but hurried ahead with preparations for sailing. As hours past, signal guns were fired from shore as a reminder of the admiral's orders but it was not until late evening that the ship made sail and began to move towards the harbour mouth and the open sea. Later, Marryat heard that Admiral Young had been watching and was heard to say of Cochrane, 'Damn his eyes! There he goes at last! I was afraid that the fellow would have grounded on his beef bones before we should have got him out!'[12]

Yet the ship was still not ready for sea and was accompanied by a storeship, one lighter loaded with ammunition and another with powder, which were to be taken aboard when out of the admiral's sight, at anchor in a secluded bay. This was done and mercifully the weather was fine and the sea calm, although it was not to last.

The wind was getting up; first to a strong breeze and then to a gale. Cochrane ordered sails to be reefed and the gun carriages secured with extra cordage to prevent them breaking loose, for one of the greatest fears in a storm was a loose cannon.

During the hasty preparations, something had been overlooked. As Marryat himself later explained, 'In the general confusion of leaving port, some iron too near the binnacles had attracted the needle of the compass; the ship was steered out of her course.'[13] This was dangerous in the extreme since the ship was nearing the north-westerly headland of France, where great rocks – some, at low water, looming large as churches; others, saw-toothed, beneath the surface – reach out from Britanny to Ushant. In consequence, as Cochrane entered in his log of 20 November: '5.15 a.m. Ship struck and beat over a shoal.'[14] Marryat was to put it more graphically:

> In a heavy gale ... so dark that you could not distinguish any object, however close, the *Impérieuse* dashed upon the rocks between Ushant and the Main. The cry of terror that ran through the lower decks, the grating of the keel as she was forced in; the violence of the shocks, which convulsed the frame of the vessel; the hurrying up of the ship's company without their clothes; and then the enormous waves, which again bore her up and carried her clean over the reef, will never be effaced from my memory.
>
> Our escape was miraculous; with the exception of the false keel [the light, outer keel designed to protect the main structure] having been torn off, the ship had suffered little injury; but she had beat over a reef and was riding by her anchors, surrounded by rocks, some of them as high out of water as her lower yards.[15]

The frigate had not only survived but remained seaworthy and was able to fulfil her orders to join Commodore Richard Keats's squadron in the Bay of Biscay. In 'squalls and fresh gales',[16] the *Impérieuse* steered south and Marryat's second experience of the realities of life and death at sea followed when a marine was lost overboard.

Yet there were moments of joy, too, when the miseries of the dark and squalid gunroom, seasickness and danger gave way to delight. Emerging on deck when a gale abated he could find 'the sun shining gaily, a soft air blowing from the shore ... and the ship slowly forging through the blue water ... The captain and first lieutenants were standing on the gangway in converse and ... the officers were with their quadrants and sextants ascertaining the latitude at noon. The decks were white and clean ... and the men were busy coiling down the ropes. It was a scene of cheerfulness, activity and order ... after the suffering, close air and confinement.'[17]

Commodore Keats, a friend of Nelson's, who had fought at Trafalgar, was commanding six ships of the line and charged with the blockading of La Rochelle, Rochefort and the Basque and Aix Roads. This complex of harbours and anchorages complemented Brest as a strategic naval base opening on to the Atlantic. But while the big ships rolled in the ocean swell off the long, low coastline and the distant clusters of masts, the task of a frigate would be patrolling south towards Bordeaux.

With such a task and such a captain, there would certainly be action. Throughout that stormy winter, Marryat was recording this almost daily in his log: 'Engaged a battery and took two prizes ... engaged a battery and received a shot in the counter ... anchored and stormed a battery ... trying to get a prize off that was ashore, lost five men.'[18] Daily, Marryat heard the drums beat to quarters and the squeal of the boatswain's calls as the ship's company made or took in sail, ran out the guns and manned boats. As he put it, he thrilled to 'the rapidity of the frigate's movements, night and day; the hasty sleep, snatched at all hours; the waking up at the report of the guns, which seemed the only key-note to the hearts of those on board; the beautiful precision of our fire ... the coolness and courage of our captain.'[19]

The boy was lucky because the gunroom, where he lived, was unusually happy and free of the endemic bullying, which could often add unnecessary stress. Lord Cochrane had brought to sea the young sons of friends and their natural leader was the Honourable William Napier, from the distinguished naval and military family. Marryat saw him as 'a giant among us pigmies' and, he was to write, 'I was for years a messmate of Napier's and, although not easy to be controlled and usually returning blow for blow, I can positively assert that I never received a blow from him; and, at the same time, he was the only one to whom I paid implicit obedience ... Well do I recollect the powerful form of Napier, with his claymore, bounding in advance of his men and cheering them on to victory.'[20]

It was Napier who taught him the brutal pragmatism of life at sea and at war. A marine had fallen overboard as the ship ploughed through heavy seas, driven by a gale. As Marryat was to write,

The cry of 'Man overboard!' was passed through the ship; many of the officers and men hastened to the boats, the lashings were cut off, the falls in hand ready for lowering. The youngsters were at the taffrail, watching with anxiety the poor fellow, who swam well and bore up against the seas, rising after they had broken over him, his eyes turned towards the ship, knowing that from thence, and thence alone, he could expect assistance.

Lord Cochrane, who was standing abaft, surveying the raging seas and compressing his lips, as if he had made up his mind, in a grave tone said, 'Hold fast'. The boats were not lowered and the poor man still struggled with the waves, gradually increasing his distance. At last he held up his hand, as if to show where he was, and shortly afterwards he disappeared ... Lord Cochrane had walked forward ... saying only, 'Poor fellow.' We still continued watching the wave, where he was last seen, full of melancholy and rather indignant thought. Napier stood by us and he appeared to have read our reflections ... He pointed out that it was hardly possible for a boat to live in such a sea; that, although there were hundreds who would have been eager to save the man's life, the attempt would only have been attended with the sacrifice of their own; that a captain of a ship was responsible for the lives of his men and that it was the duty of the captain to forbid a boat to be lowered down.[21]

With men like Cochrane and young Napier to set examples, Marryat took to warfare as to sport, remembering, 'the suddenness of our attacks, the gathering after the combat, the killed lamented, the wounded almost envied; the powder so burnt into our faces that years could not remove it; the proved character of every man and officer on board, the implicit trust and adoration we felt for our commander; the ludicrous situations which would occur even in the extremist danger and create mirth when death was staring you in the face; the hair-breadth escapes; and the indifference to life shown by all ...'[22]

In the spring of 1807, the ship returned to Plymouth and leave was granted. Marryat returned to his family in London, visited his younger brothers at their school near Sydenham and gloried in his new-found confidence reflected in the eyes of his contemporaries. The family was about to move from the City of London to Westminster because Joseph Marryat had political ambitions and was to stand as Parliamentary candidate for Horsham.

Lord Cochrane, too, was to fight the coming election, but not as member for Honiton; that had not been successful so now he and his fellow-Radical, Sir Francis Burdett, were together standing for the constituency of Westminster; there, the suffrage was relatively democratic and so vital to Radical aspirations. The campaign was rumbustious and reached a climax at a rowdy open-air meeting in Covent Garden. There, Cochrane sprang on to the rail of the platform from which the candidates had been addressing the crowd and balanced there, shouting 'with much animation that he stood upon the footing of perfect independence unconnected with any person whatsoever.'[23] He and Burdett were elected as the only two members standing for the new movement for political reform and the balladeers sang,

> All hail to the hero – of England the boast
> The honour – the glory – the pride of our coast;
> Let the bells peal his name and the cannon's loud roar
> Sound the plaudits of Cochrane, the friend of her shore ...[24]

To Marryat's disappointment, his captain was too preoccupied with demanding reforms in public and naval life to return to sea and when the *Impérieuse* sailed from Plymouth that April, she was temporarily commanded by a Captain Alexander Skene. This was a change from Cochrane's dynamism for, as Marryat put it, 'Our guns were never cast loose, or our boats disturbed out of their booms. This was a repose which was, however, rather trying to the officers and ship's company, who had been accustomed to such an active life.'[25]

There was relief when, in September, Cochrane returned. He had, as promised, belaboured his political masters in the House of Commons. So the Admiralty was again eager to be rid of him and there was no difficulty in doing so by ordering him to resume command of his ship and take her to the Mediterranean. There was, however, more change for the worse on board. The gun-room of the *Impérieuse* had, hitherto, been remarkably free from bullying; now other youths joined the mess and amongst them the son of the Radical writer, William Cobbett. Young Henry Cobbett was a truculent bully and he and Marryat were soon enemies. As at school, so at sea, the latter's cocky assertiveness – and the vulnerability suggested by his lisp – invited rough reactions. He, in turn, responded even more violently: if the lashings of a hammock were cut so that a sleeper fell, head first, to the deck, he found the answer was to do likewise, ensuring that the corner of a chest was placed to catch the bully's head; there is a suggestion that Cobbett suffered such revenge.

Survival in this rough world was, he began to learn, to laugh and meet violence with violence. As he put it himself, 'As I increased in strength and stature, I showed more determined resistance to arbitrary power ... I became a scientific pugilist and now and then took a brush with an oldster; and, although overpowered, yet I displayed so much prowess, that my enemies became cautious ... till, at last, like the lion's whelp, my play ceased to be a joke and I was left to enjoy that tranquillity, which few found it safe ... to disturb.'[26]

It was not only muscular strength that protected him for, as he would write, in the third person, 'His tongue was most powerful ... His keen and sarcastic remarks ... served him as a defence for he could always raise a laugh at the expense of the individual, whom he attacked with the formidable weapon he had inherited from his mother.'[27] He was quick-witted in banter and gunroom repartee, which was generally rough and simple, as he was to describe it when a black servant answered a midshipman's question as to what it was: 'Repartee, sir – repartee! – stop a bit – eh – I tell you, sir. Suppose you call me a dam' nigger – then I call you one dam', dirty, white-livered son of a bitch; dat a repartee, sir.'[28]

The Mediterranean was seen as 'the very focus of the war' and the ship's company began to speculate on 'what they would be able to accomplish in fine weather and smooth water after having done so much on a stormy coast and during a winter's cruise.'[29] The weather and water could also be rough and so could the opposition because all the northern littoral was now in the hands of France: Naples had been conquered again a year before and King Ferdinand and Queen Maria Carolina, whose throne had been preserved by Nelson, had once more fled to Palermo in Sicily, their second capital, which was held by the British, as were the strategic bases of Malta, Minorca and Gibraltar. So the British still controlled the sea; its fleet commanded by Nelson's old friend and second-in-command, Vice-Admiral Lord Collingwood, who had been ennobled after Trafalgar. Otherwise the Emperor Napoleon dominated Europe.

The *Impérieuse* escorted a large convoy – including troop transports bound for Sicily and Malta – and arrived at Valetta at the end of October. Next month they finally found Collingwood's flagship, the *Ville de Paris* (named after the French three-decker captured at the Saintes in 1782), and saw that the admiral himself was not another Nelson. Collingwood looked old – he was in his sixtieth year – and ill. He was known to be kind-hearted and it was said that women found him a witty and charming companion but most saw him as 'an old bear' and it did not seem that he would warm to Cochrane because, it was said, 'Old Collingwood likes *quiet people*.'[30] He was a commander, who dealt with battle-squadrons, big ships and large charts, and the exploits that excited Cochrane – the single-ship duels, cutting-out expeditions and raids ashore – and the new-fangled ideas like rockets, torpedoes and even submarines that occupied his imagination were dismissed as peripheral.

Yet, despite his conviction that the brisk little actions fought by his frigates and brigs were a waste of lives and effort, he admired his dashing captains, remarking that 'the activity and zeal in those gallant young men keep up my spirits.'[31] That there were grounds for the admiral's doubts was about to be demonstrated by the *Impérieuse*. On 14 November, gently sailing northward, past the east coast of Corsica, her lookouts sighted a promising quarry: a large polacre, a fast, three-masted Mediterranean craft with her main mast square-rigged. Yet there was something menacing about her, particularly in her fourteen open gun-ports. Scanning her through telescopes, the officers decided that she was a Genoese privateer and therefore fair game for boarding and capture. The wind was too light for the frigate to run alongside the polacre, so three boats were lowered and manned. Commanded by Lieutenant Napier, and with Marryat aboard, they pulled across the calm water to the waiting ship.

As the oars dipped and the boats were just beyond pistol-shot, British colours were hung over the polacre's side. Napier ordered his own boat to pull towards her stern, where her guns could not bear, stood up and shouted that if she was a British ship she could have no fear of being boarded by the British. A hail from her deck replied that she was a Maltese privateer – and therefore friendly – but doubted that the boats were British, so would not allow them alongside. In answer, Napier pointed to his marines, cocking their muskets, and the captain of the polacre pointed at his guns, now run out of their ports, and at the netting that had been triced up to the yardarms to prevent boarding. At this, Napier ordered his men to haul at the oars and his seamen and marines to stand by for boarding. With a cheer the boats surged forward and ran alongside in an eruption of gunfire.

'The boats then approached,' Cochrane reported later, 'but when close alongside, the colours of the stranger were taken in and a volley of grape and musketry discharged in the most barbarous and savage manner, their muskets and blunderbusses being pointed from beneath the netting close to the people's breasts.'[32]

Cutlasses slashed through the netting, pistols fired into faces and the two crews fought hand to hand: 'The rest of the officers and men then boarded and carried the vessel in the most gallant manner.'[33] The fighting had lasted ten minutes but two of Cochrane's best seamen – veterans of the *Pallas* – had been killed and thirteen others wounded, including two lieutenants. When the privateer's captain was killed, his crew surrendered and it was discovered that she was, indeed, Maltese and had been named the *King George*. It had been a costly mistake.

In reporting to Collingwood, Cochrane made the best of it, saying that the action had been against 'a set of desperate savages collected in a privateer, said to be the *King George* of Malta, wherein the only subjects of his Britannic Majesty were three Maltese boys, one Gibraltar man and a naturalised captain; the others being renegades from all countries and great part of them belonging to nations at war with Great Britain.'[34]

Taking their capture into Malta, they found that she had, in fact, been classed as a pirate and a bounty of £500 offered for her capture. However, the Court of Admiralty at Malta was notoriously corrupt and several of its members had had shares in the prize and her piracy. So, instead of being rewarded with prize-money for her capture, Cochrane was fined; as he put it, 'condemned by the Court of Admiralty to pay five hundred double sequins!*'[35] This was as blatant an example of corruption as he had encountered and he vowed revenge. 'I never saw Lord Cochrane so much dejected,'[36] noted Marryat. 'I never knew anyone so careful of the lives of his company as Lord Cochrane, or anyone who calculated so closely the risks attending any expedition.'[37]

He would be even more careful in future and the frigate's cruising over the next four months, ranging as far as the Adriatic to the east and the coast of Spain to the west, was successful and profitable. In February, they were off Barcelona and, sailing south for Cartagena, continued their routine chasing, boarding

---

* Venetian gold coins; this sum was worth more than £30,000 by the beginning of the twenty-first century.

and capturing. On 13 January 1808, Marryat was writing in his log, 'Took a settee [two-masted, single-decked ship] laden with cloth, iron and hare-skins'; on 17 February, 'Boats engaged and took 2 vessels laden with copper and hides' and, two days later, 'At night fell in with a brig and 4 gun boats. Engaged and took brig and 1 gun boat. Sunk 2 others.'[38]

After this last action, Cochrane was told by a prisoner that a 16-gun French privateer was lying off Almeria; the same ship that had beaten off the boats of the British frigate *Spartan* with heavy loss. So, before dawn on 21 February, as the sky began to lighten, the *Impérieuse* rounded the headland sheltering Almeria and, flying American colours, stood into the bay. There, in the anchorage covered by batteries on the commanding cliffs, the privateer rode at anchor, together with two brigs and three of the big, rakish xebecs traditionally favoured by Mediterranean corsairs.

The frigate was already cleared for action, boarding parties armed with cutlasses and pistols clambered down into boats alongside where, as Marryat put it, 'they found many of the younger midshipmen, who although not selected for the service, had smuggled themselves into the boats ... The Captain pretended not to see them when he looked over the side and desired the boats to shove off.'[39] Marryat himself was in the boat commanded by the first lieutenant, Caulfield. Whatever effect the American colours had had, the manning of the boats was seen by the crews of the ships in the anchorage and at once their decks were alive with men, running out the guns, hoisting the counter-boarding nets and lining the bulwarks with muskets.

Caulfield's boat was first alongside the privateer as her side burst with smoke and flame. 'Half our boat's crew were laid beneath the thwarts,' Marryat remembered, 'the remainder boarded. Caulfield was the first on the vessel's decks – a volley of musketoons received him and he fell dead with thirteen bullets in his body. But he was amply avenged; out of the whole crew of the privateer but fifteen, who escaped below and hid themselves, remained alive; no quarter was shown, they were cut to atoms on the deck and those who threw themselves into the sea to save their lives were shot as they struggled in the water.'[40]

The first shots had alerted the shore batteries and soon 'the whole bay was reverberating with the roar of cannon, the smooth water ploughed up ... while the *Impérieuse* returned the fire, warping round and round with her springs.'[41] Marryat had been bowled over by the dying Caulfield and 'lay, fainting with the pressure and nearly suffocated with the blood of my brave leader, on whose breast my face rested with my hands crossed over the back of my head to save my skull, if possible, from the heels of my friends and the swords of my enemies ... About eight minutes decided the affair ... Before it was over, I had fainted and before I regained my senses, the vessel was under way and out of gun-shot from the batteries.'[42]

The wind had now dropped and the British frigate lay becalmed and at the mercy of the batteries. Yet her boarding parties had taken all three enemy ships and, at noon, a breeze sprang up and carried her and her prizes out of the bay. Escaping a Spanish ship of the line that appeared on the horizon, Cochrane steered for Gibraltar and safety. When the fighting on the privateer had ended, the British dead and wounded had been laid out on deck; Marryat amongst the former. The surgeon of the *Impérieuse* and his mates had come aboard and with them was the bully, Cobbett. 'I was ... stretched out between the guns by the side of the first lieutenant and the other dead bodies,' Marryat was to recall, when Cobbett, 'seeing my supposed lifeless corpse, he gave it a slight kick, saying at the same time, "Here's a young cock that has done crowing! Well, for a wonder, this chap has cheated the gallows." The sound of the fellow's detested voice was enough to recall me from the grave: I faintly exclaimed, "You're a liar!", which ... produced a burst of laughter at his expense. I was removed to the ship, put to bed and bled ... but continued a long time dangerously ill.'[43]

One day, when he had recovered and was on deck, he heard a shout of, 'Man overboard!' It was Cobbett, who could not swim. Instantly, Marryat, a strong swimmer, dived over the side, kept the drowning youth afloat and helped him back on board. Later, he wrote to his mother about his surprising reaction because 'from that moment I have loved the fellow as I never loved before. All my hate is forgotten. I have saved his life.'[44] This was the first of a succession of such rescues of men overboard so that Midshipman Marryat became as renowned for saving life as for taking it in boarding enemy ships and raiding coasts.

Cochrane's cruise continued with a successful dash into the Adriatic before returning to the western basin of the Mediterranean. Already he had, in the past four months, captured and destroyed one brig, six gun-vessels, one privateer and about fifty merchantmen. There had been a cost: his first lieutenant had been killed and eleven others killed or wounded; Marryat himself had suffered three stomach wounds, one from a bayonet while boarding the enemy. Yet the boy had enjoyed a reward in being given command of a prize – a brig laden with wine – and ordered to take her into Gibraltar. It was to be an example of the unexpected to be expected by all captains, even young prize-masters. First, his men broached the cargo and were soon drunk and then the little ship was struck by a squall which, because her seamen were drink-sodden and slow, brought down her main mast. He managed to continue under improvised sail, finally reached Gibraltar, but the brig proved uncontrollable, collided with a troopship and lost her other mast. Next day, the *Impérieuse* arrived in the bay and Cochrane asked Marryat to explain his succession of mishaps. But, recalled the latter, the captain, 'so far from being angry with me for losing my masts, said it was wonderful, under the circumstances, how I succeeded in saving the vessel.'[45]

The balance of conflict had shifted: in February 1808, France had invaded Spain and, in May, the Spanish had risen against them and Britain had a new ally. Cochrane was ordered to support the guerrillas on the eastern coast of Spain and the Balearic Islands at sea and ashore, 'engaging, capturing and dismantling batteries, destroying bridges, etc.'[46] Once he launched Colonel* Congreve's newly-invented explosive rockets into Barcelona, for he was always keen to put warlike innovations into practice. This was the sort of warfare in which he excelled and offered chances

---

* The weaponry inventor was an officer in a militia regiment.

of strategic as well as tactical success when it was seen that the French army largely depended on the coastal road from France to reinforce and supply its soldiers in Spain.

First, Cochrane captured and destroyed a castle commanding a pass between Barcelona and Gerona, then cruised off Languedoc, putting his landing-parties ashore and harassing the French with broadsides and the inaccurate but alarming rockets. In November and December, his seamen and marines were committed to serious fighting ashore, when they joined the Spanish defenders of the fortress of Trinidad commanding the Bay of Rosas, just south of the border between France and Spain, which the French had besieged. Only some eighty Spanish defenders survived and were about to surrender when Cochrane arrived and at once sent half a dozen officers (including Marryat), fifty seamen and thirty marines ashore. It was an echo of the successful defence of Acre by Captain Sir Sidney Smith nine years before as the French could not afford to leave it in their rear, held by the Spaniards and with the Royal Navy offshore; the difference was that the French now had heavy siege-guns to batter down the walls. Here, too, it was ferocious fighting.

As Smith had inspired his men at Acre, so Cochrane led from the front, as Marryat recounted:

While he himself walked leisurely along through a shower of musket balls ... as an aide-de-camp, I felt bound in honour as well as duty to walk by the side of my captain, fully expecting every moment that a rifle ball would have hit me, where I should have been ashamed to show the scar. I thought this funeral pace confounded nonsense; but my fire-eating captain never had run away from a Frenchman and did not intend to begin then. I was behind him, making these reflections, and as the shot began to fly very thickly, I stepped up alongside him and, by degrees, brought him between me and the fire.

'Sir', said I, 'as I am only a midshipman, I don't care so much about honour as you do; and therefore, if it makes no difference to you, I'll take the liberty of getting under your lee.' He laughed and said, 'I did not know you were here ...

but ... I will make that use of you, which you so ingeniously proposed to make of me. My life may be of some importance here; but yours, very little; and another midshipman can be had from the ship only for the asking; so just drop astern, if you please, and do your duty as a breastwork for me!'[47]

Meanwhile the French 24-pounder guns had pulverised the walls and, on Sunday, 30 November, a thousand picked men were ordered to storm the breach. Watching from the ramparts, Marryat saw 'the black column of the enemy ... curling along the valley like a great centipede and, with the daring enterprise so common among the troops of Napoleon, had begun in silence to mount the breach.'[48] There they met not only British cutlasses and bayonets but fearsome obstacles and man-traps between the outer and inner walls. One was heavily mined with gunpowder; ships' chains were hung over the walls and covered with fish-hooks; a sloping glacis of planks was thickly greased so that those trying to scale it would slither into a chasm below: 'A very good bug trap', remarked Marryat.[49] The storming parties recoiled, leaving fifty dead – including their commanding officer – beneath the walls.

Four days later, a gale blew and, as at Acre, the ships could no longer give close support, the *Impérieuse* dragging her anchor; another assault was imminent ashore and, next day, the preliminary bombardment began. Cochrane decided that, since the Spanish defences had crumbled and the French had taken the town of Rosas, the castle could no longer be held, so sent boats ashore to evacuate the garrison; himself remaining ashore until last to fire the train of the mine. The defence had gained time for Spanish resistance to stiffen; as Marryat put it, 'A mere handful of seamen detained the whole French army for more than six weeks.'[50] The frigate had lost only three men killed and seven wounded; Midshipman Marryat was mentioned in his captain's despatch.

Just after Christmas, Cochrane again made his characteristic mark. In the harbour of Cadaques, north of Rosas, he found a convoy of eleven wheat-ships escorted by gunboats and covered by infantry ashore. As the frigate swept into the deep, narrow inlet, the French ordered the gunboats to be scuttled but had no time to sink or burn the merchantmen before Cochrane's men were over their sides. Sharpshooters behind rocks ashore opened fire but the frigate's guns fired at a cliff above, showering them with splinters of rock. The gunboats were salvaged but, instead of finding men to take the wheat-ships to Gibraltar for sale and eventual prize-money, Cochrane sold them locally and his ship's company shared the silver coins.

The day after sailing from Cadaques, Cochrane attacked another little, fortified harbour, Port Selda. There, at the height of his exchange of fire with shore batteries, the wind dropped and the frigate lay becalmed. He had, however, anticipated this and taken the precaution of laying a kedge anchor out at sea, so that his capstan could haul the ship out of the enemy's range. When safely at anchor, Cochrane saw a boat pulling from ashore; it brought a message from the enemy commander, asking for six bottles of rum. The rum was sent and, added Marryat, 'we sent in the bill about one o'clock in the morning.'[51] A few British seamen swam ashore and, finding the gunners drunk and asleep, took their muskets and a boat in which they pulled back to their ship.

In February, the frigate was back at Gibraltar, bound for England, her captain at last basking in Lord Collingwood's praise. This found no echo at the Admiralty, where he was still considered a tiresome, political troublemaker. Neither he, nor any of his officers, were accorded the promotion they were entitled to expect, Cochrane himself noting that his officers' 'fault, or rather, misfortune consisted in having served under my command.'[52] On 19 March 1809, the *Impérieuse*, unheralded, anchored in Plymouth Sound. There would be no time to grant the officers leave but Cochrane himself was urgently summoned to the Admiralty; the reason for this taxed the imaginations and inspired the speculation of those waiting and wondering on board.

CHAPTER THREE

Entering the Gates of Hell

One March morning in 1809, a messenger hurried up the stone stairs of the Admiralty in Whitehall, emerged on to the roof, climbed wooden steps to a platform among the chimney-stacks and handed a message to the lieutenant in charge of the signal station. It was a clear day and, at once, the six shutters within the huge wooden frame above them began clattering and the signal they transmitted was received and repeated by the next station on the roof of the Royal Hospital at Chelsea. Other signalmen along the line of some thirty more stations watched through telescopes as the shutter-telegraph began to transmit. On from Putney Heath, Blackdown, Portsdown, Pistle Down, High Stoy and Halton Hill the message passed until, within half an hour, it reached the signal station on The Hoe above Plymouth and, minutes later, the officer of the watch in the *Impérieuse*, at anchor far below, took down the message that the presence of Lord Cochrane was urgently required at the Admiralty.

The captain left for London immediately. He knew why he was being summoned because a letter from the Second Lord of the Board of Admiralty had awaited him at Plymouth. This told him, 'There is an undertaking of great moment in agitation against Rochefort and the Board thinks that your local knowledge and services on the occasion might be of the utmost consequence and, I believe, it is intended to send you there with all expedition.'[1]

Cochrane could guess what might be afoot. The essence of British naval strategy remained as it had been before Trafalgar: the prevention of the French squadrons at their Atlantic and Mediterranean bases escaping to the open sea and joining forces;

only then could they challenge British sea power, or mount any threat of invasion. Since the beginning of the year, the Channel Fleet, which was charged with the blockade of Brest, had been commanded by Admiral Lord Gambier, who, in 1807, had burned Copenhagen; this, Lord Nelson had been able to avoid when winning his victory there six years earlier. Cochrane was not an admirer of Lord Gambier, now past fifty, a gentle, civilised man, who had been in his element as a Lord Commissioner of the Admiralty and Governor of Newfoundland. Moreover, Gambier had become an enthusiastic Methodist and, trying to imitate John Wesley's evangelism, now seemed more interested in converting his ships' companies and distributing religious tracts than in exercising his guns' crews, or in taking risks in the face of the enemy.

In February, a French squadron of eight sail of the line and two frigates had broken out of Brest into the Atlantic and Gambier had returned to Plymouth. Free from British harassment, the French had been joined by three more ships of the line and five frigates from Lorient and together they reached the naval base of Rochefort. There lay another three ships of the line, several frigates and the *Calcutta*, once a British warship built as an East Indiaman, and when captured fitted as a fast troopship armed with 50 guns. The combined force was approximately equal to Gambier's and it was believed that, although an invasion of the British Isles – as was being prepared before Trafalgar – was unlikely, they presented an immediate threat to British islands in the West Indies. The influential landowners and planters of the Caribbean – amongst them Joseph Marryat, who was also a vocal Member of Parliament – demanded urgent preventive action. So, on 7 February, the Channel Fleet had arrived off Rochefort.

Arriving at the Admiralty, Cochrane was taken straight to Lord Mulgrave, the First Lord. Expecting a reprimand for his outspoken criticism of the Admiralty in the House of Commons, he became wary when there was none. Lord Mulgrave came straight to the point: the enemy was at Rochefort in strength, he knew Cochrane had operated in those waters when commanding the

Pallas, and then suggested a plan of attacking the enemy anchorage. All knew how difficult this would be.

Rochefort and its naval dockyard lay within the mouth of the river Charente, further from the open sea than the larger, but more vulnerable, port of La Rochelle. Between the mainland and the open sea lay the long island of Oléron, sheltering a huge anchorage that could be compared with Spithead and the Solent off Portsmouth. This water was dominated by the Île d'Aix, a fortified island commanding the channel between the more northerly Basque Roads and, to the south, the Aix Roads at the mouth of the Charente estuary. At the moment, the French fleet was lying in the Basque Roads with the British anchored far to the north-west, well out of range of shore batteries.

Cochrane had had a plan to force the French to sea by use of fireships, much as Sir Sidney Smith had planned to attack the French and Spanish fleet with rockets and torpedoes in Cadiz harbour before Trafalgar. Lord Gambier knew of this but did not approve. He had written that an attack by fireships was 'a horrible form of warfare and the attempt hazardous, if not desperate'; he was obviously reluctant but added that, if an attempt was to be made, 'it should be with secrecy and quickly.'[2]

The First Lord came to the point and said, 'You see that Lord Gambier will not take upon himself the responsibility of attack and the Admiralty is not disposed to bear the *onus* of failure by means of an attack by fireships, however desirous they may be that such an attack should be made.'[3] Therefore he was asking Lord Cochrane to take responsibility for, and command of, such an attack. 'It was now clear to me why I had been sent for to the Admiralty,' he noted afterwards; 'The Channel Fleet had been doing worse than nothing. The nation was dissatisfied and even the existence of the ministry was at stake. They wanted a victory and the admiral commanding plainly told them he would not willingly risk a defeat ... I had been sent for in the hope that I would undertake the enterprise. If this were successful, the fleet would get the credit, which would be thus reflected on the ministry; and, if it failed, the consequence would be the loss of my individual reputation as both ministry and commander-in-chief would lay the blame on me.'[4]

To Lord Mulgrave's consternation, Cochrane at first demurred, then said that he would accept on one condition: that, in addition to fireships, he would be free to employ other means to attack the enemy. He explained that, once the enemy thought an attack to be imminent, their squadron would withdraw from the Basque Roads and anchor behind the boom and shore batteries in the southerly Aix Roads; he would therefore use ships of his own devising to blast a way through the boom to make a passage for the Channel Fleet to sail through and attack the enemy, just as Lord Nelson had in Aboukir Bay. All that would be needed to ensure success would be a dark night, 'a fair wind and a flowing tide.'[5]

Cochrane voiced a further concern. Once his plan was known in the Channel Fleet, the captains of the ships of the line – all of them senior to himself – would object to a junior captain being appointed to this post of honour over their heads. 'My lord, you must go,' replied Mulgrave. 'The Board cannot listen to further refusal, or delay. Rejoin your frigate at once. I will make you all right with Lord Gambier ... Make yourself easy about the jealous feeling of senior officers; I will so manage it with Lord Gambier that the *amour propre* of the fleet shall be satisfied.'[6]

Cochrane asked for time to consider the proposal and departed to do so. However, the First Lord disregarded this and assumed that the captain had given his 'unqualified acceptance.'[7] Thereupon the Admiralty promised that twelve transports should be fitted as fireships and that another ship would be loaded with 'a large assortment of rockets and supplied with a detachment of the marine artillery, instructed in the use of them and placed under Mr Congreve's orders.'[8] Congreve was the ordnance inventor, who was pioneering the use of rockets that had been shown to be effective against enemy ships' companies rather than the ships themselves by terrifying them with the risk of fire from the descending pyrotechnics. In addition, provision would be made for the fitting out, under Cochrane's direction, of what were described as 'other engines of the kind', which he described as 'explosion vessels'; these were the secret weapons he had in mind.

Returning to the *Impérieuse*, Cochrane decided to sail immediately for the scene of impending action without waiting for his fireships and explosion-vessels and, such was his confidence in his own ship's company, not bothering to replace the recent casualties, including the first lieutenant. On 3 April, he sighted the Channel Fleet at anchor off the French coast and, miles beyond, the masts and yards of the French off Rochefort. Parallels with Aboukir Bay were immediately obvious: Lord Nelson, on sighting the enemy at anchor had crowded sail and closed with them at once; Lord Gambier had been safely anchored within sight of his enemy for nearly a month without firing a shot. So Cochrane went on board Lord Gambier's flagship, the *Caledonia*, a three-decker of 120 guns, the most powerful ship in the Royal Navy.

When directed to the admiral's great cabin, Cochrane expected a courteous, but probably frustrating meeting. As a captain, James Gambier had distinguished himself in the action of 'The Glorious First of June' in 1794, but, since then, shore and political appointments had combined with militant Methodism to blunt his aggression and his sailors nicknamed him 'Preaching Jem'. He was a courtly man with a fringe of grey hair around a bald head and refined, aristocratic looks. Yet when Cochrane was shown into his cabin he interrupted an extraordinary scene. Gambier was being hectored by one of his subordinate flag officers, Rear-Admiral Eliab Harvey, who had commanded the *Temeraire* in the thick of the fighting at Trafalgar; he was shocked by what he described as 'abuse ... to his face such as I had never before witnessed from a subordinate'; his harangue was, he said, 'incredible'.[9]

Harvey was shouting, 'I never saw a man so unfit for the command of a fleet as your lordship! Instead of sending boats to sound the channels, which I consider the best preparation for an attack, you have employed, or rather have amused yourself, with mustering the ships' companies [to preach to them]. Had Lord Nelson been here he would not have anchored in the Basque

Roads at all but would have dashed at the enemy at once!'[10]
Gambier remained silent and Harvey turned and strode out of
the cabin; Cochrane, realising this was no time for a discussion of
tactics, followed him.

Outside the cabin, Harvey began again, declaiming, 'I am no
canting Methodist, no hypocrite, no psalm-singer ...' The reason
for his outburst then became apparent: it was Cochrane's appointment to command the attack by fireships; as soon as the
latter had arrived among the Channel Fleet he had sensed his
unpopularity, which was as he had feared when given his mission. 'Every captain was my senior and, the moment my plans
were made known, all regarded me as an interloper, sent to take
credit from those to whom it was now considered legitimately to
belong. "Why could we not have done this as well as Lord
Cochrane?" was the general cry of the fleet ... "Why did not Lord
Gambier permit us to do this before?" '[11]

Harvey's outburst had begun when he had demanded to see
the admiral and presented him with a list of officers and men
who had volunteered for the fireship attack under his own command; volunteers were necessary because it was expected that
captured crews of fireships would be executed out of hand. Told
that the Admiralty had already appointed Cochrane to the command, Harvey announced that, if he himself were passed over for
the task, he would 'immediately strike his flag and resign his
commission.'*[12] Emerging on to the quarterdeck, which was
crowded with officers, Harvey continued his tirade, accusing
Gambier of 'methodistical, jesuitical conduct and ... vindictive
disposition',[13] pausing only to say that he had no personal quarrel
with Cochrane.

It was obvious that Lord Gambier had no stomach for such a
fight as was being wished upon him. He had, in Cochrane's view,
over-estimated the strength and range of the enemy shore batteries and under-estimated the navigability of the channel to
Rochefort; he also hated the idea of using fireships, which he
regarded as 'a horrible and anti-Christian mode of warfare.'[14] He

* In the event Harvey was court-martialled for his insubordination and cashiered.

had no wish to risk his fleet among unfamiliar islands, shoals, dangerous tides and currents, in the face of a strongly-positioned enemy fleet and guns ashore.

Cochrane now made his own assessment of the position. In the Aix Roads, just south of the deep channel between the Île d'Aix and the rocks of the Boyart Shoal, lay ten French ships of the line, three frigates and the *Calcutta*, the latter having the British flag hung 'under the bowsprit, near the privy'[15] as a studied insult to her former owners. They lay in three lines with the heaviest, including Admiral Allemand's flagship, *l'Océan*, which was as powerful as the *Caledonia*, in the rear and frigates patrolling ahead. Not, perhaps, realising that Gambier was no Nelson, Allemand expected a sudden attack by the whole British force, sweeping down on the flood tide; also, he suspected, fireships. To prevent this, he had ordered the Rochefort dockyard to build a massive boom nearly a mile long: bundles of spars, yards and balks of timber bound together with chains, anchored to the sea-bed with anchors weighing more than five tons apiece and kept afloat by buoys. Ahead of that patrolled some seventy oared boats to repel gunboats and fend off fireships. To Gambier, this together with the narrowness of the channel, the consequent tide-race and heavy batteries on both shores, seemed to make the French position impregnable. Working himself into a state of acute anxiety, he wrote to the Admiralty that 'such ships as might attack the enemy would be exposed to be raked by red-hot shot, etc, from the island and, should the ships be disabled in their masts, they must remain within range of the enemy's fire until they are destroyed.'[16]

It did not seem like that to Cochrane. After dark on the evening of his first meeting with Gambier, he sent boats to take soundings in the channel and survey the shores. He found that there were six fathoms of water off the Boyart Shoal and, if ships hugged its shores, they would be out of effective range of the long-barrelled 36-pounder guns on the Île d'Aix; 'Vessels of any size might go in and out,'[17] he concluded.

Cochrane set about preparing his attack. It would be in two stages: first, the boom would have to be burst open; fireships would sail through the gap and the French squadron would, he hoped, cut their cables and be driven on shore by wind and tide; then Lord Gambier's heavy ships could follow and blow the stranded ships to pieces with broadsides. The commander-in-chief seemed happy to leave this to the fiery captain the Admiralty had wished upon him. The admiral was, however, absorbed in what Cochrane described as

> '*musters*' and '*quasi*-religious practices' on board the fleet ... These 'musters' were found to relate to catechetical examinations of the men and ... the commander-in-chief sent a number of tracts on board the *Impérieuse* with an injunction for their distribution among the crew ... The fleet was in a state of great disorganisation on account of the orders given to various officers for the distribution of tracts ... I ... declined to distribute them.[18]

Cochrane's preoccupation was with fireships and other 'infernals'. Twenty-one were to be employed, a dozen of them arriving on the 10th from England; one an ex-East Indiaman, the *Mediator*. Each ship was loaded with combustibles – gunpowder, turpentine and resin – while tarred shavings were heaped on decks, tarred canvas slung from beams and tarred ropes led from square ports cut in the sides up to the yards and mastheads where as many as fifty Congreve rockets were mounted. Each ship would tow a boat into which the crew would jump when she was on course for the enemy and the fuses had been lit.

Even more fearsome were the 'explosion vessels', Cochrane's surprise for the French. These, he said, were 'simply naval mines, the effect of which depended quite as much on their novelty as engines of war as upon their destructiveness.'[19] Each hull was lined with logs, packed tightly together to concentrate the explosion; large casks were then stood upright, filled with 1,500 barrels of gunpowder and bound together with cables to form a huge mortar; on this were laid hundreds of shells and three thousand hand grenades, 'the whole, by means of wedges and sand, being compressed as nearly as possible into a solid mass.'[20]

There were to be thirteen explosion vessels, each manned by an officer, a midshipman and three or four volunteers. There was no lack of these although the commander-in-chief thought the enterprise was 'of such hazard as scarcely to admit a hope of the officers and men ever returning.'[21] It was indeed far more hazardous than manning fireships, for any spark, let alone a red-hot shot from a shore battery, would blow a ship to pieces. The three leading explosion-ships would be directly under Cochrane's control; himself commanding one and taking his brother Basil with him as a passenger; another, a brig, would be commanded by Lieutenant Urry Johnson, aged twenty-one, his crew consisting of the seventeen-year-old Midshipman Marryat and three ratings. Once the fire- and explosion-ships were ready, Cochrane awaited a dark night with a north-westerly wind and a flowing tide. All these factors came together during the second week of April.

Knowing the French were well aware of what was afoot, the whole force of thirteen explosion-ships and twenty-one fireships sailed ahead of Gambier's stationary fleet, anchored in the Basque Roads, north of Île d'Aix, eight miles from the massive boom. The admiral, having reluctantly agreed to the attack, allowed Cochrane to hold the final briefing on board the *Caledonia*. First, two light-ships were to move forward and anchor to either side of the channel between the Île d'Aix and the Boyart Shoal, while a bomb-vessel, the *Etna*, was to create a diversion by throwing her mortar-bombs into the island's batteries.

Marryat had now become familiar with the panorama of sea, shore and sky. In the oceanic haze, far to the north, the British fleet at anchor; to the south, beyond the menacing outline of the batteries on the wooded dunes of the Île d'Aix and the surf breaking on the Boyart Shoal, the French; to the south-east, the long, low shoreline of the French mainland was broken by the cranes, windmills and red roofs of the dockyard buildings at Rochefort, beyond the first loop of the Charente as it wound inland. He recalled, 'I solicited and obtained permission to go on board one of the explosion vessels that were to precede the fireships. They were filled with layers of shells and powder, heaped one upon the other ... We had a four-oared gig, a small, narrow thing (nicknamed by the sailors a "coffin") to make our escape in.'[22] Cochrane decided that the night of the 11th was ideal for the attack, the wind having driven the boats guarding the boom into Rochefort for shelter. Lord Gambier granted permission for the action to begin, the implication being that the main fleet would follow the fireships. 'Being quite prepared, we started,' Marryat continued. 'It was a fearful moment; the wind freshened and whistled through our rigging and the night was so dark we could not see our bowsprit. We had only our fore-sail set; but, with a strong flood-tide and a fair wind, we passed between the advanced frigates like an arrow. It seemed to me like entering the gates of hell. As we flew rapidly along and our own ships disappeared into the intense darkness, I thought of Dante's inscription over the portals, "You who enter here, leave hope behind." '[23] Lieutenant Johnson steered the brig, while Marryat held a lighted match of oil-soaked rope, ready to fire the port-fire fuse; the three ratings were in the gig, one holding the tow-rope from the ship, another steering, the third bailing furiously as the short, steep seas threatened to swamp her. The task of all the explosion-ships was to run alongside the boom and blow it apart to let the fireships, and then the fleet, through into the Aix Roads and the battle ahead.

> We came upon the boom with horrid crash; [Johnson] put the helm down and laid her broadside to it. The force of the tide, acting on the hull and the wind upon the foresail, made her heel gunwale to and it was with difficulty that I could keep my legs: at this moment the boat was very near being swamped alongside. They had shifted her astern, where the tide had almost lifted her over the boom; by great exertion they got her clear and lay upon their oars: the tide and wind formed a bubbling short sea, which almost buried her. My companion then got into the boat, desiring me to light the port-fire and follow.
>
> If I ever felt the sensation of fear, it was after I had lighted this port-fire, which was connected with the train ... I was

standing on a mine; any fault in the port-fire, which sometimes will happen, any trifling quantity of gunpowder lying in the interstices of the deck, would have exploded the whole in a moment ... Only one minute and a half of port-fire was allowed. I had therefore no time to lose. The moment I had lit it, I laid it down very gently and then jumped into the gig ... we were off in a moment. I pulled the stroke oar and I never plied with more zeal in all my life; we were not two hundred yards from her when she exploded.

A more terrific and beautiful sight cannot be conceived ... The shells flew up in the air to a prodigious height, some bursting as they rose and others as they descended. The shower fell about us, but we escaped without injury. We made but little progress against wind and tide; and we had the pleasure to run the gauntlet among all the fireships, which had been ignited and bore down on us in flames fore and aft. Their rigging was hung with Congreve rockets and, as they took fire, they darted through the air in every direction with an astounding noise, looking like large, fiery serpents.[24]

Cochrane's explosion-ship was aimed at the French ships of the line beyond the boom, so his fuse and train were set to burn for fifteen minutes. He himself lit the port-fire, then scrambled into the boat and then, as he said, 'urged the men to pull for their lives ... though, as wind and sea were strong against us, without making the progress calculated.' The fuses, burning in the abandoned ship, were, however, faulty and within ten minutes 'for a moment the sky was red with the lurid glare from the simultaneous explosion of 1,500 barrels of gunpowder. On this gigantic flash subsiding, the air seemed alive with shells, grenades, rockets and masses of timber ... whilst the water was strewn with spars, shaken out of the enormous boom.' Their boat had made so little head-way, that 'the shower of broken shells and other missiles' flew over their heads and fell in the darkness beyond.

The explosion of Marryat's and Cochrane's ships had heaved the great bundles of timber from their lashings and moorings and broken the boom open. A moment later, the biggest fireship, the *Mediator*, surged past and burst through its wreckage. The third explosion-ship under Cochrane's immediate command had been made fast to the *Impérieuse*, which was the most advanced of the frigates; she was ignited before casting off and Cochrane's own ship narrowly escaped destruction.

Now it was the turn of the fireships; but most of these, he said, were 'kindled too soon, no doubt to save the men the terrible pull back, against a gale of wind and a high sea.'[25] These swept past the *Impérieuse*, lying at anchor three miles from the enemy fleet. 'I could scarcely credit my own vision,' said Cochrane, 'when I saw the way in which they were handled, most of them being fired and abandoned before they were abreast of the vessels anchored as guides.'[26] It seemed a fiasco and Cochrane later declared 'four only reached the enemy's position and not one did any damage!'[27] In this, he was wrong. They presented a terrifying spectacle; a midshipman, watching from the distant British fleet, described them looking like 'a chain of ignited pyramids ... while Congreve's rockets, flying through the air in various directions, and, like comets, dragging a fiery train behind, formed a scene at once the most grand and terrific', while the French ships and batteries opened fire with 'vivid flashes glancing like electric fires through the volumes of smoke and flame emitted by the fireships.'[28]

The French captains, alarmed by the eruption of the explosion-ships, expected the blazing fireships to blow up too. So, as Cochrane reported, they 'cut their cables and were seen drifting away, broadside on to the wind and tide – whilst others made sail, as the only alternative to escape from what they evidently considered certain destruction from explosive missiles!'[29] Only two fireships directly threatened French ships but this – and the launching of a thousand Congreve rockets – was enough to throw them all into confusion. Watching the rout of the enemy, Cochrane sourly noted that Admiral Lord Gambier 'was with the fleet, fourteen miles distant.'[30]

As dawn broke on 12 April, the anchorages between Rochefort and Île d'Oléron presented an extraordinary scene. The ebbing tide had exposed long spits of rocky shoal and mud-bank reaching far out into the wide anchorage beyond the Île d'Aix. The boom had vanished and, except for two of the enemy ships, 'every vessel of the enemy's fleet was ashore. The flagship of Admiral Allemand, *l'Océan*, three-decker, drawing the most water, lay outermost ... nearest the deep water, where she was most exposed to attack ... for, whilst she lay on her bilge ... even a single gunboat might have so riddled her bottom as to have prevented her floating off with the rising tide; whilst all, by the fall of the tide, were lying on their bilge, with their bottoms completely exposed to shot and therefore beyond the possibility of resistance.'[31]

Cochrane at once sent signal flags flying up the halyards of the *Impérieuse*, telling the commander-in-chief that the enemy was at his mercy. The signal was acknowledged by the distant *Caledonia* but, watching through his telescope, he could see no sails being set by the British fleet. He made a second signal: 'The enemy's ships can be destroyed'; then a third, 'Half the fleet can destroy the enemy'; finally, a fourth, 'The frigates alone can destroy the enemy.' The signals were acknowledged but no movement could be seen. The hour hand of Cochrane's watch passed eight and nine; the tide had turned and was flooding fast. Training his telescope southward, he saw crews of stranded French ships heaving guns and stores overboard so that they could float the sooner. So he signalled to Lord Gambier, 'The enemy is preparing to heave off.'[32]

Finally, at eleven o'clock, the British fleet could be seen making sail, then slowly moved. By now, *l'Océan* and other big ships were about to heave off the mud but most were still beached and heeled and their annihilation by Gambier was still possible. Then, reported Cochrane, 'to our amazement, the British fleet, after approaching within seven or eight miles of the grounded ships, again came to anchor about three and a half from Aix, i.e. just out of range ... It was now evident that no attack was intended.'[33]

Noon passed. *L'Océan* was now afloat and others nearly so. An hour later, and the British fleet still remained at anchor, out of range. At this, Cochrane took action himself. Knowing that he could not make sail without risking an instant signal of recall from the admiral, he ordered the frigate's anchor to be slightly raised so that she would drift on the tide towards the French. As she drifted past the Île d'Aix, the shore batteries opened fire but without effect; then, after half an hour, seeing an enemy ship making sail and begin to steer for the Charente, Cochrane disingenuously signalled to Gambier, 'Enemy superior to chasing ship but inferior to the fleet.' There was no response, so, fifteen minutes later, he signalled, ' "In want of assistance", which was true enough, being a single frigate close to several enemy's ships of the line.'[34]

The French ships closest to the *Impérieuse* had, however, thrown their guns overboard to lighten themselves and float. One, still aground, that had not was the *Calcutta* and, although she out-gunned the frigate, Cochrane closed with her, at the same time raking two line-of-battle ships as he passed. This finally brought help from the British fleet and three ships of the line and five frigates came sweeping down from the north. It was a fine sight. 'One of our ships of the line came into action in such gallant trim that it was glorious to behold,' remembered Marryat. 'She was a beautiful ship in what we call "high kelter"; she seemed a living body, conscious of her own superior power over her opponents, whose shot she despised as they fell thick and fast about her ... Having furled her sails and squared her yards, as if she had been at Spithead, her men came down from aloft, went to their guns and opened such a fire as would have delighted the great Nelson himself, could he have been present.'[35]

But the intervention was too late. The *Calcutta* put up a stiff fight but in the afternoon was abandoned, took fire and blew up. 'At 3.30 p.m., the *Impérieuse* ceased firing, the crew being thoroughly exhausted,' noted Cochrane, 'whilst I was so much so as to be almost unable to stand.'[36] Then two French ships of the line surrendered and another was abandoned after being set on fire. As new reinforcements reached the channel between Île d'Aix and the Boyart Shoal, the shore batteries opened fire but only succeeded in killing a cow which, for safety, had been put in the heads – the sailors' privy – of the *Theseus*. Two ships of the line ran aground on the Boyart Shoal and could not be refloated until long after dark.

At dawn next day, 13 April, Cochrane saw three lights – the signal for recall – in the rigging of one of the more distant British ships. He proposed to ignore it, as Nelson had ignored a similar signal at Copenhagen, and seeing that British frigates, which were now anchored nearby, were preparing to obey, signalled to one suggesting that they combine forces to attack the huge *l'Océan*; but the other captain replied that he was leaving to join the fleet. Cochrane asked the captain of the next ship, his old frigate, the *Pallas*, and her captain agreed as did the captain of the bomb-vessel *Etna*. They had just opened fire at extreme range when wind and tide set against them and Cochrane realised that they must await a change in both. While they waited, a brig arrived from the main fleet at mid-day with a letter for Cochrane from Lord Gambier. It read, 'My dear Lord, You have done your part so admirably that I will not suffer you to tarnish it by attempting impossibilities ... You must therefore join as soon as you can.' In a postscript, the admiral added that he had sent three brigs and two rocket-ships to join Cochrane in case, on the way out, he wanted to attack a grounded French ship 'but I do not think you will succeed; and I am anxious that you should come to me, as I wish to send you to England as soon as possible.'[37]

Cochrane replied, acknowledging the letter and saying, 'We *can* destroy the ships that are on shore, which I hope your Lordship will approve of.'[38] Dusk was gathering and reluctantly the captains of all the British ships close to the French, excepting the *Impérieuse*, made sail to rejoin the fleet. Dawn on the 14th found Cochrane's ship alone, near the grounded French ships, three of which were unloading more guns into boats to lighten them further and Cochrane maintained that had he been allowed to attack '*even now* their destruction would have been inevitable.'[39] Instead, another recall signal was made from the *Caledonia*, to which Cochrane cheekily replied with the interrogatory signal, 'Shall we unmoor?' Gambier's response to this was another letter: 'It is necessary I should have some communication with you before I close my despatches to the Admiralty. I have, therefore, ordered

Captain Wolfe to relieve you in the services you are engaged in. I wish you to join me as soon as possible ...'[40] He added that Cochrane was to take the captain entrusted with the despatches to England. At half-past four that afternoon, Lord Cochrane sadly gave the order to weigh and make sail and rejoin the fleet.

Making straight for the flagship, Cochrane went on board and was shown into the admiral's cabin. He came straight to the point but did not accuse Gambier himself of dilatoriness, saying that 'the extraordinary hesitation, which had been displayed in attacking ships helplessly on shore' could only have arisen because of jealousy arising from himself, a junior captain, having been given command of the initial attack. He then suggested that a senior captain now be given command of a second attempt by any remaining fireships to destroy the enemy ships still vulnerable outside the Charente. 'I apologised for the freedom I used, stating that I took the liberty as a friend,' Cochrane said afterwards, 'for it would be impossible, as matters stood, to prevent a noise being made in England.' Gambier took this as a threat and, 'His lordship appeared much displeased ... then replied, "If you throw blame upon what has been done, it will appear like arrogantly claiming all the merit to yourself." '[41] At this, Cochrane pleaded to be allowed to remain off Rochefort, 'my object being alone that which has been entrusted to me by the Admiralty, viz. to destroy the vessels of the enemy.' The admiral cut him short by ordering him to sail for England next morning with the captain carrying the despatches. He had no alternative but to do so and arrived at Spithead on 21 April.

When Lord Gambier's despatches were published, it was hailed as the first great victory at sea since Trafalgar. At first sight, it seemed a success: of the ten French ships of the line off Rochefort, three had been burned and three damaged beyond repair. But gradually it was realised that all might have been destroyed, or captured; this had by no means been a repeat of the Battle of the Nile, let alone Trafalgar. All came to a head when the House of Commons was asked to pass a vote of thanks to Lord Gambier on his victory. One Member of Parliament opposed the motion: Lord Cochrane. Thereupon, Gambier demanded a court martial to clear his name and this was convened at Portsmouth in July. The admiral was well-connected and the Admiralty did not want one of its commanders-in-chief to be convicted of sloth, or cowardice. The evidence taken was selective, important witnesses were ordered abroad and there was an attempt to silence Cochrane by offering him a sought-after command in the Mediterranean. Gambier was acquitted and remained in command of the Channel Fleet. It was Lord Cochrane who realised that his career in the Royal Navy was at an end.*

The officers of the *Impérieuse* – amongst them Midshipman Marryat – were, or became, aware of this and revered – and sometimes tried to emulate – their dashing captain. They had a new captain and would move to other ships, but they would never be the same after the Cochrane years. On 10 July 1809, when Frederick Marryat reached his eighteenth birthday, he was already a man, seasoned by war and seafaring. He now stood five feet, ten inches, 'upright and broad-shouldered for his height', as one who knew him wrote; 'the firm, decisive mouth ... and thoughtful forehead ... redeemed from heaviness by the humorous light that twinkled in his deep-set grey eyes ... dark, crisp curls covered his head ... his eyebrows were not alike, one being higher up and more arched than the other, which peculiarity gave his face a look of enquiry, even in repose'; he was beginning to have to shave twice a day, with some difficulty because of the deep dimple in his chin. He was volatile and 'like most warm-hearted people, he was quick to take offence ... he quarrelled for want of something better to do ... this restless activity of spirit was visible in him indeed at all times.'[42]

This was Lord Cochrane's pupil as a young man, about to make his own way.

---

* No new appointment was offered Cochrane and, after involvement in a financial scandal in 1814, he was expelled from Parliament and the Navy; he then successively commanded the navies of Chile, Brazil and Greece in their wars of independence but was reinstated in the Royal Navy in 1832 with the rank of admiral; he commanded the American and West Indies station but was disappointed at not being offered high command in the Crimean War, when he was aged eighty. His extraordinary career, which included inventions involving gas lighting, steam propulsion, tubular boilers, smoke screens and poison gas, only ended with his death in 1860.

CHAPTER FOUR

No Longer a Place for Gentlemen

M idshipman Marryat had completed three years' intensive education under the tutelage of Lord Cochrane, a vibrant substitute for Lord Nelson, whose funeral had been such an inspiration. It was to be continued by a succession of captains – good, bad and indifferent – and began with what seemed to be an undertaking of epic proportions.

Europe seemed helpless against the power of the Emperor Napoleon. Turning on Austria, his principal enemy on the Continent, he had taken Vienna in May 1809 and, two months later, had crushed their army at Wagram. Only in the Iberian peninsula was there a glimmer of hope; although the French had expelled the British expeditionary force at the beginning of the year, it had escaped by sea from Corunna. Using sea power as had been learned in the eighteenth century, the British returned, landing at Lisbon and driving the French from Portugal. British regular soldiers, combined with Portuguese and Spanish troops and guerrillas, harried the French through the Spanish hills, defeating them in battle at Talavera. This raised the nation's spirits – the British commander, General Wellesley, being created Viscount Wellington, in gratitude* – but it had little bearing upon the main thrust of French determination to dominate Europe. Now, at last, the British conceived, and began to execute, a plan to achieve that aim.

The strategic concept was brilliant. The *Grande Armée* might rampage across Europe at will; Napoleon might still dream of invading the British Isles; but his flank was wide open to an attack that could divide the French army from France. Since the

---

* He was created Duke of Wellington in 1814.

beginning of the year, reports had reached London that the French were transforming the estuary of the Scheldt and its ports of Antwerp and Flushing into a great naval base; already, nineteen warships were building at the former and ten ships of the line lay at anchor in the river. This could be a base for the support of military operations on the German coast and in the North Sea. It was also a strategic blunderbuss aimed directly at the Thames estuary and London at point-blank range. Yet reports also suggested that the shores were lightly defended and both ports vulnerable to amphibious attack. If they could be taken and a British army put ashore, it could advance into the heart of Europe cutting Napoleon's communications between France and central Europe, where he now was. Since Sir Sidney Smith had used command of the sea to hold Acre and outflank General Bonaparte ten years before, the evacuation of Corunna and the reinforcement of Lisbon had again shown what could be done by a maritime strategy.

The Admiralty and the War Office planned and prepared the expedition with speed and efficiency. A fleet of two hundred and forty-five warships – including thirty-three sail of the line and twenty-three frigates, amongst them the *Impérieuse* – and a convoy of transports would embark forty thousand troops. These, including three thousand cavalry, would be landed along the low-lying, almost undefended shores of the Scheldt and occupy Antwerp and Flushing before Napoleon knew what was happening.

On 26 July, the *Impérieuse* – now commanded by Captain Thomas Garth – sailed from Spithead as part of the escort to some fifty troop-transports. Awaiting them in the Downs anchorage off Deal was the fleet, commanded by the capable Rear-Admiral Sir Richard Strachan, and the combined fleet steered east for the Scheldt. Next day, they sighted the sand-dunes and windmills of the Dutch coast but it was blowing hard and the ships hove to until the following morning when the wind had dropped and the sun shone on a panorama of sea and sails.

As the landings began on the 30th, and Marryat watched the cavalry put ashore: 'The weather was fine and the water smooth

... the men were first sent on shore with their saddles and bridles: the horses were then lowered into the water in running slings, which were slipped clear off them in a moment; and, as soon as they found themselves free, they swam away for the shore, which they saluted with a loud neigh as soon as they landed. In the space of a quarter of a mile we had three or four hundred horses in the water, all swimming for the shore at the same time; while their anxious riders stood on the beach awaiting their arrival. I never saw so novel, or picturesque a sight.'[1]

With the expertise the British had shown in the assault landings in Aboukir Bay eight years before and, in the past, at Quebec and Havana, the army was put ashore on the island of Walcheren between the two main channels of the Scheldt. Next day, the town of Middelburg was occupied and the siege of Flushing began with 'a tremendous roar ... with shell, shot, rockets and musketry, enough to tear the place to pieces.'[2] Two days later, the town surrendered.

Then, just as Antwerp seemed at their mercy, the army halted. Its commander was the brother of William Pitt, the great prime minister, who had died young within days of Lord Nelson's funeral; but Lieutenant-General the Earl of Chatham was more like the cautious Lord Gambier than his brother or their grandfather, the Elder Pitt, first Earl of Chatham, the pioneer of amphibious strategy during the Seven Years War. Lord Chatham decided that there was no hurry, deciding that it was necessary to consolidate their holdings before advancing further. For three weeks he waited, giving the French time to rush thirty-five thousand reinforcements to Antwerp and build a boom across the river below the port. All talk of plunging a sword into the heart of Napoleon's Europe evaporated.

As the frigates – the *Impérieuse* amongst them – began to sail up-river, they were met by fierce and accurate shooting from shore batteries, some firing red-hot shot. Cochrane's navigating master had been left ashore to give evidence at the Gambier court-martial and his replacement took the ship up the wrong channel and within range of a particularly effective battery. The ship might have been dismasted and battered into wreckage yet a touch of Cochrane's originality remained. One of his midshipmen persuaded Captain Garth to try firing shrapnel shells (explosive shot filled with musket balls, invented by an artillery officer named Shrapnel) from the main-deck guns. By luck, one burst in the shore battery's magazine; three thousand barrels of gunpowder exploded, almost wiping out the gunners.

Even before the British soldiers met the newly-arrived French, they had, each summer evening, been tormented by mosquitoes, which rose in clouds from the dykes. The mosquitoes were malarial and Lord Chatham's delay in advancing on Antwerp provided the time necessary for the fever to develop. Six weeks after the landing, almost a quarter of the army was sick and then the total approached a half; men began to die by the score, then the hundred. Landing parties had gone ashore from the ships to skirmish and, more enjoyably, to forage for farm animals and the sailors, too, went down with what became known as 'Walcheren fever', amongst them, Marryat. In October, he was evacuated to England, having decided that Walcheren 'with its agues ... was no longer a place for a gentleman.'[3]

Lord Chatham had already decided that it was no place for him and returned home in mid-September. Napoleon, who had heard news of the landings two days after his victory at Wagram, had reacted fast, thankful that 'the weakest spot and the only one at which it is possible to deal me a blow'[4] had been saved by the sluggishness of the British general. It was not until December that the British Government also decided that he was right and, on the 22nd, the fleet, laden with sick men, sailed back across the North Sea; of the four thousand soldiers who had died there, only about a hundred had been killed in action. There were immediate repercussions: the responsible ministers in London were replaced but, more seriously, the Austrians had accepted a humiliating peace, ceding huge territories to France and her allies, and joined the Emperor Napoleon's Continental System to exclude Britain from European trade. A magnificent British expeditionary force had been ruined by incompetence at the highest level of command and by 'Walcheren fever'; in all senses, wasted.

Sick as he was, Marryat was only ashore in England for one day before being appointed to the 74-gun *Centaur*, the flagship of Rear-Admiral Sir Samuel Hood, a cousin of the great Admiral Lord Hood, which was under orders to sail for the Mediterranean. Here again he served under a captain from whom he could learn. Cochrane had not only been a fighting captain of dash and originality but an innovator; currently he was beginning to devise a weapon so terrible that it was not used and its nature kept secret for a hundred years: poison gas. Captain William Webley of the *Centaur* was entirely different; a brave seaman – like his admiral, he had fought under Nelson at the Nile and had recently returned from the Baltic, where he had fought and captured a Russian ship of the line – but he was a robust dilettante. An accomplished painter in water-colours, he had painted some of the actions in which he had fought – including those under Nelson in Aboukir Bay and Tenerife – and Marryat was showing some artistic skill as, at least, a caricaturist. Webley, a bluff offspring of an impoverished squirearchal family, had, as a lieutenant, been a member of the Glass Cases Club, which had been founded in response to another group he called 'The Rough and Ugly', who maintained that the more polished lieutenants were 'too fine gentlemen to attend to the duties of our profession and were therefore only fit to be shut up in a glass-case.' The 'Glass Cases' had therefore challenged their critics to a race in reefing topsails and won. As a result, their admiral attended a celebratory dinner ashore in Newfoundland and proposed the toast, 'To the Club of Glass Cases and may they all continue to bear the character of polished gentlemen and gallant seamen, which they have now earned.'[5] To his toughness and jocularity, Marryat began to add gentlemanly attitudes and manners.

The task of Lord Collingwood's fleet was still the blockade of Toulon and the occasional skirmish when the French ventured outside. It was dull but demanding work, enlivened by an occasional emergency, as when a seaman fell from the main yard and Marryat dived into the sea to rescue him. Morale became a problem as smartness – scrubbing decks, polishing metalwork, coiling cordage and so on – filled in the long, empty hours at sea; when discontent broke out as disobedience, it was harshly suppressed with floggings. To his relief, in October 1810, Marryat was ordered home to take passage for the Caribbean and American waters in another ship of the line, the *Africa*, which had fought at Trafalgar. It was not a happy voyage: the ship was crowded with thirty other midshipmen as passengers, the first lieutenant was a drunkard and the food vile. Yet again a voyage was marked by a display of impromptu courage: Marryat dived into the sea in an attempt to save a man overboard; the attempt failed and Marryat was himself only picked up by a boat when swimming two miles astern of the ship; in recognition, he was given responsibilities over the heads of more senior midshipmen.

This was to be his first visit to the West Indies. He was always to remember his first sight of Carlisle Bay on the coast of Barbados: 'The beach of such a pure dazzling white, backed by the tall, green coconut trees waving their spreading heads to the soft breeze, the dark blue of the sky and the deeper blue of the transparent ocean, occasionally varied into green as we passed by the coral rocks, which threw their branches out from the bottom – the town opening to our view by degrees, houses after houses, so neat with their green jalousies, dotting the landscape; the fort with colours flying, troops of officers riding down, a population of all colours, relieved by the whiteness of their dress. Altogether the scene realised my first ideas of Fairyland – and "Can this be such a dreadful place as it is described?" thought I.'[6]

It could be, because tropical diseases – notably yellow fever and malaria – were endemic and the trade of the islands was based upon slave-labour. Yet society was changing; there already were moves to end slavery and freed African slaves and their mixed-race descendants were beginning to form a black middle class. This now had the self-confidence to entertain naval officers ashore, the negro and creole ladies dressing elaborately for 'dignity balls'.

Marryat could not linger here long and in April 1811 he took passage in a schooner for Halifax. It was a difficult voyage because the ship's officers were so drunken that they nearly missed their destination and, indeed, ran the ship aground at the harbour mouth. It was a relief to join his new ship, the *Aeolus*, a frigate of 40 guns, commanded by a captain Marryat could like and admire, Lord James Townshend. Although appearing to qualify more for 'The Rough and Ugly' than 'The Glass Cases', Lord James was an aristocrat, the son of the first Marquess Townshend, who had succeeded to General Wolfe's command at Quebec. Although only aged twenty-six, he was tough and weathered, stoutly-built, walking with a sailor's roll, and had been on the American station for five years. Marryat was impressed, deciding that his captain 'knew a ship from stem to stern, understood the character of seamen and gained their confidence. He could hand, reef and steer, knot and splice; but he was no orator; he read little and spoke less. He was good-tempered, honest and unsophisticated with a large proportion of common-sense. He was good-humoured and free with his officers; though, if offended, he was violent, but soon calm again; nor could you perceive any assumption of consequence from his title of nobility.'[7]

It was while the *Aeolus* was cruising off the American coast at the end of September that year that she and her ship's company were tested to the limit. A gale had been blowing but it died away, leaving a heavy ocean swell. Then, as Marryat himself described it, at 'about eleven o'clock the sky began to blacken; and, before noon, had assumed ... the most dismal and foreboding darkness; the sea-gulls screamed as they flew distractedly by, warning us to prepare for the approaching hurricane ... About noon it came with an astonishing and terrific violence.'

The sails had been taken in at the first signs of the coming storm but it was not enough because 'such was the violence of the wind that, on the moment of its striking the ship, she lay over on her side with her lee guns under water. Every article that could move was danced to leeward; the shot flew out of the lockers ... The mizzen mast and the fore and main topmasts went over the side; but such was the noise of the wind that we did not hear them fall; nor did I, who was standing next to the mizzen mast at the moment, know it was gone until I turned round and saw the stump of the mast snapped in two like a carrot.' There had not been time to batten down the hatches; enormous seas reared to be 'instantly beheaded' by the wind and broke over the ship, the water 'warm as milk' and 'the sheep, cow, pigs and poultry ... all washed overboard.'

The men clung to ropes and spars when 'a seaman crawled aft on the quarterdeck and, screaming into the ear of the captain, informed him that one of the anchors had broke adrift and was hanging by the cable under the bows.' Marryat was ordered to cut it free but, at first, could not make his way forward until 'going over to leeward, I swam along the gangway under the lee of the boats.' On the forecastle, Marryat 'found the oldest and stoutest seamen holding on by the weather rigging and crying like children' but he rallied them to help hack through the cable.

Swimming back through the surge to the quarterdeck, he found Townshend – 'as brave a man as ever trod plank' – and three seamen trying to hold the wheel. 'The violence of the gale was unabated and ... the fore and main masts still stood, supporting the weight of rigging and wreck, which hung to them and which, like a powerful lever, pressed the labouring ship down on her side ... The captain ... calling the ship's company on the quarterdeck, pointed to the impending wreck and by signs and gestures and hard bawling, convinced them that, unless the ship was immediately eased of her burden, she must go down.'

The frigate 'descended rapidly in the hollows of the sea and rose with dull and exhausted motion as if she felt she could do no more. She was worn out in the contest and about to surrender ... The men seemed stupified with the danger ... and could they have got at the spirits, would have made themselves drunk ... At every lurch the mainmast appeared as if making the most violent efforts to disengage itself from the ship; the weather shrouds became like straight bars of iron, while the lee shrouds hung over ... to leeward, or with the weather-roll, banged against the mast and threatened instant destruction ... We expected to see the mast fall and with it the side of the ship to be beat in. No man could be found daring enough, at the captain's request, to venture aloft and cut away the wreck of the main-top mast and the main yard, which was hanging up and down with the weight of the top-mast and top-sail resting upon it. There was a dead and stupid pause, while the hurricane, if anything, increased in violence ... I waited a few seconds to see if any volunteer would step forward,' Marryat recalled, 'and then seizing a sharp tomahawk, I made signs to the captain that I would attempt to cut away the wreck, follow me who dared. I mounted the weather-rigging; five or six hardy seamen followed me ... The jerks of the rigging had nearly thrown us overboard ... We were forced to embrace the shrouds with arms and legs as we mounted.' Reaching the cordage that had to be cut, Marryat hacked at the slings of the mainyard; others, the lanyards of the topmast rigging. 'The lusty blows we dealt were answered by corresponding crashes; and, at length, down fell the tremendous wreck over the larboard gunwale. The ship felt instant relief; she righted and we descended amidst the cheers, the applause, the congratulations and, I may add, the tears of the gratitude of most of our shipmates ... The gale abated every moment, the wreck was gradually cleared away and we forgot our cares. This was the proudest moment of my life.'[8]

When the ship reached Halifax, Captain Townshend presented Marryat with a certificate praising his 'bravery, intrepidity and firmness'[9] in the hurricane. Soon afterwards he was given another for saving a young seaman from drowning in the harbour. Halifax was a popular port of call as it was a settlement for loyalist Americans, eager to express their sentiments by entertaining the Royal Navy; Marryat, himself half-American through his mother's loyalist family, felt at home.

The amiability ashore was not to last. Tension between Britain and the United States of America, which had never wholly relaxed since the Declaration of Independence, had become critical. The principal disputes were at sea. The American mercantile fleet was second only in size and activity to the British and its crews included a high proportion of British seamen, often deserters from the Royal Navy – usually pressed men – and those who simply wanted the better pay and conditions offered by American ship-owners. American ships trading with European ports controlled by the French were turned away by the British blockade; the French refused to receive ships that had touched

at British-controlled ports, while the British felt justified in seizing any ship that had not done so. When British warships stopped American merchantmen, they would often illegally press
their seamen, insisting that they were British, or deserters. Since
the beginning of the century, nearly a thousand American ships
had been seized as blockade-runners and nearly six thousand,
three hundred American seamen – or those claiming to be such –
had been impressed.

That summer, an American frigate fired on a British sloop on the
suspicion that she had illegally impressed an American seaman.
The British admiral commanding the American station ordered the
captains of his squadron – the 64-gun *Africa*, six frigates and five
sloops – to avoid provoking the Americans. He was not particularly
worried by the possibility of fighting the United States Navy, which
then consisted in total of only eight frigates and eight sloops, since
he had, of course, overwhelming naval strength to call upon across
the Atlantic. The American frigates were, however, not what they
seemed. Three were rated as mounting 44 guns and four as having
36, whereas the most powerful of the British frigates was rated at
only 40 guns. The American ships were, indeed, far more powerful
than that and it was discovered that, in fact, the 'forty-fours' could
carry as many as 60 guns and the 'thirty-sixes' at least 44, and so
were virtually fast ships of the line.

As the prospect of war – with the United States in alliance
with France – darkened, Midshipman Marryat was, in November
1811, appointed to another frigate, the *Spartan*, commanded by
another such officer as he would himself have chosen. Captain
Edward Brenton had succeeded his brother Jahleel in the command and both were gentlemen of literary tastes as well as fighting captains.* The Brentons belonged to an American loyalist
family and this was a bond with Marryat as Edward Brenton
recognised the boy's latent qualities and encouraged them. The
captain was, declared Marryat, 'refined in his manner, a scholar
and a gentleman. Kind and friendly with his officers, his library

---

* Edward Brenton (1774–1839) became author of *The Naval History of Great Britain from 1783 to 1822* (1823) and *The Life and Correspondence of John, Earl of St. Vincent.*

was at their disposal; the fore-cabin, where his books were kept, was open to all; it was the schoolroom of the young midshipmen and the study of the old ones. He was an excellent draughtsman and I profited not a little by his instruction.' Marryat, profiting by this and the former influence of Captain Webley, had begun to amuse himself and his messmates with caricatures and he added what was, for him, becoming a new and exciting interest: 'He loved the society of ladies and so did I.'[10]

So when the *Spartan* was ordered 'up the spacious and majestic St Lawrence' river to Quebec in June 1812, he began to see the passing scenery with an artist's eye. 'The city ... has a very romantic appearance,' he wrote. 'The houses and churches are generally covered with tin to prevent conflagration, to which this place was remarkably subject ... When the rays of the sun lay on the buildings, they had the appearance of being cased in silver.'[11] But the frigate's mission was routine: to deliver pay for the garrison and to press men for the Navy.

Quebec was known to be a promising hunting-ground for the press-gangs because the waterfront was crowded with seamen from timber-ships, which arrived to begin loading each June; if they were delayed and caught in the autumn freezing of the river, their crews would be stranded and impoverished, so there were unemployed seamen as well as new arrivals in the ships. Marryat was given command of one of the press-gangs of ratings and marines disguised as merchant seamen. He was told that one successful trick was to send decoys ahead to taverns, where they would pretend to belong to a homeward-bound timber-ship, whose captain was offering bounties in rum and dollars for prime seamen. 'Many were procured in this manner,' it was explained, 'and were not undeceived until they found themselves alongside the frigates, when their oaths and execrations may be better conceived than described, or repeated.'[12] As warnings of the press-gangs spread, many went into hiding. 'We found more game in the interior of haystacks, church steeples, closets under fireplaces, where the fire was burning. Some we found headed-up in sugar hogsheads and some concealed within bundles of hoop-staves. Sometimes we found seamen dressed as gentlemen, drinking wine and talking with the greatest familiarity with people much above them in rank ... I ... discovered some good seamen on the rafters of an outhouse intended only to smoke and cure bacon; and, as the fires were lighted and the smoke ascending, it was difficult to conceive a human being could exist there: nor should we have discovered them if one of them had not coughed; on which he received the execration of the others and the whole party was instantly handed out. We immediately cut the strings of their trousers behind to prevent them running away.' But, he added, 'It was astonishing to me how easily these fine fellows reconciled themselves to the thoughts of a man-of-war; perhaps the approaching row with the Yankees tended very much to preserve good humour.'[13] In June 1812, they heard that war had been declared on Britain by the United States on the 19th of that month, sailed down the St Lawrence and 'arrived at Halifax full-manned and immediately received orders to proceed to sea "to sink, burn and destroy all ships, vessels, belonging to the United States".'[14]

When the *Spartan* reached the intended rendezvous with the rest of the British squadron, they had gone south and Brenton contented himself with capturing American merchantmen at sea – sometimes without their captains realising that war had been declared – and cutting out others from coastal anchorages. Coastal trade was disrupted but the Americans more than compensated for that by a succession of shocking victories over the British in ship-to-ship duels. Repeatedly, the big, heavily-armed American super-frigates beat into submission, or flight, the lighter British frigates; the *Constitution* capturing the *Guerrière* and the *United States*, the *Macedonian*. Even the bold Captain Townshend seems to have deliberately avoided action with the powerful *Constitution*. The statesman George Canning told the House of Commons in London, 'It cannot be too deeply felt that the sacred spell of the invincibility of the British Navy has been broken by these unfortunate victories'[15] and even a British success in even combat – when the more strongly-manned American frigate *Chesapeake* met the *Shannon*, the most tautly-trained ship in the British squadron, and was herself captured – failed to restore confidence.

Midshipman Marryat was kept busy, commanding his ship's boats on cutting out expeditions but, at the height of his activity, orders reached him from the Admiralty to return home immediately and take his examination for his commission as a lieutenant. On 6 October, he reached Portsmouth in a sloop and, soon afterwards, took and passed the examination by a board of captains convened in a ship moored in the harbour. His annual pay was now increased from £30 to £100 (about £3,700) and he was entitled to wear a single gold epaulette on his best uniform coat. In January 1813, it was announced in the *London Gazette* that Lieutenant Frederick Marryat had been appointed second lieutenant in the newly-built brig-sloop *Espiegle* of 18 guns. He was delighted; she was, he declared, 'a most beautiful vessel ... and sat on the water like a duck.'[16]

His pleasure was short-lived. As his boat approached the sloop at Spithead, he noticed that she flew the pennant for punishment in progress. Then, as he recalled, 'As I went up the side, I saw a poor fellow spread-eagled up to the grating ... while the captain, officers and ship's company stood round witnessing the athletic dexterity of a boatswain's mate, who, by the even, deep and parallel marks of the cat on the white back and shoulders of the patient, seemed to be perfectly master of his business.'[17] This was not enough for the captain, who shouted, 'Boatswain's mate, do your duty, or, by God, I'll have *you* up and give you four dozen yourself. One would think, damn you, that you were brushing flies off a sleeping Venus, instead of punishing a scoundrel with a hide as thick as a buffalo's.'[18]

This was Captain John Taylor, a fat, foul-mouthed brute, who, as Lieutenant Marryat was to discover, treated his officers almost as savagely as his ratings. The ship was bound for the Caribbean and the long Atlantic crossing brought boredom and the captain's excessive insistency on scrubbing and polishing the ship, enforced by floggings and beatings with a rope's end. When his first lieutenant remonstrated, he was confined to his cabin for two months and a midshipman, who was unable to report for duty because of illness, was flogged.

Captain Taylor was not only seen as a tyrant but a coward. When the American sloop *Hornet* engaged and finally sank the weaker British *Peacock*, his own ship was lying at anchor six miles away and he himself was ashore. Making only perfunctory efforts to sail, he needlessly waited overnight; when he finally set out in pursuit of the *Hornet*, his handling of his ship ensured that there was no risk of catching her. When Marryat, the officer of the watch, suggested a change of course, which would have achieved this, Captain Taylor refused, saying that his orders were to make for Barbados. 'I mentioned I thought we had better go after the *Hornet*', said Marryat later. 'He told me not to dictate to him and I held my tongue, of course.'[19]

Captain Taylor was, however, wary of Marryat, who was strongly built and had a dangerous glint in his eye. Then came an opportunity for the captain to rid himself of this possible challenge when a gale blew up and a seaman fell from the rigging into the sea. Once again, Marryat dived overboard and struck out towards the drowning man. 'Had the commonest diligence, or seamanship, been shown, I should have saved him,' said Marryat afterwards, 'but the captain, it appeared, when he found I was overboard, was resolved to get rid of me in order to save himself; he made use of every difficulty to prevent the boat coming to me.' But Marryat was popular among the sailors and the boat's crew, although delayed, pulled hard on the oars, and just managed to save Marryat, more than a mile astern, but not the man he had tried to rescue. They were only just in time because, as he was to tell his family, he was beginning to drown and 'the struggle for life once over, the waters closing round him assumed the appearance of waving green fields, which approached nearer and grew greener as his senses gradually forsook him. It was not a feeling of pain but more like sinking down, overpowered by sleep, in the long, soft grass of a cool meadow.'[20]

Yet the effort had strained Marryat to the limit and, soon afterwards, while dancing at a ball ashore in Barbados, he suffered internal bleeding and this recurred, some weeks later, when he fell while coming ashore from a ship's boat. Captain Taylor seems to have insisted that there was nothing to keep him from his duties but on 17 April 1813, the surgeon ordered him to the hospital at Halifax; soon afterwards he was sent home in his former ship, the *Spartan*. He was ashore for six months, his only duty being to attend, as a witness, the court-martial at

Portsmouth of Captain Taylor. He was charged with 'continual Acts of Severity and Cruelty, such as ... flogging persons in the sick list', the 'most unexampled tyranny and oppression towards the officers' and that 'he had failed to do his duty when in pursuit of the *Hornet*, American sloop.'[21] He was found guilty and dismissed from the service.

In January 1814, Marryat returned to the American war but in a different type of ship and captain. The ship was the *Newcastle*, a big frigate of a new class, hastily built to meet the threat of the powerful American ships. Mounting 58 guns on two decks, displacing more than fifteen hundred tons and manned by nearly five hundred men, she was built, in record time, of pitch pine because of the shortage of traditional oak. Her captain was another peer but one of a very different stamp from Lord James Townshend. Lord George Stuart was, Marryat noted, 'a smart, dapper, well-made man with a handsome but not an intellectual countenance ... and a very good opinion of himself; proud of his aristocratic birth and still more vain of his personal appearance ... He had been many years at sea but, strange to say, knew nothing, literally nothing, of his profession.'[22] Marryat soon learned to interpret his vague instructions as when, appearing on the quarterdeck, he ordered, 'Mr What's-his-name, have the goodness to what-do-ye-call-'em-the-thingumbob.' 'Ay, ay, my Lord,' replied Marryat. 'Afterguard, haul taut the weather main-brace.' But when, on receipt of such an order, he replied, 'Very good, my Lord', he was rebuked with, 'I don't suppose you mean anything like disrespect but I will thank you not to make that answer again; it is for *me* to say, "Very good" and not you.'

Unlike Captain Taylor, Lord George was brave even if, when giving chase to a supposed enemy, he commanded the first lieutenant, 'Mr Thingamay, don't you think red-hot what-d'you-call-'ems should be given in the first broadside to that thingumbob?' 'Red-hot shot, do you mean, my Lord?' 'Yes, don't you think that would settle his hash?' 'Where the devil are we to get them, my Lord?' 'Very true', said his Lordship.[23]

He was an unfeeling, rather than cruel, captain. When American prisoners were taken from captured ships, even their officers were treated harshly and Lord George seemed to have little more sympathy with his own men. Just before Christmas in 1814, when Marryat was sent with the frigate's barge in a blizzard to cut out four ships anchored in Boston Bay, he did not bother to wait offshore to pick him up but continued his cruise. As Marryat's boat approached their quarry, hidden marksmen opened fire from shore, hitting four of his men. But they boarded and captured two American ships and two, which had been run aground, were burned; Marryat sailed the largest out to sea and a midshipman took the smaller. The latter was wrecked but Marryat managed to get away and survive the storm. There was no sign of the *Newcastle* and she was not found for three days and nights, when Marryat and the other survivors sighted her and were taken aboard; eleven British lives had been lost.

'I was mad with hunger and cold,' he remembered, 'and with difficulty did we get up the side, so exhausted and feeble were the whole of us. I was ordered down into the cabin, for it was too cold for the captain to show his face on deck. I found his Lordship sitting before a good fire with his toes on the grate and a decanter of Madeira stood on the table and a wine glass and, most fortunately, a large rummer. This I seized with one hand and the decanter with the other; and, filling a bumper, swallowed it in a moment without even drinking his Lordship's good health. He stared and I believe he thought me mad. I certainly do own that my dress and appearance perfectly corresponded with my actions. I had not been washed, shaved, or cleaned since I had left the ship three days before. My beard had grown, my cheeks hollow, my eyes sunk ... As soon as I could speak, I said, "I beg pardon, my Lord, but I have had nothing to eat or drink since I left the ship." "Oh, *then* you are very welcome," said his Lordship, "I never expected to see you again." '[24]

Unlike the *Impérieuse, Aeolus* and *Spartan*, the *Newcastle* was an unhappy ship and, whenever she was close enough to shore, men deserted. She had never been up to her complement of four hundred and eighty and, once in American waters, men deserted whenever they could, knowing that pay and living conditions would be far better in American service. The number of British deserters in American service added ferocity to the fighting because deserters knew what to expect if taken prisoner, as was shown when one was identified amongst the wounded in the captured *Chesapeake*, taken to Portsmouth in irons and hanged from a yard-arm at Spithead.

Although the British were not only destroying American coastal trade but burning small seaports and seaside villages, they remained wary of facing the few, large American frigates. At the beginning of 1815, the *Newcastle* was, with another heavy frigate, the *Leander*, and a sloop, blockading Boston, where the formidable *Constitution* lay. When another deserter from Lord George's ship got ashore and told the Americans that his ship was sailing south towards Cape Cod, the American frigate escaped into the Atlantic. The British squadron gave chase but, since more than a quarter of the *Newcastle*'s crew had deserted, she was in no condition to fight a running action. They followed the American to Madeira and the Cape Verde Islands, where she was sighted. But the British ships, which should have put an end to the cruise of the *Constitution*, were clumsily handled and she again disappeared over the horizon.

Marryat was unaware of this at the time, since at Madeira he had again been taken ill with internal haemorrhages and shipped home in a passing brig. Nor did it affect the course of the war because, unknown to the British and American captains, it had been ended on Christmas Eve by the Treaty of Ghent. Nor did they know of the escape of Napoleon from the island of Elba and his restoration to power in Paris. Soon after Marryat's return home – when he was promoted to commander, or junior captain – came the climax of the war. On 18 June, Napoleon was defeated by the Duke of Wellington and Field Marshal Blücher at Waterloo and the titanic events, which had shaped the world and the lives of millions, came to an end. Commander Frederick Marryat – now entitled to the courtesy rank of captain – returned home to 6 Great George Street in Westminster to which the family had moved in 1808. This was a large, terraced house in the street linking St James's Park with the approach to Westminster Bridge, a few hundred yards from where the great strategic decisions of the war, which had given rise to all his adventures of the past decade, had been taken.

CHAPTER FIVE

Some New Comet

F ive minutes' walk from the family house in Great George
Street brought Lieutenant Marryat to the Admiralty. Up
Whitehall he walked, past Downing Street, then left
through the arch in the elegant stone screen sheltering the cob-
bled courtyard in front of the building that housed the heart and
brain of British sea power; between the pillars supporting the
pediment of the portico, across the marble-flagged hall and into a
small room, crowded with men like himself. This was the
waiting-room, where unemployed naval officers lingered in the
hope of employment.

For Marryat, and most of the others, there was none in 1815.
The war was over and the Emperor Napoleon bound for exile on
the remote Atlantic island of St Helena. At the beginning of the
year there had been some hundred British ships of the line in
commission and nearly a hundred and fifty thousand seamen
employed in the fleet. Now this was being reduced to about a
dozen sail of the line and less than twenty thousand men. There
was work for only a few of the sixty admirals, eight hundred and
fifty captains and four thousand lieutenants, who had survived
the long wars. A peacetime appointment might well depend
upon influence with highly-placed friends and past misde-
meanours might rise up to ruin expectations; in Marryat's case,
his caricatures of senior officers – notably Lord George Stuart –
acted against his prospects. Officers sought employment with the
customs and excise service, the shipping companies, foreign
navies, or tried to live on their meagre half-pay and, if they were
lucky, prize-money. The streets and waterfronts were crowded
with unemployed seamen, many of them maimed in battle, for
whom there would be no official welfare except the workhouse.

During Marryat's nine years of active service, his father had continued to prosper. He had become the London agent for the rich islands of Grenada and Trinidad and, in 1807, been elected Member of Parliament for Horsham, changing his constituency five years later for that of Sandwich. He had made his mark in Parliament, speaking for traders, ship-owners and plantation-owners in the Caribbean, on behalf of whom he was to be accused by William Wilberforce, the campaigner against slavery, of 'fanaticism'.[1] In 1811, he was elected chairman of Lloyd's in recognition of his part in fighting off rivals in marine insurance. His prosperity enabled him to buy a large country house at Wimbledon at the time of his son's return and the young man could afford to survey the scene and take time to decide upon future action. That naval officers need not be tied to their profession had already been demonstrated by two cultured captains, Webley and Brenton, and now another example was to be found in a neighbour. A contemporary of Marryat's, still in his lieutenant's uniform, was living at 12 Great George Street, near their own town house. Lieutenant William Pocock had been serving in the Adriatic, when Marryat was off the American coast, and had seen action of the same sort: captures at sea, raids ashore and cutting-out expeditions. He was a son of the fashionable marine painter Nicholas Pocock, who had himself commanded merchant ships owned by his family before becoming a professional painter, particularly in water-colours. He had moved to London from Bristol at the beginning of the war to meet the demand for elegant and accurate paintings of naval engagements, commissioned by well-to-do officers who had taken part. Nicholas Pocock had himself been present in Lord Howe's fleet at his victory on the 'Glorious First of June' in 1794 and his patrons recognised his first-hand experience; he regularly illustrated articles in what had been Lord Nelson's favourite journal, the *Naval Chronicle*, and one of his grandsons was christened Horatio Nelson Pocock.

His eldest surviving son, Isaac, had studied painting in the studios of George Romney and William Beechey and was now exhibiting himself; he also was a successful playwright. William, who had gone to sea as a midshipman with the East India

Company before transferring to the Royal Navy in the year of Trafalgar had been commissioned lieutenant a year before Marryat. A lively-minded young man, he, too, demonstrated that a naval officer could make use of other talents. Like his father, he painted skilfully in water-colours and had illustrated his own adventures in the Adriatic; as a marine surveyor, he drew charts of remarkable artistry and accuracy; he was a linguist, speaking French, Italian and Spanish; he was also an innovator and inventor. He had studied alternatives to the impressment of seamen; he was proposing the use of metal tanks, not only for the storage of liquids on board ship but, when empty, for buoyancy and this had prompted his interest in the potential of submarine warships; he was fascinated by the possibilities of developing steam-propulsion, designing an armoured, turtle-backed, steam tug for towing ships of the line into action against contrary wind and tide. So Lieutenant Pocock was not only of the school of Webley and Brenton but also of Cochrane.

Marryat began to emulate Pocock. He, too, began studying professional practice and theories such as alternatives to impressment and new, simpler methods of signalling at sea. Languages were always important to naval officers and – like Nelson, Sir Sidney Smith and many others before him – he decided to travel for this purpose and to enquire abroad into 'such branches of science as might prove useful';[2] in addition, there might be opportunity for a little espionage which could catch an eye at the Admiralty. So he set out on extended travels on the Continent, through France to Switzerland and Italy; when in England, basing himself at Great George Street and Wimbledon House.

Now, for the first time since he had been sent to sea, Marryat was directly influenced by his father. Lloyd's led the world in marine insurance and regularly expressed its gratitude to the Royal Navy for the protection of trade but Joseph Marryat was aware of one particular weakness of merchant ships: they could not communicate. The Royal Navy had developed its own signalling systems to the point where young officers specialised in signalling and, in 1816, the rating of yeoman of signals was introduced. But this concentrated upon the manoeuvres and fighting of warships, while, as Marryat put it, 'The master of a merchant vessel, who sees another steering into danger, has at present no means to warn her of it but must endure the agonising sensation of following her with his eyes till she is dashed to pieces on the rocks ... Great advantages would arise ... from the development of signals. Merchants and ship owners would know that their vessels and goods had proceeded so far on their voyage ... Underwriters would have the satisfaction of knowing the same intelligence of the vessels they had insured; and the relatives of passengers and crews would have the pleasing information that their friends were well.'[3]

Urged on by his father, Marryat devised his *Code of Signals* for merchant shipping, which could be employed in parallel with naval signals. It divided into six parts: the first two, lists of warships and merchantmen, each identified by a number; thirdly, signals representing named ports, headlands, channels and reefs; fourth, signals for sentences commonly used at sea; finally a section for vocabulary and another for the alphabet. Published in 1817, it was promoted by Joseph Marryat, through his influence at Lloyd's, prompting the sour comment from one ship-owner that, 'When it is considered that Captain Marryat is the *son* of the chairman of the Committee of Lloyd's, I am sure the ship-owners and the public will do every justice to the very ingenuous manner in which it has been brought forward.'[4] But influence, or 'interest', as it was known in the Navy, was one of the principal driving-forces of society and was taken for granted. Once the new code had been accepted by Lloyd's, all its insurance agents, every ship-owner, the master of every merchantman, every pilot, coastguard and excise officer and soon every warship had to have a copy. Its success, both practical and commercial, was assured.

Moving easily in London society, with good looks and robust wit as much a passport as his father's wealth and position, Marryat fell in with other young men of means and mettle. One of these, Joseph Ritchie, was to extend the post-war vogue for travel far beyond Marryat's own jaunts to Lausanne and Florence to Africa and the mysterious, almost mythical, Saharan city of Timbuctoo. The expedition was jointly planned by the Admiralty and the Colonial Office and was to cross the Sahara from Tripoli to Timbuctoo in the hope of discovering whether the Niger was a tributary of the Nile. Marryat was invited to join the expedition, agreed but then changed his mind. First, he feared that a long absence from the Admiralty's sight and mind might hamper his promotion. Finally, on 25 November 1818, shortly before they were due to leave, Ritchie received a note from Marryat, posted at Brighton, reading, 'My dear Sir, Courting is so expensive that I must thank you to send me down £20 to pay for my lodgings before I quit.'[5] The need to borrow ready cash suggests that he was keeping one side of his life from his family for it was the code of officers – particularly those considering themselves members of the Glass Cases Club, in spirit at least – that one did not 'speak lightly of a lady's name in the mess'; indeed, while admitting that he enjoyed female company, Marryat was always reticent about his amours.

It was not to remain secret for long. At the end of 1818, he told his parents that he intended to marry Catherine Shairp, a Scottish girl from County Linlithgow, the daughter of the British chargé d'affaires at St Petersburg, whom he had been courting at Brighton. It was a strange match. By any standards, Marryat would have been in demand as a potential husband: a well-to-do naval hero and son of a prominent financier and politician; strikingly handsome: square-jawed and merry-eyed; broad-shouldered and deep-chested. Yet she was no beauty, prim and seemingly an odd choice for such a swashbuckling, convivial sailor. Perhaps, like Nelson, he thought that a naval officer needed a ladylike wife to add poise to his vision of himself and preside over a suitably genteel household. The couple were married in January 1819.

Surprisingly, Marryat's marriage to the puritanical Kate coincided with his first venture into bohemian London. His plan to visit Timbuctoo had become a joke amongst his urban acquaintances and, shortly before his engagement, a caricature was published. This showed an African chief presenting a naval captain, who looked remarkably like Marryat, with his three naked and over-developed daughters; the caption ran, '*Puzzled which to choose; or, the King of Timbuctoo offering one of his Daughters in Marriage to Captain ---- (Anticipated result of the African*

Expedition)'. Marryat found this amusing, but his wife did not, partly because he himself had been the caricaturist and it had been engraved for publication by a new acquaintance, to whom Marryat had taken a liking, a hard-drinking contemporary named George Cruikshank.

Bohemians such as this were new to Marryat. He had long enjoyed the company of contemporaries who were witty, artistic or literary but always within the naval profession. Now, he was meeting young men whose livelihood was based only upon their wit, artistry and literacy. Having been told that he should have his caricatures published, he showed them to George Humphrey, the proprietor of a fashionable print-shop in St James's Street, who recognised their originality and also their amateurishness and introduced him to a professional engraver, who might be able to enhance them to saleable standards. This was George Cruikshank, himself the son of a caricaturist. He had wanted to become a sailor – he, too, had been inspired by watching Nelson's funeral, which he had sketched, and his younger brother, Robert, had been a midshipman with the East India Company – but his mother objected and his father refused to send him to art school on the grounds that if he was going to become a successful artist he would not need any training. But he still hankered after the sea, singing sailors' shanties when he had been drinking, and caricaturing them as Jolly Jack Tars – and soldiers as dandified poltroons, or physical grotesques. He cultivated the friendship of former sailors, amongst them John Mitford, who had been discharged from the Navy for drunkenness and written *Johnny Newcombe in the Navy*, which had been illustrated by Thomas Rowlandson, and published a scurrilous magazine for which he himself drew caricatures. Cruikshank was an amusing, eccentric companion, with his long, lugubrious face, framed with whiskers, coming alight with humour. He was amongst the wild and witty set that Marryat found increasingly agreeable as a release from the demure domesticity that had begun to envelop him.

When he had shown Cruikshank the Timbuctoo caricature and the latter had successfully engraved it, he produced others, making fun of his own life at sea and the artist agreed to engrave them, too, giving them a professional elegance. So, they began work on a set of humorous naval engravings to be called *The Sailor's Progress*, which was published in the year of Marryat's marriage. There was a growing market for such authenticity, however humorously presented; for a quarter of a century the shore-bound British had read of the exploits of the Royal Navy and hungered for details of the lives their heroes had led, wanting to be made to laugh, or cry.

Marryat himself was about to see that civilians could be as eccentric as anyone he had met in the Navy. For it was now that he was accorded the honour of being elected a member of the Royal Society, that eminent body of scientific learning. Those hearing of the distinction must have assumed it was in recognition of his authorship of the code of signals, just as his award of the Gold Medal of the Royal Humane Society in 1818 was quite clearly in recognition of his record of saving lives at sea. But this was not the case. His name had been put forward by his school-friend Charles Babbage, now a distinguished mathematician, to Sir Joseph Banks, the elderly President of the Royal Society. His reaction, as told by Marryat himself, was to exclaim, 'Marryat! Marryat! A capital fellow! Elect him by all means. *Puzzled which to choose! Puzzled which to choose!* I always have his caricatures on my table; wouldn't be without them for the world.'[6] The one that had particularly amused him was the Timbuctoo caricature and it was that – and the naval caricatures, engraved by George Cruikshank – that made him a Fellow of the Royal Society.

Soon afterwards, Babbage suggested he also be elected to the recently-founded Astronomical Society, for which there would be some justification through his professional skill in navigation. Marryat replied, 'My dear Charles, I belong to so many erudite societies that I shall soon have the whole alphabet at my heels; as, however, I like the idea of yours, I beg you will inscribe Capt. Marryat, R.N., F.R.S., F.L.S., F.G.S., F.W.S., etc., etc., among the members ... They will think me some new comet by the length of my tail ...'[7]

Perhaps his father's influence helped, perhaps the mark he was making in London society caught the eye of the First Lord of the Admiralty but on 13 June 1820, still at a time of high unemployment amongst naval officers, Marryat was given his first command. She was only an elderly, 10-gun brig named the *Beaver*, but at last he was captain of one of His Majesty's ships. His first child – a son, named Frederick after him – had been born on 6 October, the year before, but he left the baby with Kate and his parents at Wimbledon House and took the road to Portsmouth with more expectations than regrets, as Nelson had left nearby Merton for the last time fifteen years before.

There was no difficulty in manning the little ship because taverns on the Point at Portsmouth were crowded with unemployed seamen, and Captain Marryat was piped aboard and settled into his modest quarters. On 27 September, his elevation to command was followed by an invitation to dine with King George IV on board the royal yacht, which was at Portsmouth, for his first taste of the louche pomp surrounding the gross, amusing monarch. The two men had nothing in common but the King's brother, the coarse, jolly naval officer, the Duke of Clarence, laughed at his jokes; Marryat was becoming known as a humorist because his second set of nautical caricatures, *The Life of a Midshipman, or the Life of Mr Blockhead*, had been engraved by Cruikshank and just been published.

Royal connections were to be variously continued – albeit through a self-proclaimed, former sovereign – when Marryat's ship was ordered to the remote Atlantic island of St Helena, as a guardship, watching the prison of the deposed emperor Napoleon. It was a long and tortuous voyage via Madeira and Tristan d'Acunha because of the need to catch the prevailing winds. On the latter island, he met another self-proclaimed emperor, the only European inhabitant, a former British soldier, who had decided to rule his remote rock. 'His present Imperial Majesty,' noted Marryat, 'had, at the time of my visit, a black consort and many snuff-coloured princes and princesses. He was in other respects a perfect Robinson Crusoe.'[8]

On 4 March 1821, the *Beaver* reached St Helena and, soon afterwards, her captain scouring the cliffs and peaks through his telescope, saw the low-built house, Longwood, and might have seen a portly figure in white cotton trousers and wide-brimmed straw hat pottering in the garden. The prisoner was guarded by three thousand gaolers: soldiers of the garrison and the companies of warships anchored offshore. The Governor of the island, Major-General Sir Hudson Lowe, was still, after more than five years, fearful of an attempt to rescue his prisoner.

The current fear, of which Marryat would have been warned, was of an attempt by submarine. He was well aware of the experiments with submersibles by Robert Fulton and the distaste at the Admiralty for such a form of 'unmanly ... and assassin-like' warfare[9] that the American inventor had returned to the United States in 1806, unemployed. However, the rumour was well-founded. Fulton's British collaborator, a Channel pilot, smuggler and spy named Thomas Johnstone, had continued with the design and building of a submarine, funded, strangely, by the British Army. That patronage had ended with the war and the Lord High Admiral, the Duke of Clarence, refused to meet Johnstone's demands for support, despite warnings that he would otherwise seek patrons abroad. He had done so and Bonapartists had reportedly offered him an initial payment of £40,000 to build a submarine capable of being towed to St Helena, rescuing Napoleon from the beach and carrying him beneath the surface to a ship, which would carry him to South America. It was not known on St Helena that the submarine had indeed been completed at a secret boatyard on the upper Thames in November 1820, and was being brought down-river to the sea when she became jammed in under an arch of London Bridge, was captured by the authorities and burned on the foreshore.

There was another rescue being planned and of this Marryat would not have been aware. His first captain, Lord Cochrane, now commanding the Chilean fleet, had hatched a characteristically melodramatic scheme to snatch Napoleon from the island and proclaim him Emperor of South America once it had been freed from Spanish rule.

Any rescue would now be too late, however, for Napoleon was ill and thought to be dying. On 1 May, Marryat, too, was taken ill with dysentery and a fever that was first thought to be cholera.

But he made a quick recovery and five days later was on deck in bright sunshine to read a signal from shore: 'General Bonaparte is in imminent danger.'[10] Before dark, that evening, he died. Early next morning Marryat was invited to accompany Sir Hudson Lowe and other officers to Longwood to attend the lying-in-state. There, lying on the camp-bed, on which the Emperor had slept the night before his victory at Austerlitz, lay the man who had dominated Europe and their lives since they were children. They were surprised to find him so small and plump with such feminine hands, fine face and pale, translucent skin. None of the skills and materials needed for casting a death-mask were available on the island, so Marryat, who was known as an amateur artist, was asked to draw the dead man. He concentrated on the profile of the head, sketching the body and the bed, making several copies, one of which was sent in a despatch ship to England that evening with the official report of the death. Four days later, he also drew the funeral procession of French and British officers and, in a last reminder of lost, imperial dreams, Napoleon's charger, Sheikh.

On the day of the funeral, Marryat was ordered to exchange his command for that of another sloop, the *Rosario*, and return home. Taking a dozen of his best seamen with him, he found an unhappy ship that had been commanded by an incompetent captain, named Hendry, whom he described as 'a harsh, unpleasant officer'[11] and 'just like a winter's day, short and dirty.'[12] He was sly and suspicious, and with reason, for his ship's company was on the edge of mutiny. Once Hendry had left, Marryat, although weakened by dysentery, set about restoring morale. He saw that there was parallel authority among the ratings, who had even begun to bully the midshipmen. The worst was a sergeant of marines, who had been given privileges by Hendry for acting as his informer; Marryat reduced him to the ranks, had another troublemaker flogged for drunkenness and insolence and clapped a third in irons.

On arrival off Portsmouth early in July, Marryat was ordered to join a squadron escorting the body of Queen Caroline, the unstable, estranged wife of King George IV, to Cuxhaven on its way to the funeral. On his return, he found that he had not heard the last of the troublesome Captain Hendry, who seeing himself as having been deprived of his command by Marryat and hearing of the latter's disciplinary actions, complained about him to the Admiralty. An official enquiry was held at Portland in November and witnesses proved that it was Hendry himself who was to blame for the troubles and Marryat was cleared, his professional prospects enhanced.

In wartime, this might have led to a more prestigious command but, in peacetime, the best to be expected was a form of active service in the campaign against smuggling, which was then at its most virulent. Not only did this mean patrolling 'the chops of the Channel' west of the Isle of Wight in all weathers, but the chance of having to fight fellow-countrymen, fine seamen, with whom the Navy had some sympathy. Finding the revenue cutters, with which he operated, slackly commanded and inefficient, Marryat determined to show what could be done. A favourite trick of the smugglers was to tie tubs of contraband to a weighted, buoyed cable and throw them overboard offshore, where they could be retrieved later by a local fishing-boat. Marryat trawled for such caches off the Dorset coast and hauled them to the surface. He also summarised his opinions in a memorandum, suggesting the captured smugglers should be drafted into the Navy and their ships broken up. The final answer would be to blockade Cherbourg, from which most of this contraband seemed to originate. He wrote this without enthusiasm because he hated the work and was thankful when on 7 February 1822, the *Rosario* was declared unseaworthy and paid off.

Ashore again, he saw himself in print as an author rather than an illustrator, or an innovator of signals, when his pamphlet, *Suggestions for the Abolition of the Present System of Impressment for the Naval Service* was published. Deploring the tension, amounting to hostility, between the Royal Navy and the mercantile marine and increasing opposition to impressment by libertarians, he had been particularly shocked by a story of Cruikshank's. His brother Robert, when a midshipman in the East India Company's fleet, had returned home in a small merchant ship; mooring in the Thames, near the Tower of London, a butcher's boat had run alongside, apparently trying to sell mutton; the butchers had been invited on board, when they drew cutlasses, revealed themselves to be a disguised press-gang and impressed the crew; Robert Cruikshank, had, despite his uniform, also been taken and was only released when the Admiralty received a forceful complaint from East India House. Marryat now made a number of suggestions, amongst them the granting of immunity from impressment to a given number of apprentices in each merchant ship, a limit to the time that was served in the Navy by pressed merchant seamen; better conditions in the Navy itself. But this was not the whole answer, he knew, and, for the bulk of recruits, he proposed a form of conscription, which was a less obviously brutal method of impressment. The pamphlet was widely circulated in the Navy and reached the Lord High Admiral, the Duke of Clarence himself, who disliked the very idea of reform, although his intervention did have its effect on more liberal politicians; however, fearing that he was only muddying the already murky waters of the controversy, he asked for his pamphlet to be withdrawn.

Yet it was a remarkable document, including a social survey of the Royal Navy. This began with the premise that 'Our fleets were never so well manned as at the action of Trafalgar. Every good seaman had been gleaned from the merchant service and had been a sufficient time in His Majesty's Navy to be in a high state of discipline.'[13] It included a breakdown of the former occupations of the ship's company of a particular ship of the line: about half had been seamen all their working lives but some sixty other trades and skills were represented, including eight shoe-makers, one gardener, three tobacco-manufacturers, one mattress-maker, three pedlars, six hatters, one sieve-maker, three joiners, one umbrella-maker, four silk-spinners, one nail-maker, seven masons, three coach-makers, fifteen farmers and one violin-maker.

Now, most of Marryat's contemporaries were retiring into obscurity, many to live frugally on half-pay, but he himself was to be given another chance to attain professional heights.

CHAPTER SIX

Happy Jack, Great War Dog, and Billy Bamboo

B y an irony of fate, which would not have escaped Captain Marryat, his first chance of high command on active service came nearly eight years after the Great War had ended. On 31 March 1823, he was appointed to command the *Larne*, a small, fir-built frigate of 20 guns, hurriedly ordered for operations off the American coast in the War of 1812; her size suited the work the Admiralty had in mind.

India and what were known as the East Indies were increasingly seen as replacing the West Indies as the principal source of overseas profit. The threat to this from France had been eliminated but there was another, which, once removed, could present vast opportunities for trade and the exploitation of natural resources. Among the wooded hills and rivers of Burma was the almost mythical kingdom of Ava, ruled by a self-confident and aggressive monarch. Regarding the European merchant adventurers in India with contempt, the King of Ava was known to be planning to extend his boundaries into Bengal – the province of the East India Company – and as far afield as Assam. To contain, or pre-empt, such aggression, the British Government were preparing an expeditionary force, for which three frigates would provide the naval escort with Commodore Charles Grant, the senior officer, flying his broad pennant in the *Liffey* of 50 guns.

The three ships sailed from Portsmouth; Marryat on 3 July, having – with another touch of irony – brought his ship's company up to strength by the impressment of thirteen smugglers. Also on board was Kate Marryat and their second son, William, who were to be put ashore in Madras before the force made its final approach to war. It was a long voyage via Madeira, the Cape of Good Hope, Bombay and Colombo and incidents worth recall were rare. One, which Marryat liked to tell, was when calling at Falmouth, when he and one of his midshipmen were being rowed out to the sloop by an old bumboat woman. It was choppy and, in coming alongside, the boat capsized. Marryat was a strong swimmer and, as they bobbed to the surface, the woman clasped him in her muscular arms. 'Go to the boy, go to the boy!' he shouted. 'He can't swim!' 'Go to the boy?' she yelled back. 'What, hold up a midshipman when I can save the life of a captain! Not I, indeed!'[1] And she clutched him like an octopus until all three were rescued.

The *Larne* was a cramped ship and her captain was careful to avoid upsetting his wife and little boy. So he waited until he could send them ashore for a day at Colombo before ordering floggings to which several of his men had been sentenced during the voyage: one to forty-eight lashes for desertion and drunkenness; four to thirty-six each for theft; and two with a dozen each for neglect of duty. Marryat disliked flogging but thought that there was no practicable alternative at sea. Had his wife and child remained to board, they could not have avoided hearing the roll of the drums; the order, 'Boatswain's mate, do your duty'; the hiss of the cat o'nine tails and, probably the yells and gasps of pain that followed.

Ashore in Indian ports, they found that Marryat was already known for his caricatures engraved by Cruikshank, notably the Timbuctoo joke and also a shipboard scene entitled 'A Lee Lurch on Board an Indiaman' with passengers flung from the dining-table in a rough sea. Leaving Kate and William at Madras, the ships made for the Kedgeree roadstead off the mouth of the Hooghli and, arriving at the beginning of April, the little *Larne* was sent up-river to Calcutta, where the coming operations were being planned. War had been officially declared in March, the immediate cause being the invasion of Bengal by the King of Ava in January 1824, and the *Larne* escorted a troop convoy down-river and across the Bay of Bengal to the forward base in the Andaman islands. Once assembled under command of Colonel Sir Archibald Campbell, a veteran of the Peninsular campaigns, the force seemed irresistible: nine thousand troops, about half of them European, half Indian and more than sixty ships, escorted by the *Liffey*, the two smaller frigates and a variety of lesser warships, mostly manned by the motley crews of the East India Company's Bombay Marine.

There was one remarkable ship, of which Marryat had high hopes. This was the East India Company's paddle-steamer *Diana*, the first warship powered by steam to be sent on active service. When she had been launched at Kidderpore the year before, only two steam-ships – both of them tugs – had been in service with the Royal Navy. Traditional naval officers hated the idea of the new, noisy, dirty form of propulsion being developed; not only might it eventually lead to the obsolescence of their beautiful sailing ships but it would most certainly spoil the scrubbed decks in which they took such pride. But Marryat, like the other innovators Captain Lord Cochrane and Lieutenant Pocock, foresaw that they could be decisive when sails could not be used. One such theatre of war might well be the rivers of Burma, facing the King of Ava's huge war-canoes, which relied on muscle-powered paddles when there was no wind. The *Diana*'s wood-burning steam engine could command sixty horse-power, she drew only five feet of water and she could mount both light guns and Congreve's alarming rockets. Marryat had successfully insisted, against opposition, that she accompany the force.

At Port Cornwallis, in the Andaman Islands, officers pored over charts and the sketchy maps of the great Burmese rivers. The plan was to move up the estuaries of the Irrawaddy, take Rangoon and then, capturing the King of Ava's riverside fortresses, forge upstream and occupy his capital to the north near Mandalay. Morale was high, military bands played on deck and optimism prevailed. The expedition sailed at the beginning of May, the sunlit sails of the convoy forming an elegant setting for the new-fangled steamer, her tall, thin funnel pouring smoke and her twin paddle-wheels thrashing, as they steered for Burma.

On the 10th, they anchored within the sand-bar of the Rangoon river, one of the innumerable channels of the Irrawaddy delta.

Yet, as had become traditional in British military operations in the tropics, bungles and disasters lay ahead. The monsoon season had been chosen for the campaign in the belief that heavy rain would raise the levels of the rivers and enable the bigger ships to navigate farther upstream. The accompanying humidity had been overlooked and the soldiers would be expected to fight in their red serge coats and high, black shakos in the steaming jungle. Drinking water was an immediate problem and what there was was tainted, producing dysentery; Commodore Grant was taken ill, Marryat took over the naval command, shifting to the *Larne*, and made the collection and distribution of clean water from springs ashore his priority.

On the 11th the *Larne* began to lead the fleet up the river, first between the dark green of mangrove swamps and then flooded paddy-fields and clumps of jungle. The Bengali pilot ran the ship aground and the convoy had to wait for the next high tide to float her off; meanwhile, as darkness fell, beacons began to flare ashore in warning of their approach. Next morning, twenty miles from the sea, they rounded a bend and there, ahead, lay Rangoon; roofs of palm leaves clustered around the gilded spires of pagodas, all surrounded by little wooded, lumpy hills.

Not knowing what to expect, the expeditionary force prepared for an opposed landing. The *Larne* and *Liffey* beat to quarters and, cleared for action and with guns run out, sailed inshore. As they approached the sixteen-foot bamboo palisade along the waterfront, a sputter of musket-fire greeted them and both ships loosed a broadside. Then, the soldiers clambered aboard ships' boats and sat, shoulder to shoulder, their muskets between their knees; the seamen hauled at the oars and pulled for land. As the boats grounded on the beach, the infantry scrambled ashore, bayonets fixed, running between the bamboo stilts of flimsy wooden houses. But the town was deserted, except for stray dogs, scavenging pigs and fifteen European missionaries found locked in a warehouse. In twenty minutes, Campbell's soldiers had occupied Rangoon without a fight.

Once the troops were ashore, Marryat followed and found an unkempt town with a few brick buildings, its only distinction, an avenue lined with small pagodas, gold or whitewashed, leading to the biggest, the glittering Shwe Dagon. There, the bronze doors had already been forced and, within, soldiers had planted the British flag in the arms of the huge golden Buddha, gazing down at them with a mysterious little smile. Already the shrine had been commandeered as a billet for Highlanders by an assistant adjutant, Lieutenant Henry Havelock,* who dismissed the temple as, 'a haughty hill of devil-worship.'[2]

It had been an easy victory but, as night fell, the British felt uneasy. Rangoon offered none of the expected provender: fruit, vegetables and fish; the only stores found was a cellar filled with brandy and soon many soldiers were incapably drunk. The town was surrounded by savannahs of tall grass, swamps – from these arose the mist, believed to spread malaria, and clouds of mosquitoes, which, although they did not know it, actually did so – and thick jungle beyond; over all, the heavy, damp heat. Rations had to be unloaded from the transports and, at once, squabbling began between their skippers and the naval officers and between soldiers and sailors over the division of responsibility for the heavy work. At the back of all minds was the knowledge that the Burmese – 'Burmahs', as Marryat called them – who had fled from the stockade and vanished were still somewhere in the wall of greenery that surrounded them on three sides.

Nobody knew what to expect. Most thought that the Burmese would be something like Bengalis: delicately-built and fighters only when well-led, as, they liked to think, were their sepoys under British officers. Certainly, they did not expect the enemy to be well armed because the inaccuracy of the initial fusillade had, they discovered, been caused by the musket-shot being roughly hammered into balls and by the weakness of the gunpowder. They were soon to meet with the reality.

---

* The future Major-General Sir Henry Havelock, who defended Lucknow during the Indian Mutiny 1857.

After a few anxious days and nights at Rangoon, preparing perimeter defences, confidence was beginning to return. Then, after dark, the anchorage was lit by a sudden blaze and that instantly reminded Marryat of the Aix Roads. As he described it, blazing fireships, each of some forty large canoes, lashed together and loaded with jars filled with inflammables – 'they have wells of petroleum up the country',[3] Marryat explained – drifted down-river towards the British ships and 'blazed as high as our maintop, throwing out flames, heat and stink.'[4] Boats, guarding the roadstead, fended them away but the British now realised that conquest might not be so easy as expected.

Soon afterwards, the British first saw the Burmese war-canoes and Marryat, once he had overcome his surprise, was admiring. 'The Burmah war-boats are very splendid craft, pulling from eighty to one hundred oars; the Burmahs manage them very dextrously and will pull them from seven to eight miles an hour.'[5] This meant that they could nearly always out-run and out-manoeuvre the British warships, as they were soon to demonstrate. Their armament was variable: 'The gun mounted on the boat's bow is of little effect but their spears are really formidable. At a night attack upon some of our vessels ... I had evidence of the force with which they are thrown. The sides of the vessels were covered with them, sticking out like porcupines' quills and they entered the plank with such force that it required a very strong arm to pull them out. We lost some men to them; the effect of a hundred spears hurtling through the air at the same time was singularly appalling to our men, who were not accustomed to the sound, especially during the night ... Some of these spears were sixteen feet long with an iron head, sharp at both sides ...'[6]

It was only after these attacks, the capture of a few Burmese warriors and the first contacts with the population, that they could assess their enemy. 'The Burmahs are decidedly a brave nation', declared Marryat. 'They are peculiarly a warlike nation; indeed, they are fond of war.'[7] Their weaponry might be inadequate – two-handed swords, spears, home-made muskets, bullets and gunpowder and even wooden cannon bound with iron hoops and only capable of being fired two or three times – but the warriors were another matter. 'The Burmahs are a very powerful race, very muscular in their limbs ...', he noted. 'They are rather taller than Europeans. They have the high cheek bones of the tartar ... strong hair and beards and certainly would remind you of a cross between the Jew and the Tartar.'[8] He even repeated the theory that the Burmese were descended from a lost tribe of Israel. Although he described them as 'semi-barbarous', he admitted that he had never met an illiterate Burmese and that they were 'the most even-tempered race I ever met with ... They work very hard and with the greatest cheerfulness. They have a high respect for the English ... and the superiority of our warlike instruments, and our ships, was a subject of wonder ... They perceive how far they are behind us and are most anxious to improve. From this reason ... it was a pity we ever made war with the Burmahs ... for they have every quality necessary to become the first nation in the East.'[9]

As the smaller British craft began to patrol up the wide, smoothly swirling Irrawaddy, they saw what they had to face on their way to the King of Ava's capital, far to the north. The Burmese had built stockaded forts at strategic points on the banks, or at the confluence of rivers and creeks from which their war-canoes debouched with a flash and flurry of paddles. These would have to be taken. At first, it seemed that a few broadsides from the frigates would bring them down. This was tried and it failed for, as Marryat reported, 'Their stockades are usually built of thick teak timber, or rather squared trees, which are much too strong to be penetrated by other than battering cannon. Some of them are built of bamboos, running from a foot to two feet in diameter. These are equally strong with the peculiarity that, if you fire cannon at them, the bamboos yield, admit the shot, then close again.'[10]

So the forts would have to be taken by storm. Often the stockades were surrounded with ditches set with sharpened and poisonous bamboo stakes, a scratch from which could cause lock-jaw. There were several such forts within a day's march of Rangoon and these were attacked by columns of soldiers, dragging cannon through swamps and scrub and around paddy-fields. Sometimes they could be supported by ships' boats with guns mounted in the bows. In May, the principal base of the war-canoes at Pagoda Point, four miles from the capital, was attacked but no scaling-ladders had been provided and the infantry had to retreat into the jungle. Another, at Kemmendine, was attacked by three columns while the *Larne* provided covering fire; when, at last, the signal, 'Breach practicable' was run up her halyards and the troops burst through the palisade they found the fort deserted but for one old woman.

Whenever he could, Marryat led attacks such as one described in the log of the *Larne*: 'May 29. A party of 34 men under the Captain and 2nd lieutenant and midshipman went away in the Steam Boat on Service with a division of the Army. Fired a salute of guns being the anniversary of King Charles' restoration. Heavy rain. May 30. Captain and party returned, p.m.'[11] The *Diana*, puffing and thrashing her way ahead of the flotilla, towing becalmed sailing ships and striking fear into the Burmese, had proved her worth but only thanks to Marryat's practical skill in maintaining new-fangled machinery. She had been towing a frigate, when, as he reported, 'The *Diana* Steam vessel ... had been run down by a transport and her engine broken and thrown out of its level and the only engineer had fallen under the traversing beam and had undergone the amputation of his leg. I had re-paired the *Diana*, re-levelled her engine and now worked her myself, or she would have been rendered useless.'[12]

Sometimes his landing parties joined the assaults, cutlasses in hand, heaving each other over the palisades, goaded by both musket fire and the taunts of the Burmese. Particularly galling were those calling themselves 'The Invulnerables' who 'stood above the timbers of the stockade, dancing and capering as the boats advanced and continued their extravagance amidst a shower of bullets.'[13] As a talisman against shot, they had sewn precious stones under their skin and one of them – recognisable by the red jacket he wore over his loincloth – was nicknamed by the sailors '*Happy Jack*, from his capers which he used to cut ... for taking stockade after stockade, at every fresh attack there was Happy Jack to be seen capering and shouting as usual ... It was quite amusing to hear the men shout out with laughter, "By heavens, there's Happy Jack again." '[14]

Commodore Grant had sickened further and been evacuated to Penang, where he died in July. Marryat now officially assumed the naval command, but he, too, was sick with malaria. Indeed, the whole expeditionary force was sickening to the point of re-calling the disastrous campaigns of the eighteenth century when European armies in the tropics were almost wiped out by epidemics. By July, the ship's company of the *Larne* had had a hundred and seventy cases of cholera and dysentery, thirteen had died, fifty were currently ill and the convalescents were too feeble to work; only three officers and twelve men were fit for duty. To give them cooler air, Marryat took the ship down-river and out to sea for a fortnight and this helped recovery; but not for long.

On their return to Rangoon, Marryat himself led three more assaults: on an old Portuguese fort and a pagoda at Syriam, four miles east of the town; at Dala, just across the river, which cost seventy-six men killed and wounded; and up a creek, where thirty war-canoes were moored. The first attack was with drawn cutlasses; the second, a charge through 'remarkably stiff and thigh-deep' mud;[15] the third, to rescue a brig, which was found with her sides bristling with spears, ladders still hanging in her rigging and the netting, rigged to deter boarders, slashed through.

By early September, only about half the European soldiers and sailors of the force were still fit for duty and a third of the officers were dead. The crew of the *Larne* had been further weakened by scurvy and, as Marryat wrote to his brother Samuel, 'My head is so shattered with the fever ... that it swims at the least exertion and I am obliged to lay down my pen every four, or five, lines. I have also a touch of the liver.'[16] In November, he took his ship, manned by 'the remnants of a fine ship's company',[17] across the Bay of Bengal to recuperate and replenish at Calcutta.

After loading bread, flour, suet, raisins, sugar, tea, vinegar, lime juice and fresh water and resting his men, Marryat returned to war, anchoring off Rangoon on Christmas Eve. During his month's absence, much had happened. The British had cleared the coast and river banks around the town, its inhabitants had begun to return and its markets had begun trading again. The next move was the advance up-river to where the King of Ava was said to be concentrating his forces under its commander – named Bandoola – some thirty miles away.

General Campbell (as he now was) was aware of the risk of being outflanked and having his communications cut. So he planned three separate offensives: a riverine force would sail up the Irrawaddy to make a frontal attack; three columns, accompanied by himself, would advance overland; a third, amphibious force would move by sea to the mouth of the Bassein river – the most westerly of the mouths of the Irrawaddy – make its way nearly eighty miles up-river to take the town of Bassein and so cut off Bandoola's retreat. Captain Marryat was to command the latter expedition with a Major Sale leading the soldiery.

Embarking some eight hundred troops in the *Larne*, two East India Company ships and three transports, they sailed on 19 February 1825. The sea passage, across the width of the Irrawaddy delta, was rough but, once in the river, all went smoothly; the Burmese had been taken by surprise and the few stockades they passed were seldom defended. 'Our progress was therefore easy,' reported Marryat. 'After a few broadsides, we landed and spiked the guns and then, with a fair wind, ran about seventy miles up one of the most picturesque rivers I was ever in.'[18] Sometimes there were brisk little actions and sometimes the ships ran aground but were refloated without difficulty.

Then the wind began blowing down-river and the ships had to be warped upstream while the commander of the land force, Major Sale 'grumbled ... because there was no fighting. He grumbled when we passed the stockades at the entrance of the river because they were not manned; and he grumbled at every dismantled stockade that we passed. But there was no pleasing Sale; if he was in a hard action and not wounded, he grumbled; if he received a slight wound, he grumbled because it was not a severe one; if a severe one, he grumbled because he was not able to fight the next day. He had been nearly cut to pieces in many actions, but he was not content ... But notwithstanding this mania for being carved, he was an excellent and judicious officer.'[19] The major favoured Indian troops, although Marryat noted that the enemy fought against them with more confidence than against the British. During the advance, a strong force of sepoys was cut off and assumed to have been killed, or captured; later the British found them dead, strung by the feet, naked, from trees and dreadfully mutilated. All were warned against surrendering after the corpse of a British sailor, also mutilated, was found floating down the river.

When they reached Bassein, they found the town burning and undefended: 'Here again, the Major was disappointed.'[20] Band-oola's main force – ten thousand warriors, supported by artillery and war-elephants, it was reported – waited at the huge fortress of three interlocking stockades at Danubyo. Although Sale's force numbered less than a thousand, he attacked with his British troops. They took the first stockade and were then cut off by Burmese from the second and slaughtered, the survivors retreating to the river, leaving more than two hundred dead. Next day, reported Marryat, 'their bodies, crucified on rafts, were floated down among the English boats by the triumphant Bandoola' after 'the only defeat by the white troops during the whole war.'[21] Then Campbell's overland columns reached Danubyo and both forces launched a co-ordinated assault. 'After some hard fighting, in which elephants played their part, the troops gained possession,' Marryat wrote, 'and Bandoola having been killed by a shell, the Burmahs fled.'[22]

Despite the victory, the British were isolated, their communications by the Bassein and Irrawaddy rivers now vulnerable to Burmese forces that had not yet been committed. Marryat's task was now a form of rough diplomacy. One Burmese chief was brought on board the *Larne* and ordered to tell Marryat where he had concealed his artillery; when he refused he was told he was to be beheaded; marines were drawn up and the chief made to kneel before a pile of sand; still he refused. 'However', remarked Marryat, 'as it is not the custom to cut off people's heads on the quarterdeck of His Majesty's ships, we very magnanimously reprieved him.'[23]

On another occasion, Marryat was invited to a Burmese entertainment ashore at Naputah. Although seeming to be unarmed, but fearing treachery, the officers carried pistols and the accompanying marines left their muskets on board but carried bayonets inside their trouser-legs. They sat in 'a sort of covered circus, brilliantly lit up with oil in coconut shells' when 'about twenty men struck up a very barbarous kind of music, in which the bells and drums made the most noise. After a few minutes of discordant sound, the play began ... The dialogue was constantly interrupted by an actor, who appeared to be ... the Jack Pudding of the piece, and several of his jokes were not very delicate.'[24] After the performance, the guests were given pickled tea to eat but 'we could not swallow it, so it remained like a quid of tobacco in our cheeks until we had an opportunity of getting rid of it.'[25] The chief's daughter, who did not attend the performance, was curious about the foreigners and asked for one to be sent to her hut. 'My clerk was the favoured party,' noted Marryat. 'She examined him very closely, pulled his dress about, made him bare his legs to see how white they were and then dismissed him. The clerk reported her as very handsome and quite as white as he was.' Finally they departed and 'the chief walked with us down to the boats and we were not sorry to find ourselves on board again; for the population was much more numerous than we had imagined and, had any treachery been attempted, we must have fallen a sacrifice.'[26]

Marryat's charm and humour was effective. At one riverside town, the chief was won over by being presented with a little brass cannon and he responded by giving the captain – to his delight – the title of 'Great War Dog'. Marryat was particularly fond of children and one of the chiefs, who submitted at Bassein, was accompanied by his eight-year-old daughter. 'I generally made her little presents,' he said, 'She became very much attached to me but she never appeared without a little wax candle' – a symbol of submission – 'which she dropped at my feet before she threw herself into my lap.'[27]

Indeed, so successful was the diplomacy combined with shows of force, that several chiefs offered their services against others, who had not submitted and Marryat found himself commanding eight war-canoes as well as his sloops and a steamer. Finding themselves under attack by an Anglo-Burmese force with Burmese warriors firing on their stockades with British muskets from the warships' rigging, they, too, surrendered. Marryat had evacuated Sale's surviving troops and, early in April, returned to Rangoon. There, Marryat transferred into the 26-gun *Tees*, classed as what the lower deck called a 'jackass frigate', which should entitle him to immediate promotion to post-captain, although this would have to await confirmation from London. That would be the ultimate hurdle in his career for, once on the list of post-captains, his advancement to the highest ranks in the Royal Navy would – subject to his good behaviour – be automatic, its speed governed by the death, or resignation of his superiors.

When orders reached Marryat to return to Madras, he recorded some mixed feelings, despite severe casualties from battle and disease and the miseries of the climate. While he found the King and chieftains of Burma 'despotic, cruel and treacherous ... the people are neither ... on the contrary ... it is singular to find ... a people so active, so laborious, so enterprising as the Burmahs. The English seamen are particularly partial to them and declared they were "the best set of chaps they had ever fallen in with".'[28] Several Burmese had come to live on board, the favourite being a three-year-old boy, they nicknamed 'Billy Bamboo', who could speak English 'and was quite as amusing as a monkey';[29] there was real grief when he suddenly sickened and died in the unhealthy confines of the mess-decks.

On 16 May 1825, the *Tees* sailed, Marryat leaving General Campbell and his own successor to begin the main advance up the Irrawaddy to the capital of the King of Ava*.

Anchoring off Madras, Marryat had Kate and the six-year-old William brought out to his ship in a surf-boat, the child 'dressed in imitation of a man-of-war's man ... a light, narrow-brimmed straw hat on his head.'[30] They set sail for England and shortly before the end of the year, they saw the hills of Dorset on the port bow.

---

* The King did not submit until February 1826, when he agreed to abandon his claims to Assam, pay indemnity and grant teak logging concessions to the East India Company. Even so, it was not until the Second Burma War in 1852 that the country was taken under British rule.

CHAPTER SEVEN

A New Region of Fiction

C aptain Marryat paid off the *Tees* on 11 January 1826, and came ashore to face a conflict of emotion. His father, the domineering but supportive Joseph Marryat, had died of a stroke on 12 January 1824, leaving him a handsome share of a bequest to his children of £250,000 (more than £14 million in 2000). Soon afterwards, he inherited a share of another fortune from his uncle, Samuel, a lawyer, who had left £180,000 (about £10 million). He himself had been appointed a Companion of the Bath for his services in Burma, the third-ranking honour in the order after the Knight and Commander and so no great distinction. He had been promoted to the rank of post-captain, which should ensure his automatic rise through the higher ranks, but only after delays during which twenty-six were promoted over his head.*

There had been a third bereavement. One night, months earlier, when Marryat had been lying, sleepless on his bunk in the *Larne*, his brother, also named Samuel, who was close to him, seemed to enter the cabin and say, 'Fred, I am come to tell you that I am dead.'[1] So vivid was this vision that Marryat noted the time and date; now he heard that Samuel had indeed died at that very time. More grievous than these losses, and the professional disappointment, was the illness of little William. As was so usual in childhood illness – his was fever, accompanied by intense thirst – there seemed little hope of recovery and his mother began telling him stories about the delights that awaited him in heaven. William interrupted her with the plaintive protest, 'Mother, I don't want to go there. I want some beer!' A few days

---

* His commission as post-captain was dated 25 July 1825.

later, he was dead. Marryat concentrated his hopes on their surviving children, two boys and a girl.

He was now well-to-do and, with his charm, looks and amusing London friends, could, at the age of thirty-five, set himself up as a man-about-town. The house in Great George Street had been given up on the death of his father and he now took a lease of another large house at an even grander address, 5 Cleveland Row, opposite St James's Palace. They also stayed at Brighton, which Kate enjoyed and where she had been living during their courtship. King George IV was often there at his grandiose, oriental pastiche, the Royal Pavilion, and the Marryats were frequent guests at soirées, or 'swarries', where he was a popular guest from his anecdotes, jokes and tales from Burma.

Soon after his return he lent his Burmese trophies and curios for an exhibition at the Royal Asiatic Society, the most spectacular exhibit being a golden statue of the King of Ava set with rubies. Friends visiting his mother's house at Wimbledon, where he sometimes stayed, were shown jewels cut from the bodies of The Invulnerables – but not Happy Jack, who seemed to have survived – and he was as prodigal as the traditional sailor with his generosity in giving such valuable souvenirs to friends. The most unusual gift was that of an eight-year-old Burmese boy, whom he had brought home in his ship; said to be a chieftain's son, Sofar was presented to the King's brother and sixth son of King George III, the Duke of Sussex, as a page and was soon to be seen at Kensington Palace and Windsor Castle, where he was known as Mr Blackman.

The Duke would be a useful friend. A portly dandy of fifty-three, he had literary tastes and liberal views, supporting the abolition of slavery. He might not be able to promote Marryat's naval career directly but he could mention his name to his brother, the Duke of Clarence, who was Lord High Admiral, and could ease the couple's progress into smart society. He was well-read and mildly eccentric, one of his smaller pleasures being the synchronisation of all the chiming clocks in the house. One visitor described meeting him for breakfast at nine when 'As the clock struck that hour, its tones were responded to by a host of loud-sounding timepieces, to be found in every nook and corner of the Duke's suite of apartments. Some of them played martial tunes, others the national anthem. This bell-metal chorus was half-drowned by the yapping of a pack of little dogs, which came scampering down the stairs. At the same moment would appear the Duke's page, Mr. Blackman ... whose diminutive form set off to advantage the truly imposing presence of the royal master, whom he preceded.'[2]

Marryat's new friend brought him another change in his life by inviting him to become a gentleman-in-waiting, an appointment described as 'light and agreeable' as it involved little more than occasional attendance on the Duke at social functions. There was a consequent change of scene, too, when the Duke offered him a lease of Sussex House,* a fine suburban house in a large garden, which would be convenient for appearances at both Kensington Palace and Windsor Castle. So Marryat let his house in Cleveland Row – at an annual rent of £200 – to one of his bohemian friends, Theodore Hook, a novelist, journalist and wit, with whom he attended convivial parties, where the Duke would have been out of place.

A man of his means could afford more than one residence and, since Kate loved Brighton and the sea air would be good for the children, he took a house there, too, but found little to do during the days but look out of the window at terraces of stucco-fronted houses and the sea beyond. So Captain Marryat began to write a novel. When commanding the *Beaver* he had whiled away lonely hours in the captain's cabin by planning stories, roughing out the plots and conjuring characters from his own memory. Now it was all coming together. His central character would be a young naval officer, such as he himself had been, having the same initials, being named Frank Mildmay. For his adventures at sea, he would draw upon his own up to the year 1821, beginning with Cochrane and continuing with the gallery of good, bad and indifferent captains. As he began to write his hero began to assume a life of his own and, increasingly, seemed to be a hard, vengeful

---

* Standing on the east side of what is now Fulham Palace Road.

young man, as well as a philanderer. Marryat did not see himself like that but he had been brought up in the rough nursery of a frigate's gunroom, where hardness was a necessity to survival, bullies had to be resisted and humiliations survived through cunning and resilience. So he wrote what came into his imagination and let his own adventures tumble on to the pages in his tiny, almost unreadable, handwriting. Perhaps the self-indulgence of Brighton and the Royal Pavilion spurred him to tell truthful tales of the sea and spurn the sentimentality that drenched the comfortable landsman's vision of Jolly Jack Tar. While admitting that his descriptions of seafaring and fighting were accurate accounts of his own experiences, he denied that Mildmay was a self-portrait, although he admitted in the novel that 'we had sowed our wild oats; we had paid off those who had ill-treated us.'[3]

In November 1828, before he had written the last chapter of his book, he was told by the Admiralty that he had been chosen for another command, albeit a modest one. His ship was to be another 'jackass frigate', the *Ariadne*, of 28 guns, currently lying at Plymouth. Packing his manuscript, he travelled to Devon, taking his family with him. One of his sons, the ten-year-old Frederick, was to sail with him as 'Boy, Second Class', with the prospect of early promotion to 'Volunteer, First Class'. Another son, Frank, aged three, was dressed in a sailor suit to be presented to the port admiral, who patted his head and declared, 'Well, you're a fine little fellow.' In style worthy of his father, Frank replied, 'And you're a fine old cock, too'![4]

Whatever Marryat's expectations of his first command as a post-captain may have been, the reality was disappointing. The *Ariadne* herself was, although a small ship, adequate for peacetime when frigates and ships of the line were relatively few; true he had become a fashionable captain and the Duke of Sussex had asked him to take a young friend, the Honourable Tom Keppel, to sea as a supernumerary midshipman. But there were distractions and disadvantages. Now that he was a rich, married man, moving in the smart circles of London and Brighton and was making new literary and artistic friends, the cramped quarters of the frigate and the company of the usual mixed collection of officers were less appealing. His ship's company had a gang of troublemakers: he managed to get rid of his cook but both the carpenter and the master-at-arms seemed likely to cause problems. Such adventures as he had shared with Lord Cochrane could not, of course, be expected in peacetime.

There was satisfaction, however, in completing his first novel, *The Naval Officer, or Adventures in the Life of Frank Mildmay*. It was to be published anonymously in three volumes, in March 1829, by Henry Colburn, who had a reputation for picking fiction that would satisfy popular demand for realistic stories of the Great War, and paid the author a fee of £400. It told an exciting story but it left a sour taste since the hero was so violent and amoral a young man, who reaped unearned rewards. Other characters were as sharply drawn and it seemed probable that senior officers would identify themselves, particularly when the secret of its authorship finally emerged; then it would not help Marryat's professional prospects.

The first tasks given to the *Ariadne* were uninspiring. When she sailed on 6 June 1829, her captain's instructions were to locate and survey a dangerous, submerged rock off the west coast of Ireland. Arriving at the position where the hazard had been reported, they found nothing and Marryat complained of the waste of time searching for 'a rock in the Atlantic, which never existed except in the terrified, or intoxicated, noddle of some master of a merchant vessel.'[5] But he had made use of some of the six-week cruise to begin another novel, describing the scene; 'I am seated in the after cabin of a vessel endowed with as liberal a share of motion as any in His Majesty's service; whilst I write, I am holding on by the table, my legs entwined in the lashings underneath, and I can barely manage to keep my position before my manuscript. The sea is high, the gale fresh, the sky dirty ... I have just been summoned from my task in consequence of one of the battens, which secured my little library, having given way to the immoderate weight of learning that pressed upon it.'[6] This book was also to be about the sea, drawing upon the author's own experience. It began with an execution for mutiny and a flogging round the fleet and told the story of the mutineer's child and the fight to claim his inheritance. Again the reader was to be excited by action at sea, then surprised by the climax, which, despite the promise of a happy ending, was tragic. It was to be called *The King's Own*.

In August, orders were received for a diplomatic mission. Revolution had broken out in Portugal and its islands in the Atlantic and Marryat was ordered to the Azores to report on the current situation. There were two claimants to sovereignty in Lisbon: the seven-year-old heiress to the throne, Donna Maria, and the regent, Don Miguel, the latter having sent the former into exile and, with the support of the military, been crowned; however, some of the islands had proclaimed the queen. Marryat was quick to come to the conclusion that 'the Portuguese ... are perfectly indifferent as to the point whether Don Miguel, or Donna Maria are seated on the throne It is the Constitution which they require and I do not think that Portugal will ever be in a settled state until it is obtained. The torch of Liberty has been lighted and, although it may be smothered for a time, the flame will reappear.'[7]

His weary appraisal of foreign politics was blotted out for eight days by one of the tremendous storms that were to mark his memory. It struck the ship eleven miles south-east of Madeira, tearing her sails from the yards and throwing her on her beam ends. As Midshipman Keppel recalled, 'all hands had given themselves up for lost ... they kicked off their shoes and stockings and rushed into the rigging, there to await the expected catastrophe.'[8]

Weathering the storm and bound for Madeira, the *Ariadne* called at the most southerly of the Azores and there, beached in a little bay, lay an American schooner, the *Samuel Smith*. She was an elegant little ship of a hundred and eighty tons, built of oak and cedar, with raked masts and hermaphrodite rig – a square-rigged foremast and a square sail on her main mast above a schooner's gaff sail and he was 'surprised at the beauty of her model'[9] and fell in love with her. She had struck a wreck and leaked so badly that she had had to be run aground. Now, as there were no carpenters on the island, she could not be repaired and was to be sold. Marryat surveyed the wreck with his first lieutenant and both his own carpenters and found the damage relatively slight and easily repairable. He knew that the Admiralty often bought such craft to act as tenders and that this ship was so well built that she might well be copied in British shipyards; even if she was resold at home port, a profit would be made. There was no time to seek authority from the Admiralty, so he decided to buy her for a mere £240.

By working on her all day and at night by torchlight, the schooner was quickly made seaworthy, floated over the reef and anchored near the *Ariadne*. She was to be sailed home directly, so there was no shortage of volunteers for the prize crew of eleven and Marryat ensured that the troublesome carpenter was amongst them. She was provisioned for five weeks but, before she could load ballast, or Marryat could give her captain his orders and the ship's documentation, a gale blew. The schooner dragged her anchor into deep water and 'the weather then boisterous, blowing hard',[10] as Marryat put it, had to put out to sea. Next day, she reappeared but wind and tide were contrary and she could not reach the anchorage and again headed out into the stormy sea. 'From that time,' reported Marryat to the Admiralty, she 'has never been seen, nor heard of.'[11]

What had happened to the *Samuel Smith*? Had she simply capsized or foundered in the storm? The *Ariadne* searched for her in vain and, as Marryat reported, 'no wreck has appeared, which, as she was "flying light" ... would in all probability have been the case.'[12] There was another possibility that came to mind when she never returned to a British port. The carpenter had been on board and captains usually made sure that any persistent miscreants be drafted into prize crews. 'It is impossible for me to state either where the schooner went down, or if she went down at all,' he told the Admiralty. 'There have been various reports since. One was that she was seen off one of the West Indian islands and subsequently off the African coast as a pirate, or a slaver.'[13]

That was not the end of it. The Admiralty demanded to know why Marryat had bought the schooner without authority and then manned her from his own ship's company. The Navy Board held an enquiry and questioned his officers, deciding that he had not been justified in buying her without authority, nor in risking the lives of her crew, for which he would be held responsible. What was particularly galling was that if the Admiralty had repudiated his purchase and the ship had not been lost, he himself could have sold her at a profit. At Plymouth, whither the *Ariadne* had returned, the bereaved families demanded compensation, followed Marryat in the streets, shouting abuse and even attacked his servant. He himself was outraged at what he saw as an injustice: he had taken a sensible initiative in buying the ship on behalf of the Navy and the fact that she had, presumably, been lost at sea was a familiar risk of the service.

This came on top of a series of grievances. His promotion to post-captain had been a year late. He considered the reward for his command in the Burma campaign to have been tardy. He knew his code of signals had benefited the Navy but his suggestions for the reform of impressment had aroused what he thought undue hostility at the Admiralty. Also, his caricatures and witticisms had offended the higher ranks. In peacetime, his prospects would be poor, so, he wondered, was this the moment to retire?

Ashore, there was his own fortune, his family, a grand suburban house, a wide circle of amusing friends and a possible career as a novelist for, when homeward-bound and three days out from Plymouth, he had completed *The King's Own*. 'I remember ... I was as happy as a pedestrian who has accomplished his thousand miles in a thousand hours,' he remembered. 'What could I do? Why, I could dance; so I sprang from my chair and, singing the tune, commenced a quadrille movement.'[14]

Because of the enquiry into the purchase and loss of the *Samuel Smith*, Marryat had to remain in London and hand over the command of the *Ariadne* to a temporary captain. There was plenty to occupy him ashore, notably the publication of his second novel on 15 April 1830. It was well received and he was delighted by a letter from the American author and traveller Washington Irving, who told him, 'You have a glorious field before you and one in which you cannot have many competitors, as so very few unite the author to the sailor. I think the chivalry of the ocean quite a new region of fiction and romance and, to my taste, one of the most captivating that could be explored.'[15] So inspired, he planned to write not only more novels – one about seafaring with the East India Company, to be called *Newton Forster* and a much longer naval story, *Peter Simple* – but also naval biography, starting with a life of Nelson to be followed by Collingwood.

Despite this new horizon, Marryat did not intend to rush into retirement from the Navy. So when the Admiralty enquiry concluded in the autumn, he returned to Plymouth to resume command of the *Ariadne*. He was restless and torn between the two ambitions, writing to Colbourn on 28 September, 'I am again ready for sea and waiting for orders and I shall be very glad to receive them as I am so unsettled at present that I cannot do much. When once I am completely miserable, i.e. at sea, I shall work hard that I may forget my unfortunate situation. I have made a few memorandums for the Aera of Nelson but have not, as yet, commenced serious operations, indeed I am puzzled between the variety of works, which I have commenced, upon which to finish. I therefore go adding up matter for *Peter Simple* one day, for the present work, which I intend to call *Newton Forster* and for the biography before mentioned ... I have not the least idea where I am going, but I hope to Lisbon, or that quarter – as, when I come back, I shall resign the command and come on shore, probably for an indefinite period and then I shall get on a little faster.'[16]

A week later, he was writing to the port admiral, asking leave to resign his command temporarily because, he explained, 'Since rejoining my ship, I find that in consequence of the death of both my father's executors I am likely to sustain a great loss of property if I do not remain in England to attend to my interests.' When his ship's company heard of this so many of them applied for discharge that the Admiral noted, 'My opinion is that the crew of the *Ariadne* have been actuated to the above state of insubordination from their preference to Captain Marryat.'[17]

Soon afterwards Marryat heard that his son Frederick had been confirmed in the rate of first class volunteer and so was on the way to becoming a naval officer himself. Finally on 11 November 1830, Marryat wrote formally to the Secretary of the Admiralty, 'I beg you will be pleased to solicit the Right Honourable Lords Commissioners of the Admiralty to direct the insertion of my name in the Half Pay List.'[18] For the time being, at least, his naval career was over.

There was another reason for wanting to be ashore. In London one night, over a bottle of champagne and, perhaps, either in tipsy bravado, or in a gamble, with a rich builder and architect, Alexander Copland, he had exchanged the handsome Sussex House, for a farm of a thousand acres on the coast of Norfolk. That he did not seem to regret this suggests the seafarer longing to put down roots; or, knowing himself to be a spendthrift, he decided to invest in land and live more modestly in London; or it may have been that he simply sought some tranquillity. Whatever the reason, this, too, marked 1830 as the watershed of Marryat's life.

He visited his new domain at the village of Langham as soon as he could. It meant a journey of some hundred and thirty miles, taking two days by carriage, or coach, via Cambridge, Norwich, the market town of Holt and then five miles of lanes to Langham. Alexander Copland had bought the estate from the second Marquess Townshend, father of Marryat's former captain, in 1810 and built there a charming *cottage ornée* in the style of a house designed for King George IV at Windsor with a thatched roof, leaded windows and tall, mock-Tudor chimney-stacks. Copland was both rich – he had made his fortune building barracks during the Great War – and restless; he had already built himself a grand house, Gunnersbury Park, but that had been inconveniently far to the west of London and he was now moving to Sussex House. He had also built Manor Cottage as a rural retreat, supported by the income from two farms, which he let. The snag was its distance from London and the poor communications, which, in winter, were sometimes quicker by sea than by road.

When Marryat finally arrived, he was enchanted. The house stood on a low ridge two miles from the coast and three from the open sea beyond Morston salt-marshes and the sand-dunes of Blakeney Point. It was sheltered by a belt of trees, surrounded by gardens and woodland – 'pleasure grounds, shrubberies and plantations'[19] – and some seven hundred acres of farmland, with coach-houses, barns and cottages nearby; from the house, his land stretched half a mile to the village of Langham and its fourteenth century church. Despite its mock-cottage appearance, it was a roomy house with handsome reception rooms opening on to a terrace, four large bedrooms upstairs and four more for the children and guests. From the windows could be seen the sea to the north and, to the south, across the shallow valley of the little Stiffkey river, the billowing treetops along the ridge beyond. He determined to make this his home, staying at his mother's house at Wimbledon when visiting London.

Marryat's ambitions were confused. The authorship of his first two novels had been anonymous but there was the possibility of making a name in writing, or even journalism; he had been dabbling in the life of a courtier, but found this unsatisfying; he did not rule out a return to the Navy, if prospects again seemed bright; or, he could settle for the life of a country gentleman. He had introductions to the landowning Norfolk families from his old commanding officer Captain Lord James Townshend, who now lived ten miles to the south at Bintree. Lord James's grandfather had been Lord Lieutenant of Norfolk and one of his successors was Lord Wodehouse, who invited Marryat to become his deputy and a magistrate and introduced him to Freemasonry. Marryat enjoyed such company and their shooting parties but their outlook seemed limited by the East Anglian horizon, wide as that was.

There was another reason for the move to Norfolk. Marryat had resigned from the Duke of Sussex's household. At first it had seemed exciting, offering the entrée to both royal circles and fashionable society. It mostly involved sitting at the royal table and, realising that 'the smiles of princes are by nature evanescent,'[20] he recognised the reality of the self-indulgent Hanoverian court. He knew that an officer who reached the rank of post-captain had established either his 'family connections, or personal merit', or both. But he was aware that naval officers, who owed far less to social position and private means than did army officers, seldom blended with the Hanoverian households. 'One cannot touch pitch without tar,' he mused, 'but there is a moral pitch, the meanness, the dishonesty and servility of a Court with which, I trust, our noble service will never be contaminated.'[21]

This left Marryat with the view that English society consisted of 'froth at the top, dregs at the bottom and in the middle, excellent.'[22] By making the move to Norfolk his reason for resignation, he could avoid offence, notably to King William IV, himself a former naval officer and Lord High Admiral, who had come to the throne in June 1830, and whose patronage might prove useful.

But country life was not what he had hoped. He let the two farms and so was free to lead the life of a country gentleman. Yet amusing company was scarce and what there was widely scattered. He invited friends to stay, but they were daunted by the prospect of the journey from London. Washington Irving, who worked part-time as an American diplomat when on his travels, replied to such an invitation, 'I again repeat I shall be delighted to pay you a visit at your new place, not only from the description you give me of it, which has something wild and engaging, but also from the strong inclination I feel to be on sociable and intimate terms with you;'[23] he later stressed that he would be happy to accept an invitation to visit the Marryats when they were at Wimbledon. His was the sort of company Marryat craved: amusing, well-travelled men of the world; writers, artists and wits, all ready for conviviality and within a mile or two in some comfortable salon, assembly rooms or in one of the new clubs that were opening in London; it had become clear that Langham was far too remote.

It was not only sophisticated conversation that he missed but politics, which, in Norfolk, revolved around the merits of the Whig and Tory landowners. 'I have buried myself in the country,' he wrote in a journal he had begun to write, 'but it has all been in vain ... The farmyard with its noisy occupants, what was it but the reality so well imitated by members of the Lower House, who would drown argument in discord? I thought I was in the lobby at the close of a long debate. Every tenth field, every tenth furrow (I could not help counting), every tenth animal and every tenth step reminded me of the Irish tithes; and when I saw a hawk swoop over a chicken, I thought of the Appropriation Bill – so I left the country.'[24]

Kate Marryat enjoyed the country even less than her husband. She could not join the shooting parties and such social gatherings as there were involved long, jolting journeys along muddy, or dusty lanes. She found the Norfolk servants difficult to manage and a manservant had to be dismissed for being rude to her. The remote village did not seem the ideal place to bring up children and mostly she had only her husband for company. They did not seem a particularly well-matched pair: she was puritanical and sharply critical; his jollity was combined with a violent temper and his humour was occasionally touched with coarseness and cruelty. Beneath the charming, well-to-do gentleman still lurked a spark of the boy determined to survive the ordeals of seafaring and war.

At first, Marryat just visited London to see friends and his publisher. He was writing a new novel about naval life, *Peter Simple*, which, like *Newton Forster*, would be published under his name. It would be a long book and less autobiographical than *Frank Mildmay*. Instead, he would conjure up the heroes, villains and eccentrics he had known at sea, introducing them to a readership that had regarded seafarers as a curious but fascinating race apart. Both Lord Cochrane and Captain Taylor inspired characters in the story but the most compelling were those drawn from life amongst those that most readers would never have met ashore.

One such was William Chucks, the boatswain with pretensions to gentility and so known as 'Gentleman Chucks', 'who held his head up and strutted as he walked ... He declared "that an officer should look like an officer and *comport* himself accordingly." ... He wore rings on his great fingers and a large frill to his bosom, which stuck out like the back fin of a perch and the collar of his shirt was always pulled up to a level with his cheek bones. He never appeared on deck without his "persuader", which was three rattans twisted into one, like a cable; sometimes he called it his ... Trio Juncto in Uno.' Sighting a miscreant, Mr Chucks then said, 'Allow me to observe, my dear man, in the most delicate way in the world, that you are spilling that tar upon the deck – a deck, sir, if I may venture to make the observation, I had the duty of seeing holystoned this morning. You understand me, sir, you have defiled His Majesty's forecastle. I must do my duty, sir, if you neglect yours; so take that – and that – and that – (thrashing the man with his rattan) – you d ---- d hay-making son of a sea-cook. Do it again, d ---- d your eyes, and I'll cut your liver out.'[25]

To Midshipman Simple, he explains, 'I think coolness is the great character-stick of a gentleman. In the service, Mr Simple, one is obliged to appear angry without indulging the sentiment. I can assure you that I never lose my temper, even when I use my rattan.' 'Why then, Mr Chucks, do you swear so much at the men? Surely that is not gentlemanly?' 'Most certainly not, sir. But I must defend myself by observing the very artificial state in which we live on a man-of-war. Necessity, my dear Mr Simple, has no law. You must observe how gently I always commence when I have to find fault. I do that to prove my gentility.'*[26]

On the surface of his life, Marryat seemed effortlessly proving his gentility. But, beneath, there still simmered the ambitious, hard-edged, restless man, whose shadow had been Frank Mildmay, straining his eyes and imagination beyond the horizons of Norfolk farmland and the sea.

---

* The original Boatswain Chucks seems to have enjoyed a long post-war career as he was known to Commander Charles Pocock (1829–99), who joined the Navy in 1840. The latter's son, Roger, himself a writer and traveller, wrote many years later, 'Read all Marryat's books, the best ever written about the Navy in sail. One character, Boatswain Chucks, my father knew well as a shipmate. The books are roaring fun.'

CHAPTER EIGHT

A *Tumult of Applause and Disapprobation*

L
ess than two years after acquiring the Langham estate, Marryat had let the Manor Cottage as well as the farms and returned to London. Taking a house, 38 St James's Place, off St James's Street, he plunged into the metropolitan life he had missed so much. An instinctive club-man, he mingled with senior officers at the United Service Club in Waterloo Place and with the literati at the Garrick Club, which opened in 1831 with the Duke of Sussex as its patron, in King Street, near Covent Garden.

Captain Marryat's only involvement with business was through *The Metropolitan*, subtitled 'The Monthly Journal of Literature, Science and the Fine Arts', which had run his novels as serials before publication, with *Newton Forster* about to appear. Its editor was Thomas Campbell, a popular poet and the author of *Ye Mariners of England*; its proprietor was named Cochrane. The more he saw of these two the more Marryat was beguiled by magazine journalism and the less confidence he had in their conduct of it. He put some of his own money into the publishing company and became increasingly involved in editorial policy. As the inefficiency and insolvency of the magazine increased, so he became more involved, finally, at the end of 1832, himself taking over as editor – on an annual salary of £400, rising to £600 – and then as proprietor.

In 1819, *The Naval Chronicle*, every sea-officer's favourite reading, had closed after twenty years and Marryat now thought of making *The Metropolitan* its successor. There were other former naval officers who were supplementing their half-pay by writing and he knew most of them: Captain Walter Glascock, who had written *Sailors and Saints* and *Tales of a Tar*; Captain Frederick Chamier, who was writing *Ben Brace* and had also invested in *The Metropolitan*; Captain Basil Hall, who wrote travel books; and Lieutenant the Honourable Edward Howard, whom Marryat was advising on his novel *Rattlin the Reefer*.

The idea did not materialise but the magazine continued, changing its name to *The Metropolitan Magazine* and he engaged Howard as assistant editor. Related to two dukes and two earls, Howard remained essentially a naval officer* and his editor treated him as such; he regarding Marryat as his captain. Marryat's letters to Howard are rough, bluff but affectionate, just as a captain might reprimand but encourage a junior officer. 'The pride that apes humility is to me delightful', he wrote about a humorous article of Howard's. 'I am very fond of touching people up in the *raw*. Now, listen to me. You say you chuckled over your own performance. I don't doubt it ... Your error is *straining to be very witty*. However, you improve fast and some day or another (about 90 or 95) you will write passably well ... I know you will d---n me in your heart for my overbearing but I don't mind that. People have a right to scream under punishment.'[1] Sometimes the editor's jocularity verged on the bullying, as when he added to some instructions, 'Mind you don't forget, or I'll thump you when I meet you.'[2]

Since retiring from the sea, Marryat had shown that he could adapt superficially to various social roles: from naval officer to man-about-town, paterfamilias, novelist, or country gentleman. When his practicality, charm and humour proved unable, or inappropriate, he could, like 'Gentleman Chucks', become harsh, even violent and the fuse of his temper was short. Like many who have overcome fear and taken initiative under stress, Marryat was undaunted by any person, or circumstance. There was sometimes a coarse edge to his humour, too, as when he wrote a letter about 'the most remarkable circumstance in the

---

* His naval career was to continue and he died an admiral in 1874, having also been a Liberal Member of Parliament and becoming a peer himself.

Great expectations: leaving home for the first time. Marryat's self-caricature, later engraved by George Cruikshank.

Harsh reality: introduction to his future home in the gunroom of his first ship; also engraved for the 'Midshipman Blockhead' series.

At war: boarding and 'cutting out' an enemy ship; a hitherto unpublished drawing by Marryat.

At peace: the midshipman 'mastheaded' – sent aloft for many hours – as a punishment, drawn by Marryat from memory.

The timid admiral: Lord Gambier, who failed to destroy the French fleet off Rochefort.

The bold captain: Lord Cochrane, who presented Gambier with the opportunity to do so.

The opportunity taken and missed: Lord Cochrane in the *Impérieuse* attacks the stranded French ships off Rochefort, while Lord Gambier holds back his main fleet.

Best behaviour: naval officers enjoying a 'dignity ball' in the West Indies; drawn by Marryat's friend R W Buss as an illustration for *Peter Simple*.

Private practice: naval officers drinking in their ship's wardroom; drawn by Marryat.

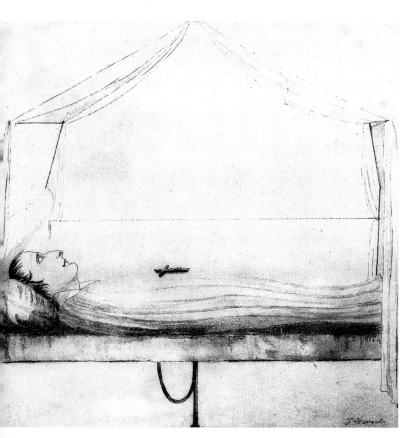

The end of the great war-maker: Napoleon on his death bed, drawn at the time by Captain Marryat at Longwood on St Helena. The beginnings of peace, below: unemployed naval officers in waiting-room at the Admiralty, engraved by George Cruikshank after a drawing by Marryat, showing himself leaning against the wa on the left.

War in Burma, opposite, top: the steam gunboat *Diana* with the squadron attacking the for at Dala on the Rangoon river; engraved after a drawing by L Joseph Moore of the 89th. Regiment. Amphibious warfar below: British troops and the squadron's boats attacking Burmese war canoes and the fortress of Danubyo; engraved after a drawing by Marryat.

Marryat's maternal homeland: the City Hall in New York as it looked at the time of his tour of the United States.

The new locomotion: a train passing Little Falls in the Mohawk Valley.

Rebellion in Canada: the blazing American steamer *Caroline* plunging over Niagara
Falls after her capture by Marryat's friend, Captain Drew.

The rebellion put down: British troops attack the rebels' stronghold in the church at
St Eustache, near Montreal, on 14 December 1837; after a drawing by Lord Charles Beauclerk.

The famous author: Captain Frederick Marryat painted by John
Simpson in London, *c.* 1833.

The hostess: Lady
Blessington, who entertained
Marryat, Charles Dickens and
other literary celebrities.

The patron: the liberal,
literate Duke of Sussex,
whose gentlemen-in-waiting
Marryat briefly became.

The caricaturist, top left: the hard-drinking George Cruikshank, who became a temperance crusader.

The novelist, above: Charles Dickens, Marryat's friend and rival, drawn by Samuel Laurence in 1837.

Pondering his future, left: Captain Marryat drawn by William Behnes in 1827 as he was considering his future as a naval officer, courtier, magazine editor, or novelist.

The unlikely farmer, above: Marryat – with manuscripts in his pocket – and his pony, Dumpling, in Norfolk; caricatured by his son Frank.

The unexpected friend, right: Lieutenant George Thomas, RN, of the Mortson coastguard station, caricatured by Frank Marryat.

The inexperienced countrywoman, above: Marryat's daughter Augusta in trouble with her chaise in Norfolk, drawn by her brother Frank. The divided family, below: Marryat as a placid dog and his wife Kate as an angry cat, caricatured by Frank Marryat.

The final haven: Langham Manor Cottage, the *cottage ornée*, where Marryat and his children settled in Norfolk.

Pencillings in Langham.

Langham on a Foggy Day

Stock on a rainy day.

Pigs on a Snowy Day.

Far from the turbulent past: Langham, the remote Norfolk
village, seen at its bleakest by Frank Marryat.

episode of the History of Mr Cochrane', whom he had succeeded as publisher. He named another backer who 'went into partnership with him and was intended to be the active partner [but] being found in bed with Cochrane's wife [became] a sleeping partner ... Cochrane gets rid of a b---h of a wife and obtains capital.'[3]

Busy as he now was, he remained restless, seeking activity – the more turbulent the better – and a place in the public eye. Politics might be the answer, an election was in the offing and he decided to stand as a Parliamentary candidate. Lord Cochrane had shown how stimulating this could be; so, for his former midshipman, the idea of a political campaign was full of dash, epitomised by Cochrane leaping on to the rail of the election platform to symbolise his independence.

In the autumn of 1833, Marryat stood in the Tower Hamlets constituency, close to his childhood home on Tower Hill, which could elect two Members of Parliament. There were three other candidates, Colonel Leicester Stanhope,* William Clay and Stephen Lushington, Marryat describing himself as 'a liberal and a reformer but not a radical'.[4] As one newspaper reported, 'He denied being either a Tory or a Radical; he belongs to no party. He would oppose the crown, or the aristocracy, if he saw either exceeding their constitutional authority.'[5] Rowdy election meetings were held in East End taverns, notably the Britannia and the Mermaid.

Like Cochrane and Nelson, he held strong views on subjects with which he was familiar as a naval officer; otherwise his opinions were vague. At a packed meeting of eight hundred at the Britannia in Limehouse on 25 October, a timber merchant named Richardson introduced him as 'a bluff, honest and honourable man'[6] at which some cheered and waved their hats and a few hissed. Marryat began his speech on safe ground: he was against corruption and against monopolies in general, excepting the Bank of England and the East India Company; he was also

---

* A future Earl of Harrington

against free trade and therefore in favour of protectionism. If elected, he would return to active service in time of war.

He asked if there were any questions. When asked whether he opposed slavery, he replied that 'the old adage was perfectly true, "Real charity begins at home". He detested slavery as much as any man could but he could never consent to give his sole attention to the negroes across the Atlantic, while he knew that his own countrymen were being dragged into slavery ... he would redress that grievance and protect the British seaman before he thrust his philanthropy upon the African negro. Again, when he looked to our manufacturing districts – when he looked to the factory and found infants working in penury and misery for seventeen hours a day – how could he, as a man with a heart in his breast, pass by such a scene and think only of the black slave?' In any case, 'immediate emancipation would be starvation and misery to the slaves themselves.'[7]

This led him into an attack on impressment for the Navy, declaring that 'there was nothing in which reform was more required than in the degrading, unjust, repressive system of the impressment of seamen. When he was a junior officer in the service, when he knew that to meddle with a subject he knew the Ministers wished to keep quiet was to risk his promotion, perhaps to blight his prospects in the service, even then he wrote the work he held in his hand, pointing out the unjust and oppressive character of the practice and suggesting measures for its remedy;'[8] and he waved the pamphlet about impressment he had written in 1822.

Several voices shouted, 'What about flogging?' Marryat replied that he himself reduced its application to 'within the narrowest compass known in the Navy ... but did not see how it could be done without.'[9] At this, the chairman of the meeting, Thomas Wilson, a former Member of Parliament for the City, asked if he or his sons went to sea and came under 'the gallant captain's' command they would want to know whether or not he was opposed to flogging. 'If ever you, or one of your sons, should come under my command and deserve punishment,' he replied, 'if there was no other effectual mode of punishment, I would flog you.'[10]

As the meeting ended 'amidst a tumult of applause and disapprobation',[11] Marryat was given an opportunity of emulating Cochrane's memorable acrobatics when the floor began to collapse. 'The shouting and noise was tremendous', ran the newspaper report, 'Captain Marryat, who had been standing on the table, sprung into the centre of the room and conjured the people not to be alarmed ... and to quit the room as quickly as possible ... The windows were broken and one person dropped from the sill to the street ...' Despite his histrionics, Marryat was unsuccessful; Clay and Lushington were elected.

Failure increased Marryat's restlessness. As proprietor and editor of *The Metropolitan Magazine*, there was plenty to occupy him but, as he wrote in a letter from the Garrick Club, 'Being editor of a magazine is very hard work and rather harder than I like.'[12] He enjoyed dealing with contributors in his bluff, occasionally rough, way; but handling the magazine's finances was another matter. In the Navy, this had been the realm of the ship's purser, the store-keepers, book-keepers, the commissariat ashore and the Admiralty; now he was dealing with circulation, advertising, paying printers and balancing the books. Like many sailors, he was a spendthrift; gambling, giving lavish presents (including most of the treasures he had brought home from Burma), spending his inheritances as if they were inexhaustible and complaining of 'another bill, which I had forgot and hoped the tailor had also ... I am being devoured alive.'[13] He was soon writing to a friend, '*Metropolitan* goes on well ... but I am obliged to sail very near the wind, bad debts are so very plentiful these days.'[14]

He found increasingly that he could leave day-to-day editorial decisions to Edward Howard, whom he saw as his first lieutenant, but the letters by which he gave his instructions were not always encouraging. While staying with the Townshend family at Raynham Hall in Norfolk, he wrote of the magazine, 'I am quite tired of it and, rather than lose money, will throw it up altogether.'[15] In 1834, he took his family to Brighton for a lengthy stay, Kate preferring the smart seaside town to London; they lived in style at Montpelier Villa, the air was good for the children and King William IV and Queen Adelaide were in residence at the Royal Pavilion. Marryat had heard that the King had been vastly entertained by *Peter Simple* and closer acquaintance might prove valuable. So it seemed to be as both shared naval interests and a salty humour. Sometimes the Marryats were guests at 'swarrys' in the oriental saloons of the Royal Pavilion, where relatively easy manners now prevailed. Once, one of the King's illegitimate sons asked, while escorting Kate into the ballroom, 'Has dad bussed you yet?'[16] The King did not recognise Marryat and when he asked an equerry who he was, the latter said, 'Tell His Majesty I am Peter Simple.'[17] When Kate was wilting towards the end of the long and exhausting evening, the King noticed her glancing at her watch and asked why she did not leave if she was so tired. 'Your Majesty must be aware that we cannot move until Her Majesty and yourself have taken your departure,' she replied. 'Oh, damn,' replied the King, 'I'll smuggle you out.'[18]

The King's memory was variable in length. Some time after this, while Sir James Graham, who was friendly towards Marryat, was First Lord of the Admiralty, he was recommended for a knighthood and the royal honour of the Star of Guelph, for his professional services in Burma and in devising the code of signals. The King seemed well disposed but then, as Marryat put it, 'Some kind friend informed His Majesty that I had once written a pamphlet on Impressment. And when Sir James ... saw His Majesty ... the King said to him, "By the bye, Marryat wrote a work on Impressment, I hear" – whether for or against, His Majesty did not deign to enquire – "I won't give him anything", adding in his wonted free and easy style, "I'll see him d--d first." '[19]

Marryat received no honours from the King but did so from an unexpected quarter. In 1833, King Louis Philippe of France had appointed Marryat a *Croix Officier* of the *Légion d'Honeur* in recognition of his authorship of the signalling system that the French called *La Langue Télégraphique Universelle*. When he asked Lord Palmerston, the Foreign Secretary, for permission to wear the insignia of the order, it was refused. But he did give himself the distinction of having his portrait painted in oils by a favourite pupil of Sir Thomas Lawrence, John Simpson. This showed him in civilian clothes with a fashionably high, black stock and captured his good looks: the steady, quizzical gaze beneath slightly drooped eyelids, the determined, cleft chin and the mouth that seemed about to laugh.

Marryat needed all his resilience when, that year, litigation involving his dead father's dealings came to court and the judgement was adverse. Whatever penalties there were, they seemed light and Marryat wrote to his mother, 'It is easy to impute motives and difficult to disprove them ... I did not, therefore, *roar*, I only smiled. The effect will be nugatory. Not one in a thousand will read it; those who do, know it refers to a person not in this world and, of those, those who knew my father will not believe it; those who did not will care little about it and forget the name in a week ... but it's no use crying; what's done can't be helped.'[20]

All the while, Marryat was writing his fiction, pouring forth stories in his small, cramped scrawl: next *Jacob Faithful*, the story of a Thames waterman, wrongly accused of deserting from both the Navy and the Army, which finally ends happily; then, *The Pacha of Many Tales*, a collection of his short stories inspired by the *Arabian Nights* that had appeared in the *Metropolitan Magazine*. He also began work on two short novels, designed to be printed together, entitled, *The Pirate* and *The Three Cutters*; for this he found an ideal illustrator in a former able seaman, now a painter of theatrical scenery, named Clarkson Stanfield, who had moved into George Cruikshank's lodgings in Mornington Crescent; the former novel would be remembered for coining a phrase: 'It's just six of one and half-a-dozen of the other.'[21] This steady output maintained the fame that had reached a climax with *Peter Simple* but did not keep pace with his aspirations.

There was some satisfaction in being taken up by the literary hostess, Lady Blessington, who had just written her own first novel, and the smart dilettante, the Count d'Orsay – said by some to be her lover; by others, her homosexual confidant – but this only increased his extravagance when visiting London. But lack of royal recognition, the worries of owning and editing a magazine and a growing lack of mutual sympathy in his marriage left Marryat irritable and occasionally seething with frustrated and unfocused anger. In 1834, a clergyman named Frederick Maurice, whom he had never met, wrote a novel, naming his villain 'Captain Marryat'; the real Marryat's response was to challenge the author to a duel, which was declined – 'my cloth forbids my accepting his challenge'[22] – and profuse apologies. Worse was to follow over what should have been a trivial and easily-resolved misunderstanding with a contributor. Johnson Neale was an undistinguished writer but he had tried to emulate the currently popular naval novelists, describing Marryat as 'the witty naval writer, head of the English marine novelists'[23] and defending one of his books against criticism. He himself tried his hand anonymously with *Cavendish, or the Patrician at Sea* and then with *The Port Admiral*. Marryat had been friendly to Neale until, in his second novel, he and other former naval officers read what they saw as a hostile and lightly-disguised portrait of Admiral Troubridge. Former naval officers, who had turned novelist, felt it appropriate for themselves to attack their former shipmates, or superior officers, but that it was outrageous for a younger man, a civilian, to make a personal attack upon a gallant officer, a friend of Lord Nelson's, who had fought at St Vincent and the Nile. The review of the book in the *Metropolitan* described it as 'a rascally work ... an infamous libel upon one of our most distinguished officers'[24] and Marryat himself revealed the name of the anonymous author.

Neale politely reproved Marryat for breaking the confidence but also congratulated him on the success of the serialisation of *Peter Simple* in the *Metropolitan*. Marryat responded with a snarl: he told Neale that when they first met he had expected to meet a patrician, instead he met someone like a schoolmaster's assistant: 'you are aware that the situation of master's assistant is never held by anyone who has any pretentions to be a *gentleman*.'[25] Neale therefore challenged Marryat to a duel, the latter refusing on the grounds that he would only fight another gentleman. However, the two did fight, on 5 November 1834, as was reported in the newspapers.

That afternoon, Neale and his brother Melville, a clergyman, suddenly and by chance met Marryat, face to face, as they were walking across the north side of the newly-named Trafalgar Square, 'the very name of the spot being calculated to inspire high courage and noble daring',[26] as a newspaper report noted with sarcasm. Neale called on Marryat to stop. 'Well, sir?' asked Marryat and accused him of libelling Troubridge and mocking the Navy. 'Keep your distance!' cried Neale, brandishing his walking-stick. 'You are a liar and a scoundrel and only want the courage to be an assassin!'[27] Marryat took off his cloak and hung it on the railings of the National Gallery but, as he did so, Neale 'hit him with his stick.'[28] Another newspaper reported that Melville Neale joined the fight, giving Marryat 'a tremendous blow on the back of the head' and Neale, struggling to his feet, tried to 'put an end to the encounter by a twenty-four-pounder in the shape of a paving-stone.'[29]

Now Marryat began to get the better of Neale. A crowd had gathered and finally pulled the men apart. Neale picked up his hat, put it on, said 'Good morning' and walked away, while Marryat 'gave full vent to his wrath and endeavoured to turn the multitude in his favour; but those who had seen the whole affair called out in terms neither flattering to his feelings, nor his courage.'[30] The police had been called and both men later appeared at Bow Street, charged with causing an affray. No reconciliation was possible but the affair was treated light-heartedly by the sarcastic newspaper, which concluded, 'We cannot dismiss the affair without a hearty guffaw at the cool but spanking broadside poured by Captain Marryat into his suspicious-looking enemy ... in return for his shower of stink-pots.'[31]

There were occasional rumours about Marryat's morals. Little evidence was to survive but he referred to a letter he had received from a woman, identified only as 'M---', when writing to Howard: 'It is very violent and very loving, telling me that it is her farewell letter and that if I meet her walking the streets I may exult and say it was my doing. I beg leave to differ from her. I have done all I can to prevent her from walking the streets but she is determined to do anything rather than work.'[32] At this

time, the streets of the West End were thronged with pros-
titutes, many of them young women from respectable back-
grounds, desperate to support their families. He tells Howard
that, should he happen to meet the woman, he is to tell her that
he, Marryat, is shortly leaving for Italy.

Public mockery combined with private unhappiness, lack of
the recognition he thought was his due and ever-increasing financial problems led Marryat to a drastic decision: he would take
his family to live abroad.

The Marryats escaped to the Continent at the beginning of
April 1835. For Kate there was relief in the prospect of living
comfortably abroad, where her husband was less likely to become embroiled in madcap enterprises; for the children, there
was the adventure of travel; for Marryat himself there was escape
from creditors and, at the start, the thrill of again treading a deck,
albeit a heaving one as the passage to Ostend was rough. They
sailed in one of the new passenger paddle-steamers that had
been developed from the early tugs, and gunboats like the *Diana*, but she was not comfortable.

'Paddle, paddle – splash, splash – bump, thump, bump,' he
jotted in his journal. 'What a leveller is sea-sickness. All grades,
all respect, all consideration are lost. The master may summon
John to his assistance but John will see his master hanged before
he will go to him; he has taken possession of his master's great
coat and intends to keep it ... Decorum and modesty ... fall
before the dire prostration of this malady. A young lady will
recline unwittingly in the arms of a perfect stranger and the bride
of three months, deserted by her husband, will offer no resistance to the uncouth seaman, whom in his kindness, would
loosen the laces that confine her heaving bosom ...'

'Paddle, paddle, splash, splash, bump, thump, bump – one
would really imagine that the passengers were so many pumps,
all worked at once with the vessel by the same hundred horse-
power, for there were a hundred of them about me, each as sick
as a horse. "*Sic omnes*", thought I. I have long passed the ordeal
and even steam and smoke and washing-basins, and all the
various discordant and revolting noises from those who suffer,

have no effect upon my nervous system – but still was I doomed to torment and was very sick indeed.'[33]

Finally it was over. 'I looked over the bows and perceived that we were close to the pile entrance of the harbour of Ostend. Ten minutes later there was a cessation of paddle, paddle, thump, thump, the stern-fast was thrown on the quay, there was a rush on board of commissionaires with their reiterated cries, accompanied by cards thrust into your hands. "Hotel des Bains, monsieur"; "Hotel de'Angleterre", *ad infinitum* – and then there was the pouring out of the Noah's Ark, with their countenances wearing a most paradoxical appearance, for they evidently showed that they had had quite enough of water and, at the same time, that they required a great deal more. I looked at my children, as they were hoisted up from the ladies; cabin, one after another; and, upon examination, decided that, with their smudged faces, the Hotel des *Bains* would be the most appropriate to their condition; so there we went.'[34]

The Marryats arrived in Brussels to live expensively and be received at the court of King Leopold, the first King of the Belgians. They were just in time for a ceremony heralding the age of steam, presided over by Robert Stephenson, the son of George Stephenson, the inventor of railways. On 5 May, three new locomotives, which he called 'steam tugs', named the *Stephenson*, the *Arrow* and the *Elephant*, were to haul 'thirty-three omnibuses, diligences, or cars, which are attached to the said three steam-tugs' from Brussels to Malines and back with the King of Belgium, his ministers, ambassadors and 'everybody else who can produce a satisfactory yellow ticket.'[35] It was a triumphal progress, noted Marryat: 'we were tugged through twelve miles of the most fertile pasture in the universe, the whole line of roads crowded with spectators ... We arrived safe at Malines and I was infinitely amused at the variety of astonishment in the five hundred thousand faces, which we passed ... I beheld a crowd of Roman Catholic priests, who looked at the trains in such a manner as if they thought that they were "heretical and damnable" and that the chemin de *fer* was nothing but the chemin *d'enfer*. For the return journey, Mr Stephenson attached all the cars, omnibuses and diligences together and directed the *Elephant* to take us back without assistance from the other two engines ... We arrived safely at Brussels, much to the delight of those who were in the cars and also of His Majesty and all his ministers and all his authorities and all the mercantile classes, who consider that the millennium is come, but very much to the disappointment of the lower classes, who have formed the idea that the *chemin de fer* will take away their bread and therefore longed for a blow-up. And Mr Stephenson himself, having succeeded in bringing back his decorated cars, has been *decoré* himself and is now a *Chevalier de l'Ordre Léopold*. Would not the *iron* order ... have been more appropriate as a Chemin de *Fer* decoration?'[36]

Despite his levity, Marryat was as aware of the importance of the new form of propulsion as he had been on the Irrawaddy. 'It is impossible to contemplate any steam engine,' he wrote in his journal, 'without feeling wonder and admiration at the ingenuity of man; but the feeling is raised to a degree of awe when you look at a locomotive engine – there is such enormous power compressed into so small a space – I can never divest myself of the idea that it is possessed of *vitality* that it is a living as well as a moving being – and that idea, joined up with its immense power, conjures to my mind that it is some spitting, fizzing, terrific demon, who, if he could escape control, would be ready and happy to drag us by thousands to destruction. And will this powerful invention prove to mankind a blessing, or a curse?'[37]

From Brussels, the family moved to Liège and then to spend the summer at the nearby resort of Spa, which he described as 'a very beautiful and a very cheap place,'[38] noted for its mineral waters. Throughout their travels Marryat proved a practical father: 'Like most sailors, he was very kind and tender-hearted with children and especially so with his little ones,' wrote one who knew him, 'and when, at the close of a day's travelling, they were tired and fractious and refused to shut their eyes, he would wrest the servants' duty from their hands and enact the part of head nurse himself. He could not sing but ... it was by means of telling stories that he used to lull his children to sleep.'[39]

He continued to edit the *Metropolitan* by letter and was running a discursive account of his travels as a serial, which he regarded as 'very good magazine stuff.'[40] He kept in touch with London and Norfolk friends with jolly letters, one beginning, 'I am alive and when I am dead and gone I'll write and let you know, that is if my communication is not stopped at the Dead Letter Office. I have been to Paris and did a little business at Frascati's ...'[41] It was a more relaxed life than he had been able to lead in England and he wrote to his new friend, Lady Blessington, 'I am like a horse, which had been worked too hard, turned out to grass and I hope I shall come out again as fresh as a two-year-old. I walk about and pick flowers with the children, sit on a bench in the beautiful *allées vertes*, smoke my cigar and meditate till long after the moon is in the zenith. Then I lie on the sofa and read French novels, or I gossip with anyone I can pick up in the streets. Besides which I wear out my old clothes ...'[42] It was not quite like that because he was busy writing a new novel, *Mr Midshipman Easy*: more naval adventures, peopled, like *Peter Simple*, with a rich gallery of characters, a favourite being Jack Easy's humorous black servant, Mesty.

Kate was pregnant again so she and the children remained in Spa while Marryat visited London that autumn. This was partly to oversee the publication of a novel called *Japhet in Search of a Father* with the popular theme of the search for a lost inheritance, which had been serialised in the *Metropolitan* two years before and also of his latest book, which he hoped would first be published as a serial. Returning to Spa and again restless, he moved his family again, this time up the Rhine to Switzerland, finally stopping at Lausanne on Lake Geneva, where they rented a splendid house from a nobleman.

Marryat was not always the charming companion. Once, when on their Continental travels, he was invited to dine with a party of notables, who were keen to meet the famous author and wit. He sat silent throughout dinner and when his host later asked the reason, Marryat replied, 'If *that's* what you wanted, you should have asked me ... Did you imagine I was going to let out any of my jokes for those fellows to put in their next books? No, that is not my plan. When I find myself in such company as that I open my ears and hold my tongue, glean all I can, and give nothing in return.'[43]

His manners could be even worse when in such a mood and he did decide to speak, as happened in Lausanne. A friend of Marryat's* was to hear the story when he, too, visited the town and wrote, 'There was, staying there at the time, a stately English baronet and his wife, who had two milksop sons, concerning whom they cherished the idea of accomplishing their education into manhood consistently with such perfect purity and innocence that they were hardly to know their own sex.' The Marryats were invited to meet them at dinner at the house of a mutual friend, who did not, perhaps, realise that the captain was, although 'a man of many sterling fine qualities but with a habit of free indulgence in coarseness of speech, which, though his earlier life had made it as easy to acquire as difficult to drop, did always less than justice to a very manly, honest, really gentle nature.'

So it was that 'our ogre friend encountered these lambs at dinner with their father ... and, as if possessed by a devil, launched out in such frightful and appalling impropriety – ranging over every kind of forbidden topic and every species of forbidden word and every sort of scandalous anecdote – that years of education in Newgate would have been nothing compared with their experience of that one afternoon. After turning paler and paler and more and more stoney, the baronet, with a half-suppressed cry, rose and fled. But the sons – intent on the ogre – remained behind instead of following him; and are supposed to have been ruined from that hour.'

To this, the friend added comment that illuminated Marryat's strained relations with Kate. 'Poor fellow!' he wrote. 'He seems to have had a hard time of it with his wife. She had no interest whatever in her children and was such a fury that, being dressed to go out to dinner, she would sometimes, on no other provocation than a pin out of its place, or some such thing, fall upon a

---

* Charles Dickens, whom Marryat was to meet in 1841, was writing to John Forster in 1846.

little maid she had, beat her till she couldn't stand, then tumble into hysterics and be carried to bed. He suffered martyrdom with her ...'[44]

This source of stress, added to the others, convinced Marryat that change was necessary. He was writing *Snarley Yow, or the Dog Fiend*, a violent historical novel about smugglers, which was not so well received but did include a narrative verse, describing a sea battle, of such gusto that it was said to be amongst his best writing; it seemed to encapsulate the spirit of the old Navy, with which he had first been to sea, and it began,

> *The captain stood by the carronade – 'First lieutenant', says he,*
> *'Send all my merry men aft here, for they must list to me;*
> *I haven't the gift of the gab, my sons – because I'm bred to the sea,*
> *That ship there is a Frenchman, who means to fight with we.'*
> *Odds blood, hammer and tongs, long as I've been at sea,*
> *I've fought against every odds – but I've gained the victory.*

And, the battle fought and won, it ends,

> *Our captain sent for all of us: 'My merry men', said he,*
> *'I haven't the gift of the gab, my lads, but yet I thankful be;*
> *You've done your duty handsomely, each man stood to his gun.*
> *If you hadn't, you villains, as sure as day I'd have flogged each*
> > *mother's son.'*
> *Odds blood, hammer and tongs, as long as I'm at sea,*
> *I'll fight 'gainst every odds – and I'll gain the victory!*

Then, in October 1836, he heard that his loyal deputy, Edward Howard, had been recalled to duty and given command of a sloop. His own editorship could not, therefore, continue and he sold his interest in the *Metropolitan Magazine* to its publishers for £1,050. His property at Langham had been let, his family was comfortably settled at Lausanne and he was now free for whatever enterprise took his fancy. He began to write a biography of his admired former shipmate William Napier, who had retired as a post-captain, succeeded to his father's barony and recently died in China; he had written half when Napier's widow changed her mind, withdrew permission to consult family papers and the project was dropped.

Another, far more ambitious project came to mind; one that might mean a year or two away from his family. He returned to Lausanne to make his farewells and marked the occasion with 'a large and brilliant entertainment consisting of private theatricals and a ball';[45] he had written the play, *Ill Will*, himself and took the leading part with expatriate English men and women in supporting roles. Assured that his family would be happy in Lausanne – 'Kate likes it ... and says she could live all her life there,' he wrote to his sister, Fanny – so he returned to London, taking rooms at 8 Duke Street in St James's. A final worry arose with news from Norfolk that his tenant at Langham was 'behaving very ill ... cutting down my timber and allowing people to shoot my game.'[46] He was able to find a new tenant – 'a good, responsible man'[47] – to rent Langham for twelve years at a satisfactory rent, so could depart for lengthy travels with an easy mind. He was increasingly curious about countries he had yet to visit. He had found the Swiss selfish, mercenary and puritanical. 'Avarice rules over the beautiful country of Helvetia,' he wrote in the last chapter of his Continental journal. 'Do the faults of this people arise from the peculiarity of their constitutions, or from the nature of their government? To ascertain this, one must compare them with those who live under similar institutions. I must go to America, that's decided.'[48]

CHAPTER NINE

The Americans ... a Restless, Uneasy People

'All hands, up anchor!' shouted the captain of the transatlantic packet *Quebec*, lying at Spithead, her upper deck heaped with baggage and swarming with crew and passengers, amongst the latter, Captain Frederick Marryat. Pushing his way through the crowd, he seated himself forward, where he could look, listen and remember the scene and the sounds, notably the sea shanties sung by the sailors – this morning it was *Sally Brown* – that was forbidden in ships of the Royal Navy. He noted what he heard.

'Heave away there, forward.'
'*Sally Brown – oh! my dear Sally*!' (single voice)
'*Oh! Sally Brown*!' (chorus)
'*Sally Brown of Bubble -Al-ley*!' (single voice)
'*Oh! Sally Brown*!' (chorus)
'Avast heaving there; send all aft to clear the boat.'
'Aye, aye, sir. Where are we to stow these casks, Mr Fisher?'
'Stow them! Heaven knows; get them in at all events.'
'Captain H! Captain H! there's my piano still on deck; it will be quite spoiled – indeed it will.'
'Don't be alarmed, ma'am; as soon as we're under weigh, we'll hoist the cow up and get the piano down.'
'What! under the cow?'
'No, ma'am; but the cow's over the hatchway.'
'Now then, my lads, forward to the windlass.'
'*I went to town to get some toddy*!'
'*Oh! Sally Brown*!'

'*T'wasn't fit for anybody*!'

'*Oh! Sally Brown* – '

'Out there, and clear away the jib.'

'Aye, aye, sir.'

'Mr Fisher, how much cable is there out?'

'Plenty yet, sir. Heave away, my lads.'

'*Sally is a bright mulatter*'

'*Oh! Sally Brown*!'

'*Pretty girl, but can't get at her.*'

'*Oh! –*'

'Avast heaving; send the men aft to whip the ladies in. Now, miss, only sit down and don't be afraid and you'll be in in no time. Whip away, my lads, handsomely; stead her with the guy; lower away. There, miss, you're safely *landed*.'

'*Landed* am I? I thought I was *shipped*.'

'Very good, indeed – very good, miss, you'll make an excellent sailor, I see.'

'I should make a better sailor's *wife*, I expect, Captain H.'

'Excellent! Allow me to hand you aft; you'll excuse me – Forward now, my men, heave away!'

'*Seven years I courted Sally.*'

'*Oh! Sally Brown*!'

'*Seven more of Shilly-shally –*'

'*Oh! Sally Brown*!'

'*She won't wed –*'

'Avast heaving. Up there and loose the topsails; stretch along the topsail-sheets – upon my soul, half these children will be killed. Whose child are you?'

'I – don't – know.'

'Go and find out, that's a dear – let fall, sheet home; belay starboard sheet; clap on the larboard; belay all that – now then, Mr Fisher.'

'Aye, aye, sir. Heave away, my lads.'

'*She won't wed a Yankee sailor*'

'*Oh! Sally Brown*!'

'*For she's in love with the nigger tailor.*'

'*Oh! Sally Brown*!'

'Heave away, my men; heave and in sight. Hurrah! my lads.'
'*Sally Brown – oh! my dear Sally.*'
'*Oh! Sally Brown!*'
'*Sally Brown of Bubble Alley.*'
'*Oh! Sally Brown!*'
'*Sally has a cross old granny.*'
'*Oh! –*'
'Heave and fall – jib-halyards – hoist away.'
'Oh, dear! Oh, dear!'
'The clumsy brute has half-killed the girl – don't cry my dear.'
'Pick up the child, Tom, and shove it out of the way.'
'Where shall I put her?'
'Oh, anywhere just now; put her in the turkey-coop.'
'Starboard!'
'I say, clap on, some of you *he* chaps, or else get out of the way.'
'Sailor, mind my band-box.'
'Starboard!'
'Starboard it is; steady so.'[1]

Then, Marryat, delighted and amused by this fresh view of the world he understood, quipped, 'Thus, with the trifling matter of maiming half a dozen children, unsetting two or three women, smashing the lids of a few trunks and crushing some band-boxes as flat as a muffin, the good ship *Quebec* was at last fairly under weigh and standing out for St Helen's.'[2] That was the anchorage under the lee of the east point of the Isle of Wight, where sailing ships awaited a wind. The *Quebec* did not have to wait, for the wind got up that afternoon and she plunged down-Channel into a rising sea. At four o'clock, a cold dinner was served and, Marryat noted, 'Dinner over, everybody pulls out a number of *Pickwick*; everybody talks and reads *Pickwick*; weather getting up squally; passengers not quite so sure they won't be seasick.'[3]

The Pickwick Papers, currently being serialised, were rivalling Marryat's own novels and outstripping them in popularity. The author was a young man of twenty-five named Charles Dickens, a former newspaper reporter, who had already made a success with his collected writings, published as *Sketches by Boz**; he was a friend of Cruikshank's but Marryat and Dickens knew each other only by reputation. *Sketches by Boz* was of particular interest to Marryat because, following his *Diary on the Continent*, he was planning the same sort of reportage in America. He had mined his memory for naval anecdotes for his first novels and now he needed fresh material. Two women, Frances Trollope and Harriet Martineau, had recently visited the United States and published their journals to acclaim in London but resentment by Americans, sensitive to any criticism by the British. His objective was to travel more widely, research more deeply and write a thoughtful, occasionally humorous, account of the new nation, bearing in mind that he himself was half-American. The expedition was also an escape from money troubles and a muddled career as an editor and magazine proprietor; also from his wife. Kate seems to have been disapproving, and probably envious, of her husband's popularity, which she did not share. A literary undertaking provided a perfect excuse for a long separation.

In March that year he had walked down Tower Hill – his birthplace – to the new St Katherine's Docks and found that the *Quebec* was to sail for New York on 1 April. Thinking the day unlucky, he had booked a passage but arranged to join the ship three days later off Portsmouth. The voyage lasted the usual four weeks; the sea was rough, there was much sea-sickness; influenza broke out and there were the deaths of an old woman and a boy of twelve amongst the thirty-eight passengers.

Arriving at New York early in May, his first sight was of spires and tall buildings clustered on Manhattan Island; his second was shocking. Looking over the side of his ship, he saw 'fastened by a rope yarn to the rudder chains of a vessel next in the tier at the wharf where the packet had hauled in ... the body of a black man, turning over and over with the ripples of the waves.' He continued, 'I was looking at it, when a lad came up ... he looked ... turned away with disdain, saying, "Oh, it's only a nigger." '4

---

* A Dickens family nickname.

Soon he was ashore and writing in his diary, 'On the 4th of May in the year of our Lord 1837, I found myself walking up Broadway among the free and enlightened citizens of New York.'[5] At once the egalitarianism of America was demonstrated by the porter carting his baggage to his lodgings. The man had gone ahead, Marryat could not see him or his cart until as he was 'looking round for him in one direction, when I was saluted with slap on the shoulder ... I turned and beheld my car-man, who had taken the liberty to draw my attention in this forcible manner.'[6]

He took his first walk along the wide streets lined by a mixture of new buildings of six or seven storeys, the classical facades of public buildings and narrow-fronted houses built in the last century in the mixed style of Georgian London and Amsterdam. 'New York is not equal to London,' he decided, 'nor Broadway to Regent Street, although the Americans would compare them. Still, New York is very superior to most of our provincial towns and, to a man who can exist out of London, Broadway will do very well for a lounge – being wide, three miles long ... besides which it may almost challenge Regent Street for pretty faces ... Many of the shops, or *stores*, as they are here called, have already been fitted up with large, plate-glass fronts, similar to those in London ... At the corner of many of the squares, or *blocks* of buildings, as they are termed here, is erected a very high mast with a cap of liberty in top.'[7]

New York was, he noted, built on a narrow island some ten miles in length, three of which were built upon to house its three hundred thousand inhabitants. 'Building lots were marked out for the other seven miles; and, by calculation, these lots, when built upon, would contain an additional population of one million and three quarters. They were first purchased at from one hundred to one hundred and fifty dollars but ... they rose to upwards of two thousand dollars.'[8] He had 'never seen any city so admirably adapted for commerce'. The island, between the Hudson River and the East River had Broadway 'running up it like the vertebrae of some huge animal and the other streets diverging from it at right angles, like the ribs; each street running to the river and presenting to the view a forest of masts.'[9]

It was spring and he was surprised by the climate. 'On 5th May, the heat and closeness were oppressive. There was a sultriness in the air, even at that early period of the year, which to me seemed equal to that of Madras. Almost every day there were, instead of our mild, refreshing showers, sharp storms of thunder and lightning ... While I was throwing off every garment which I well could, the females were walking up and down Broadway wrapped in warm shawls. It appeared as if it required twice the heat we have in our country, either to create a free circulation in the blood of the people, or to stimulate nature to rouse after the torpor of a protracted and severe winter. In a week from the period I have mentioned ... the belles of Broadway were walking about in summer dresses and thin satin shoes and the men calling for ice ...'[10]

Always having had an eye for a pretty face, Marryat watched the young women with a connoisseur's eye. 'The women are very pretty and very delicate,' he wrote, 'but they remind you of roses which have budded fairly, but which a check in the season has not permitted to blow. Up to sixteen or seventeen, they promise perfection; at that age, their advance appears to be checked ... The women are affected by the climate ... if you transplant a delicate American girl to England, she will, in a year or two, become so robust and healthy as not to be recognised on her return home; showing that the even temperature of our damp climate ... is more conducive to health than the sunny, yet variable, atmosphere of America. The Americans are fond of their climate and consider it, as they do everything in America, as the very best in the world. They are ... most happy in their delusions. But, if the climate is not a healthy one, it is certainly a beautiful climate to the eye: the sky is so clear, the air so dry ... at night, the stars are so brilliant ... that I am not surprised at the Americans praising the *beauty* of their climate.'[11]

Climate apart, Marryat had arrived at a bad time and a good one. That spring the United States was in recession, a financial slump following several years of booming speculation; it was, he said, 'like bursting into a friend's house with a merry face, when there is a death in it.'[12] He was also determined to face and, if possible, reform piracy in publishing: his books, which were earning him a comfortable income in London, were here being reprinted and sold without the publishers having the rights to do so, or paying him royalties.

The positive side was that he was a literary celebrity; he was lionised as the guest at dinners, he was being interviewed by newspaper reporters and his books were so famous that strangers would ask him about the final outcome of the story they were then reading. He was not quite what many expected, one New Yorker observing, 'The lion, Captain Marryat is no great thing of a lion, after all ... a very every-day sort of man ... more of a sailor than an author ... savours more of the binnacle lamp than of the study.'[13] So it was gratifying to him that half a dozen seamen – all from American merchant ships or warships of the United States Navy – called at his hotel each day to remind him that they had been shipmates in the Royal Navy; another reminder of the outflow of the best seamen from the latter to the former.

He was reconciled to living in hotels for most of his stay. These were a startling change from the coaching inns and converted town houses, in which he had stayed in England. The 'first-rate American hotel' – such as the Globe Hotel and Astor House in New York – 'is very spacious,' he wrote and, at busy times, up to three hundred guests could be seated in the dining-room. 'The upper storeys contain an immense number of bedrooms, with their doors opening upon long corridors, with little variety in their furniture, or arrangement, except that some are provided with large beds for married people and others with single beds.'[14]

An important and, to him, unusual public room in American hotels was the bar, 'generally a very large room in the basement, fitted up very much like our own gin palaces in London ... A long counter runs across it, behind which stand two or three bar-keepers.' Behind them were shelves of 'masses of pure crystal ice, large bunches of mint, decanters of every sort of wine, every variety of spirits, lemons, sugar, bitters, segars and tobacco; it really makes one feel thirsty, even going into a bar.' There, he said, 'you meet everybody and everybody meets you. Here the senator, the member of Congress, the merchant, the store-keeper, travellers from the Far West ... all congregate. Most of them have a segar in their mouths, some are transacting business, others conversing, some sitting down together, whispering confidentially. Here you obtain all the news, all the scandal, all the politics and all the fun ... The consequence of the bar being the place of general resort is that there is an unceasing pouring out and amalgamation of alcohol.'

There was a wide variety of such amalgamations: 'slings in all their varieties; cock-tails – but I really cannot remember ... the whole battle-array against one's brains.'[15] A Westerner offering a drink might ask, 'Stranger, will you take in wood?', inspired by a steam-boat travel: 'The vessels taking in wood as fuel to keep the steam up, the person taking in spirits to keep *his* steam up.'[16]

'What shall it be?' he heard in a bar. 'Well, I don't care – a gin-sling'; and again, 'What shall we have?!' 'Well, I don't care; I say brandy cocktail.'

He overheard one woman say to another (although not in a bar) that 'If I have a weakness for one thing, it is for a mint julep.' This, he decided, was 'one of the most delightful and insinuating potions that was ever invented ... I learnt how to make them and succeeded pretty well. Put into a tumbler about a dozen sprigs of the tender shoots of mint, upon them put a spoonful of white sugar and equal proportions of peach and common brandy so as to fill up one-third, or perhaps a little less. Then take rasped, or pounded, ice to fill up the tumbler. Epicures rub the lips of the tumbler with a piece of fresh pineapple and the tumbler itself is often encrusted with stalactites of ice. As the ice melts, you drink.'[17]

New York was hot and his need to maintain a smiling public face was wearing, so he set out for his ancestral home, Boston, first travelling up Long Island Sound by a big paddle-steamer to Providence, going ashore and covering the last forty miles in two hours by the new railway. He found the journey tiring 'as the constant coughing of the locomotive, the dazzling of the vision from the rapidity with which objects are passed, the sparks and ashes which fly in your face and your clothes become very annoying; your only consolation is the speed with which you are passing over the ground.'[18] He thought American railways inferior to the British and more dangerous because 'nothing is made in America but to last a certain time; they go to the exact expense considered necessary and no further; they know that in twenty years they will be better able to spend twenty dollars than one now. The great object is to obtain quick return for the outlay ...'[19]

During the War of 1812, Marryat had often been at sea off Boston, and his mother and her family had lived there, so he did not feel a stranger, particularly after a newspaper announced his arrival beneath the headline, 'MARRYAT A BOSTON BOY.'[20] Just as the Bostonians were eager to see the famous novelist, half of whose ancestry they could claim, he was curious to see his mother's birthplace so that he could tell her about it. He found it 'a fine city' with a population of eighty thousand and, although it had lost much of its trade to New York since his grandfather's time, he found it more cultivated. 'The Bostonians assert that they are more English than we are,' he wrote in his journal, 'that is, that they have adhered to the old English customs and manners as handed down to them previous to the revolution ... certainly ... I feel at home with them ... You meet here with frequent specimens of the Old English Gentleman, descendants of the best old English families, who settled here long before the Revolution ... The society of Boston is very delightful; it wins upon you every day.'[21]

Returning to New York, he was dined by the mayor and corporation on Independence Day and surprised when toasts were proposed to the Americans who had defeated the British at the battles of Bunker Hill and New Orleans. But he was delighted by the mixture of patriotic ceremonial and domesticity; as the military parade marched up Broadway, the cheers were punctuated by such cries as 'Ma! Ma! There's pa!' and 'Look at uncle on his big horse!'[22] On the night of 4 July, he watched the firework display filling the sky, which, he said, 'exceeded anything that I had witnessed in London, or Paris. What with sea-serpents, giant rockets scaling heaven, Bengal lights, Chinese fires, Italian suns, fairy bowers, crowns of Jupiter, Tartar temples, Vesta's diadems, magic circles, morning glories, stars of

Columbia and temples of liberty, all America was in a blaze ... and all America was tipsy.'[23]

His own activities were being reported so widely that the *New York Transcript* published a parody by a 'Mr Toadey'. A long and detailed account of his day began, 'Captain Marryat dined yesterday on roast beef, which he ate very heartily – accompanying each mouthful with a plentiful coat of mustard, a sizeable piece of potato and a large bit of bread-and-butter. He did not use any cayenne pepper and he was observed to turn up his nose very perceptibly at a dish of buttered turnips that were tendered to him. Why he should object to buttered turnips – not being in the secrets of the gallant captain – I really cannot pretend to say.' Describing his every mouthful, his picking his teeth 'deliberately but with infinite grace'[24] and reporting half-heard witticisms, it was a comic writing worthy of its subject.

Another newspaper report was more serious, sympathising with his complaints of literary piracy. Beneath the headline 'CAPTAIN MARRYAT AND THE BOOK PUBLISHERS', the New York *Mirror* declared sarcastically, 'How a man who has seen so much of the world as Captain Marryat could have conceived that he had any natural right of property in his own productions, we cannot imagine.' Then, naming the guilty publishers, it continued, that 'we consider it our duty to expose their underhand and oppressive conduct.'[25]

He made several more excursions; first, up the Hudson to the Military Academy at West Point. Transport was by river and Marryat watched with delight when he saw the big passenger paddle-steamer 'sweep round the Battery with her two decks, the upper one screened with snow-white awnings – the gay dresses of the ladies – the variety of colours – it reminded me of a floating garden and I fancied that Isola Bella, on the Lake of Como, had got under weigh ...'[26] The voyage took him up the 'noble stream, flowing rapidly through its bold and deep bed', past Sing Sing prison, 'where people are condemned to perpetual silence ... a very fine building of white marble, like a palace – very appropriate for that portion of the *sovereign people*, who may qualify themselves for a residence in it.' Arriving at West Point after dark it was not until morning that he was thrilled – 'a more beautiful view I never gazed upon' – by what he saw as the Rhine as it once had been 'when the lofty mountains were clothed with forests and rich in all the variety and beauty of undisturbed nature.'[27] He was impressed by the Military Academy, particularly because all the cadets were trained as engineers.

A few days later, he returned to New York on the night steamer. Flinching from the huge, stuffy dormitory, where some five hundred passengers were sleeping, he passed the night on deck, musing, 'The moon sank down and the sun rose and ... gilded the spires of New York, as I ... enjoyed the luxury of being alone ... in America, where the people are gregarious and would think themselves very ill-bred if they allowed you one moment for meditation.'[28] He was noting American curiosity, too, and not only in himself and his opinions of their country. 'The Americans are excessively curious,' he wrote, 'they cannot bear anything like a secret – that's *unconstitutional.*'[29]

After an expedition to admire the Passaic Falls in New Jersey, he prepared for a long tour. He would again sail up the Hudson but this time as far as Albany and thence to Saratoga Springs and, via the Niagara Falls, to Buffalo and Detroit and the Great Lakes.

After 'once more flying up the noble Hudson,'[30] Marryat reached Albany, where he declared, 'American women are the *prettiest* in the world.'[31] This was prompted by a visit to the Albany Female Academy, where, he wrote, 'as young ladies are assembled here from every State of the Union, it was a *fair* criterion of American beauty.'[32] He had already noticed in New York that women's looks reached their zenith in adolescence.

Invited to attend a French language class, the teacher, an elderly émigré count, seated him beside the blackboard as one girl after another was summoned to write upon it answers to questions in French. As the first girl stood beside him and the question was asked she wrote the wrong answer. 'I perceived it and, without looking at her, pronounced the right word so that she could hear it. She caught it, rubbed out the wrong word with the towel and rectified it.' Congratulated by the teacher, she sat down, blushing, and, one by one, the rest of the class were called to the blackboard and each time Marryat whispered the correct answer without the teacher hearing. 'What amused me,' he recalled, 'was the *tact* displayed by the sex, which appears to be innate ... Had I prompted a boy, he would most likely have turned his head round towards me ... but not one of the whole class was guilty of such indiscretion ... but never by any look or sign made it appear that there was any understanding between us ... It was really beautiful. When the examination was over, I received a look from them all, half comic, half serious, which amply repaid me for my assistance.'[33]

He became fascinated by American women and the differences between them and their menfolk. 'The women of America,' he declared, 'are unquestionably physically, as far as beauty is concerned, and morally of a higher standard than the men; nevertheless they have not that influence which they ought to possess.'[34] Before marriage, young women were subject to 'universal adulation' that made the time between leaving school at marriage 'the happiest of her existence.'[35] He was surprised at the language used in such gallantry as when he heard a young man say, 'She's the *greatest* gal in the whole Union', and another remarked that of his girl, 'With her yellow hat and feathers, wasn't she in *full blast?*'[36]

However, such attention sharply diminished on marriage. 'All men in America are busy,' he continued, 'their whole time is engrossed by their accumulation of money; they breakfast early and repair to their stores or counting-houses; the majority of them do not go home to dinner but eat at the nearest tavern, or oyster-cellar ... It would be supposed that they would be home to an early tea; many are but the majority are not. After fagging, they require recreation and the recreations of most Americans are politics and news, besides the chance of doing a little more business, all of which, with drink, are to be obtained at the bars ... The consequence is that the major portion of them come home late, tired and go to bed; early the next morning they are off to their business again ... The women do not have much of their husband's society ...'[37]

Looks apart, he decided that 'their principal fault ... is that they do not sufficiently modulate their voice'; when he asked one Southern lady why she drawled her words, she replied sharply, 'Well, I'd drawl all the way from Maine to Georgia rather than *clip* my words as you English people do.'[38] In attitudes, he concluded that they showed 'a remarkable apathy to the sufferings of others, an indifference to loss of life, a fondness for politics, all of which are unfeminine.'[39] They showed 'a virtue, which the man have not, which is moral courage. The independence and spirit of an American woman, if left a widow without resources, is immediately shewn; she does not sit and lament, but applies herself to some employment so that she may maintain herself and her children.'[40]

Marryat was shocked by what he saw as the over-indulging of children. 'There is little or no parental control,' he decided. 'At the age of six or seven, you will hear both boys and girls contradicting their fathers and mothers and advancing their own opinions with a firmness, which is very striking.' He quoted, verbatim, such a confrontation, which ended with the father commanding his small son, 'I tell you, come in directly, sir – do you hear?' 'I won't.' Then the father, 'smiling at the boy's resolute disobedience', turning to Marryat and saying 'A sturdy republican, sir.'[41]

He was finding the Americans 'restless, uneasy people – they cannot sit still, they cannot listen attentively unless the theme be politics, or dollars – they must do something ... their curiosity is unbounded and they are very capricious. Acting upon impulse, they are very generous at one moment and without a spark of charity the next. They are good-tempered and possess great energy, ingenuity, bravery and presence of mind ...'[42] The theme of restlessness kept recurring: 'The love of excitement must, of course, produce a love of gambling ...' [43] and 'one very remarkable point in the American character ... is that they constantly change their professions.'[44] Half-American that he was, he felt a foreigner.

From Albany onwards, Marryat's principal form of transport was the stagecoach and soon he found that 'you long for the delightful springing of four horses upon the level roads of England.'[45] The American stagecoach was not sprung but 'hung upon leather braces ... when the roads are bad ... the motion is very similar to that of being tossed in a blanket.'[46] Inside, nine passengers sat on three seats, the backs of those seated in the centre being supported by a broad leather strap. The side-panels were open in warm weather and, when it was wet, or cold, covered with leather aprons, 'a very insufficient protection as the wind blows through the intermediate spaces, whistling in your ears.'[47] Once, when rain was driving through the sides, Marryat complained to the driver, who replied, 'Well, now, I reckon you'd better ask the proprietors; my business is to drive the coach.'[48]

By such means, he travelled through Saratoga Springs and to Niagara Falls and he was not disappointed by what he was told was the greatest natural spectacle in North America, describing it as 'the thunder of the Almighty ... the majesty ... is far too great for the mind to compass.' Indeed, his own was overwhelmed, as he wrote, 'I stood on the brink above the falls ... to watch the great mass of water tumbling, dancing, capering and rushing wildly along and if in a hurry to take the leap ... I continued to watch the rolling waters and then I felt a slight dizziness and a creeping sensation come over me ... a craving desire to leap into the flood of rushing waters. It increased upon me every minute; and, retreating from the brink, I turned my eyes to the surrounding foliage until the effect of the excitement had passed away.'

When he looked again, a bizarre thought came to him: 'I wished myself a magician, that I might transport the Falls to Italy and pour their whole volume of waters into the crater of Mount Vesuvius ... and create the largest steam boiler that had ever entered the imagination of man.'[49] After writing more than a thousand dramatic words in his journal, his mordant humour reasserted itself, as if he felt ashamed at having been so impressed and, when asked to write his impressions in a visitors' book, jotted down, 'Upon a patient and careful examination of the Falls called Niagara, I have come to the conclusion that if any person were to be taken down in them, he would be in consider- able danger of receiving serious injury.'[50]

It was at Niagara that he learned more about the character of American women and how, forthright as they were, they could be surprisingly prim. Walking to the Falls with a young woman he knew, she slipped on a rock and grazed her shin. 'As she limped a little in walking home, I said, "Did you hurt your leg much?" She turned from me, evidently much shocked ... and I begged to know what was the reason for her displeasure. After some hesitation, she said that, as she knew me well, she would tell me that the word *leg* was never mentioned before ladies ... the word *limb* was used. "Nay", continued she, "I am not so particular as some people are, for I know those who always say a limb of a table, or limb of a piano-forte." '[51]

Continuing to Buffalo, where he found that 'the main street is wider and the stores handsomer than the majority of those in New York' and mused upon a difference between America and Eng- land: in the shops of Buffalo and Cleveland could be bought 'articles for which, at Norwich, you would be obliged to send to London. It is the same thing in almost every town in America ... Would you furnish a house in one of them, you will find every article of furniture – carpets, stoves, grates, marble chimney- pieces, pier-glasses, pianos, lamps, candelabra, glass, china, etc., in twice the quantity and in greater variety than at any provincial town in England.'[52] There he boarded a steamer for the voyage across Lake Erie to Detroit. He felt at home upon water and even began to keep a log: '5 a.m. Light breezes and clear weather, land trending from South the S.S.W. Five sail in the offing.'[53]

Stopping only two nights at the National Hotel, Marryat began a five day expedition by birch-bark canoe on Lake Huron and then by way of the St Clair river to Lake Superior, when he was 'devoured by the mosquitoes.'[54] His guide was an Indian agent, Henry R Schoolcraft, in whose company he realised that he was not universally liked. Schoolcraft said later that he found his guest 'a perfect sea-urchin, ugly, rough-mannered and conceited beyond all bounds'. At the end of their cruise on Lake Huron, during which they came close to disaster in a sudden gale, he enlarged upon this, saying, 'His manner and style of conversation appeared to be those of a sailor and such as we should look for in his own *Peter Simple*. Temperance and religion, if not morality, were to him mere cant words and, wherever he was observed, either before, or after dinner, in the parlor or out of it – his words and manners were anything but those of a quiet, modest English gentleman.'[55] But it was Schoolcraft who inspired Marryat with a fascination with the American Indian.

Returning to Detroit, he was again lionised. Staying with Governor Stephen T Mason, he made a close friend of an actress, Charlotte Cushman, and, while enjoying the hospitality, he sharply observed his surroundings. Although the capital of the new state of Michigan, Detroit had not one paved street and 'in rainy weather, you are up to your knees in mud; in summer, practically invisible from dust.' So, when ladies went calling 'a small, one-horse cart is backed against the door of a house; the ladies, dressed, get into it and seat themselves upon a buffalo-skin at the bottom of it; they are carried to the residence of the party upon whom they wish to call.' But its population was fast growing and, he wrote, 'Detroit will soon ... become one of the most flourishing cities in America.'[56]

Boarding another steamer, he returned to Buffalo and the pace of his tour became even more hectic. Crossing into Canada, he visited Toronto, becoming aware of the convoluted, interlocking geography of the Great Lakes. There, 'mist, arising like curling smoke' from the spray from Niagara Falls and 'the roar of the water as it falls ... is sometimes distinctly heard at Toronto, a distance of fifty miles.'[57] Here, he remarked that 'the minute you put your foot on shore you feel that you are no longer in the United States ... You do not perceive the bustle, the energy and activity at Toronto that you do at Buffalo, or the profusion of articles in the stores ... The hotels and inns at Toronto are very bad.'[58]

But he felt confidence in the future of both the United States and Canada not only because of what he saw about him but after meeting an English friend, with whom he had attended shooting parties in Norfolk soon after he acquired the Langham estate.

The young man had failed in a business enterprise so his father had sent him to Canada with £1,000 and the promise of an annual allowance of £200. He had arrived in Canada seven years ago and now, Marryat recorded, 'I found him located on a beautiful farm of about four hundred acres ... His house was a very elegantly-built *cottage ornée* ... He had married a beautiful woman of one of the first families ... He was really living in luxury ... We returned the next day and the whole road from his farm to Toronto was lined with similar farms and handsome houses belonging to gentlemen who had emigrated, forming, among themselves, a very extensive and most delightful society.'[59] So Marryat himself became a landowner, writing to his mother that, as land doubled its value in five years, he had been 'fortunate in purchasing some very fair land from the Government opposite to Detroit on the Canada side – about 600 acres.'[60]

After a short stay in Toronto to pay the deposit on his purchase, he continued to Montreal – partly by the new railway – then headed south and back into the United States, through New England to New York; there his play, *The Ocean Wolf, or The Channel Outlaw* was about to open at the Bowery Theatre. By the end of September, Marryat was in Philadelphia, apparently tired of his own public performances as a famous novelist. One of his hosts, Samuel Breck, who had long connections with his family for he had introduced his parents to each other, now saw their son with undazzled eyes, remarking that he was 'a frank, plainspoken man ... There is in him no ambition to shine. He observes with a quick eye everything around him and speaks his thoughts ... with an off-hand, seaman-like positiveness.'[61] His stay was to be cut short by news that arrived from Montreal in November. It was terse and dramatic and presented him with a decision he had no difficulty in making. A rebellion had broken out in Canada. That was something he understood far more than writing or publishing and his duty was clear. He would postpone further research into American politics, economics and social customs; together with his new interest in the Indian tribes. He would return to Montreal and volunteer his services to his King.

CHAPTER TEN

These Deeds of Blood

T he first news that reached Philadelphia from Canada had
been of rioting in Montreal by French-Canadians. Worse
followed as Marryat hurried north through New England, where it was reported that British troops and Canadian
militia had been mobilised and that fighting had broken out.
During the first week of December 1837, he crossed from the
wooded hills of Vermont, where the red and gold leaves had
begun to fall, sleet was turning to snow and stagecoaches were
giving way to horse-drawn sleighs.

The trouble was not unexpected. It was nearly eighty years
since General Wolfe had taken Quebec and all Canada had come
under British rule, but the French-Canadians had never fully
accepted this. Of the two provinces, Lower Canada, along the St
Lawrence river, remained overwhelmingly French; Upper Canada, bordering the Great Lakes was predominantly British since
they made up almost all of the new immigrants, who had increased the population tenfold over the past quarter-century. In
the governing Assembly, the upper house was dominated by the
British; the lower, by the French, who felt that their interests
were being neglected by the colonial government there and in
London. A French movement for reform, if not independence,
grew but its leadership was divided, the more militant following
Louis Papineau, a forty-eight-year-old intellectual filled with unfocused French patriotism. Without any policy, or plan, his revolution was undisciplined and soon became violent.

When Marryat reached Montreal on 7 December he found the
city 'knee-deep in snow and the thermometer below zero' but
'all alive – mustering here, drilling there, galloping everywhere ...
Every hour brings fresh intelligence of the rebels, or patriots –

the last term is doubtful, but may be correct.'[1] Although the city was securely held by the British, many of the surrounding villages supported the *patriotes* and skirmishing had begun as one side, or the other, occupied them. The loyalist forces were commanded by Major-General Sir John Colborne, a bewhiskered, fifty-eight-year-old veteran of the Great War, who had routed the Imperial Guard at Waterloo and was now Lieutenant-Governor of Upper Canada. Captain Marryat met Colborne, who explained the gravity of the crisis and that he awaited reinforcements from Quebec before beginning major operations; and he made the captain a supernumerary member of his staff. 'Our defeat would be serious,' mused Marryat with a touch of his old ruthlessness, 'that is certain, for the loyalty of thousands depends upon their contiguity with bayonets.'[2]

Inevitably, violence had escalated as the rebels achieved minor successes and Colborne's particular worry was that the Americans might become involved. The United States had always been sympathetic towards the French-Canadians and there were reports that volunteers and arms might be smuggled across the border from New England. So the General sent columns across the Richelieu river to attack the villages of St Denis and St Charles, to the east of Montreal, which were held by the rebels and which commanded communications with Maine.

At St Denis, the rebels had fortified a stone house and the troops, lacking heavy artillery, were beaten off. Meanwhile communications between the two columns was to have been made by a courier, Lieutenant Jack Weir of the 32nd Regiment, who was to make his way through rebel-held country with despatches either with his uniform hidden, or in civilian clothes. On 23 November, Weir had been stopped by rebels near St Denis, questioned and forced to admit his name and rank. When the attack on the village began, the lieutenant was bound and was being taken to the French-Canadian headquarters at St Charles by cart. As this lurched over frozen slush along woodland tracks, he tried to escape and, although pinioned, jumped to the ground and stumbled towards the trees. His guards shot him and hacked him with sabres but Weir managed to struggle to his feet and

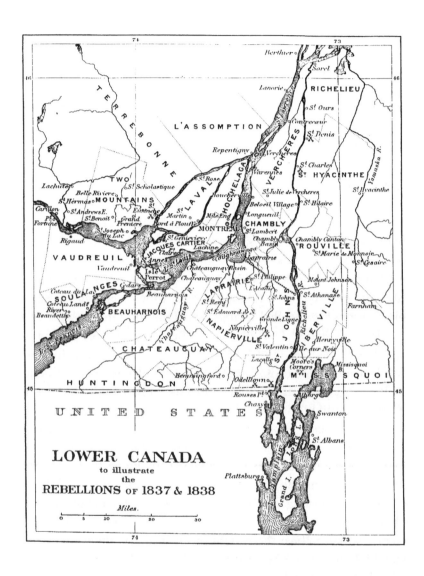

LOWER CANADA
to illustrate
the
REBELLIONS OF 1837 & 1838

take refuge beneath the cart; he was dragged out and killed; his mutilated body was then weighted and thrown into the Richelieu river.

News of the killing sharply increased the ferocity of the war, as Marryat put it, 'when an English soldier swears to show no mercy, he generally keeps his word.'[3] When the second British column reached St Charles, they instantly attacked with the bayonet; although outnumbered two to one, they routed a thousand rebels, killing nearly sixty. St Denis also fell, Weir's body was found in the river and a reward was offered for the capture of his killers. The soldiers began to sack and burn with fresh ruthlessness, chalking on walls the words, 'Remember Jack Weir.'[4]

Now that there was little chance that American aid could reach the rebels from the east and south-east, Colborne proclaimed martial law and turned his attention to the west of Montreal. There, early in December, some eight hundred rebels had gathered at the little town of St Eustache, about twenty miles from the city, and at St Benoit beyond, which commanded communications up the St Lawrence towards the Great Lakes and the United States. The rebels' two field commanders, Chenier and Girod, had fortified St Eustache and the general himself would lead his main force of two thousand regular troops and volunteers against them. The cold was intense and painful and Marryat, muffled in furs, felt and serge, was offered one of the general's horses – 'supplying the place of a groom who was better employed'[5] – but it was too cold to ride; so he set out in a sleigh drawn by two horses in tandem to what was to be his first battle since those along the Irrawaddy twelve years before.

'On the morning of the 7th, the ice on the branch of the Ottawa river, which we had to cross, being considered sufficiently strong to bear the weight of the artillery, the whole force marched out,' wrote Marryat in his diary. 'The snow ... lay very deep but, by the time we started, the road had been well beaten down by the multitudes which had preceded us. The effect of the whole line of troops, in their fur caps and great coats, with the trains of artillery, ammunition and baggage-wagons, as they wound along the snow-white road was very beautiful. It is astonishing how much more numerous the force and how much larger the men and horses appeared to be from the strong contrast of their colours with the wide expanse of snow.'6 They crossed the frozen river but one of the ammunition wagons crashed through the ice, the drivers saving the horses by cutting them from the traces and hauling bridles tightly round their necks so that their lungs inflated and they could float to be hauled ashore.

Reaching St Eustache next day, Marryat scanned their objective as he had the Burmese stockades. The village, he wrote, was 'very pretty situated on the high banks of the river, the most remarkable object being the Catholic church, a very large, massive building, raised about two hundred yards from the riverside upon a commanding situation. This church the insurgents had turned into a fortress and ... there was never one so well calculated for a vigorous defence, it being flanked by two long, stone-built houses and protected in the rear by several lines of high and strong palisades running down to the river ... The troops halted about three hundred yards from the town to reconnoitre; the artillery were drawn up and opened their fire but chiefly with a view that the enemy, by returning their fire, might demonstrate their force and position.'7 Colborne was unaware that two-thirds of the rebels, including Girod, had fled.

Mounted on his charger, the General ordered the infantry to surround the town; as they did so, 'the insurgents, perceiving this, many of them escaped, some through the town, others by the frozen river. Those who crossed the ice were chased by the volunteer dragoons, and the slipping and tumbling of the pursued and the pursuers afforded as much merriment as interest; so true it is, that anything ludicrous will make one laugh in opposition to the feelings of sympathy, anxiety and fear. Some of the runaways were cut down and many more taken prisoners.'8

The fortified church was the core of the *patriotes'* defences and troops, marched down the main street towards it and when 'within half-musket shot were received by a smart volley, which was fired from the large windows of the church', which wounded a few soldiers; Marryat remembered hearing 'bullets whizzing about my ears.'[9] The infantry were then ordered 'to make their approaches under cover of the houses; and, the artillery being brought up, commenced firing upon the church; but the walls of the building were much too solid for the shot to make any impression and, had the insurgents stood firm, they certainly might have given a great deal of trouble and probably have occasioned a severe loss of men ... but they became alarmed and fired one of the houses which abutted upon and flanked the church – this they did with the view of escaping under cover of the smoke. In a few minutes the church itself was obscured by the volumes of smoke thrown out; and at the same time as the insurgents were escaping, the troops marched up and surrounded the church. The poor wretches attempted to get away, either singly or by twos or threes; but the moment they appeared a volley was discharged and they fell. Every attempt was made by the officers to make prisoners but with indifferent success; indeed, such was the exasperation of the troops at the murder of Lieut. Weir that it was a service of danger to attempt to save the life of one of these poor, deluded creatures. Fire from the house soon communicated to the church. Chenier, the leader, with ten others, the remnant of those who were in the church, rushed out; there was one tremendous volley and all was over.'[10] The fighting had lasted an hour; about seventy rebels had been killed and a few soldiers and volunteers wounded; for Colborne, this could not have been more different from facing the Imperial Guard at Waterloo.

Accustomed to war, Marryat found it an ugly little battle. 'It has been a sad scene of sacrilege, murder, burning and destroying,' he wrote to his mother later. 'All the fights have been in the churches and they are now burnt to the ground and strewed with the wasted bodies of the insurgents. War is bad enough, but civil war is dreadful.'[11]

The fire spread from the church and presbytery to other houses and, to escape the fire, Marryat's sleigh had to be driven through a narrow street lined with blazing houses: 'one side of each of the horses was burnt brown and yellow before we could force them through ... the poor animals were more frightened than hurt.'[12] The soldiers turned their attention to fire-fighting, pulling down buildings to halt the spread of the flames, not so much to save the town but to preserve houses as billets for themselves. 'The night was bitterly cold,' wrote Marryat, 'the sky was clear and the moon near to her full: houses were still burning in every direction but they were as mere satellites to the lofty church, which was now one blaze of fire and throwing out volumes of smoke, which passed over the face of the bright moon and gave her a lurid, reddish tinge as if she, too, had assisted in these deeds of blood. The distant fires scattered over the whole landscape, which was one snow-wreath, the whirling of the smoke from the houses ... which, from the melting of the snow, were surrounded by pools of water, reflecting the fierce, yellow flames, mingled with the pale beams of the bright moon – this, altogether, presented a beautiful, novel, yet melancholy panorama. I thought it might represent, in miniature, the burning of Moscow.'[13]

At midnight, when all was quiet, Marryat and an officer were walking up to the church, when they heard cries, then found and saved a wounded rebel lying in a blazing house. Reaching the church, Marryat reflected on what it had been – 'the solemn music, the incense' – and what he saw: 'nothing but bare and blackened walls, the glowing beams and rafters and the window-frames, which the flames still licked and flickered through. The floor had been burnt to cinders.'[14] There he saw the ghastly scorched and charred remnants of the dead.

It was over: Chenier had been killed, Girod committed suicide and St Benoit fell without a fight. On the 16th, Captain Marryat rode sadly back to Montreal. Brief as his participation had been, he was shaken, having experienced nothing like this before. 'We have been fighting in the deep snow,' he wrote to his mother, 'and crossing rivers with ice thick enough to bear the artillery; we have always been in extreme – at one time, our ears and noses frost-bitten by the extreme cold; at others, roasting amidst the flames of hundreds of houses.'[15]

The rebellion was not quite over because the French-Canadian's American sympathisers began smuggling arms and volunteers across the frontier and this seemed impossible to stop. The wide, fast-flowing rivers of North America had not frozen solid, although cluttered with ice-floes and so difficult to navigate, but could be crossed. The border followed the St Lawrence and Niagara rivers for many miles and the surest way to cross was by one of the rare, new paddle-steamers. One of these, the American-owned *Caroline*, manned by rebels and several Americans, was being used for gun-running, shipping weapons and ammunition – said to be from United States arsenals – to a thousand French-Canadian rebels occupying Navy Island in the Niagara river. The forty-six ton ship did not, of course, depend upon the wind and that, combined with the current and the ice, made it impossible to intercept her with sailing or rowed gunboats.

A friend of Marryat's, Captain Andrew Drew, Royal Navy, had already arrived on the Canadian bank of the river. Drew, a con-temporary and former shipmate of Marryat's – they had both taken part in the Walcheren campaign – was asked to find a solution to the problem of the *Caroline* and her gun-running, a challenge that would have delighted his friend. From Chippawa on the low-lying Canadian shore of the river above the Falls, he could see the thickly wooded Navy Island, where the rebels were entrenched and firing their cannon at the Canadian bank six hun-dred yards away; from the vantage-point of the Pavilion Hotel, could even watch through his telescope as the *Caroline* landed field-guns and muskets on the beach. But when the steamer re-turned to the far shore, trailing smoke from her tall funnel, her berth on the American shore was masked by the trees of Navy Island. But Drew was told that she would moor close inshore, beneath the guns of Fort Schlosser, where she would be, he was assured, invulnerable. The loyalist force assembled at Chippawa numbered three thousand but could only watch helplessly.

For a naval officer of Drew's and Marryat's generation there was an immediate response: the ship would have to be cut out. It would be a night action, exactly like so many they had fought around the coasts of Napoleon's Europe. Drew chose three of-ficers – including a British infantry captain – and called for sixty volunteers from the loyalist militia. Then, on the night of 29

December 1837, he and his men, armed with pistols, pikes and cutlasses, clambered aboard seven boats on the Canadian shore, upstream of Navy Island, and pulled out into the freezing darkness. It was an expedition of which Lord Cochrane would have been proud.

So strong was the current that the oars were needed only for steering across to the far side of Navy Island and thence to Fort Schlosser, where the steamer lay. As Drew's boat ran silently alongside her, the rebel crew opened fire, hitting several of the boarding-party as they scrambled on to her deck and fought hand to hand. The fight was short but fierce, one – perhaps more – of the rebel crew was killed, the rest escaping ashore, or surrendering; then it was over and the guns of Fort Schlosser were still silent; three of the attackers had been wounded. Drew had hoped to take his prize back across the river but it was obvious that the current was too strong for oared boats to tow her and, by the time they could have fired her boiler and got up steam, the gunners of Fort Schlosser would be in action.

There was one other course open to a cutting-out expedition that failed to carry its prize away. Cutting the *Caroline*'s cable, tow-ropes were made fast and she was hauled from her moorings and into the main stream of the Niagara river. There, Captain Drew set her on fire and jumped into his boat to watch as he 'sent her flaming over Niagara Falls.'*[16] It was a spectacle that would have delighted Marryat, something to remember, like the bursting of the boom off Rochefort. American opinion was outraged: the *Caroline*, an American ship, had been seized from moorings in United States waters and at least one American citizen had been killed; what the British hailed as a glorious little victory was condemned by Americans as piracy.

Marryat had left Montreal by coach shortly before Christmas for New York on his way to resume his stay in Philadelphia.

---

* In fact, she grounded, blazing, on a reef near Goat Island just above the Falls, her bow breaking away and plunging over the edge. Her figurehead was found off Lewiston next day and is now in the collection of the Buffalo Historical Society; the steamer's flag was taken by the British and is now in Toronto Public Library; the remains of the ship's engine and paddle-wheels lay rusting in the shallows off Goat Island for at least three decades.

Crossing the St Lawrence was made hazardous by ice-floes sweeping down-river on the current – next day, the river froze solid enough to bear ox-drawn wagons – then, uncomfortably, by sleigh over ridges of frozen snow 'as the sleigh jumps from hill to hill, like an oyster-shell thrown by a boy to skim the surface of the water.'[17] It was agonisingly cold and Marryat wore under his cloak and coat 'a wadded black silk dressing-gown ... I afterwards discovered that I was supposed to be one of the rebel priests escaping justice.'[18]

Travelling towards the American frontier he passed through Lower Canada, which was mostly French-speaking and hostile and when he crossed into the United States, he realised that American opinion had supported the French-Canadian *patriotes*. 'It is strange how easily the American people are excited,' he noted. The sleigh stopped at the inns in Vermont towns and he wrote, 'I always got out to warm myself at the stove in the bar and heard ... the most absurd lies, which the very people who uttered them knew to be such but which produced the momentary effect intended. They were even put into the newspaper ... and, when the truth was discovered, they still remained uncontradicted ... The majority of those who travelled with me were Americans, who had crossed the St Lawrence in the same boat, and who must have known well the whole circumstances attending the expedition to St Eustache; but, to my surprise, they declared that there had been a battle between the King's troops in which the insurgents had been victorious ... I never said one word.'[19]

At St Albans in Vermont, fifteen miles from the border, he was interviewed about the rebellion by the editor of the local newspaper in a private room at the inn. As Marryat began to expound, the door opened and, unbidden, patrons of the tavern trooped in, sat down and listened. Eventually, the room was packed with more than a hundred silent men. When Marryat stopped talking, the editor departed and there was silence until one of the audience thumped his stick on the floor, and declared, 'I believe, sir, that you are Captain Marryat?'

He then accused Marryat of 'trying to prove to us that we are totally ignorant. You will oblige us by an explanation of your assertions.' Marryat assessed the position and concluded, 'Thinks I to myself, I'm for it now and if I get away without a broken head, or something worse, I am fortunate; however, here goes.' He then began to speak again, telling in laborious detail the story of British Canada from the fall of Quebec, through the American revolutionary war and the Declaration of Independence. 'Having spoken for about an hour and observing a little impatience on the part of some of my company, I stopped.' Questions followed and were answered at length, with compliments to the institutions of the United States. The audience began to relax. 'Perceiving this, I ventured to introduce a story or two, which made them laugh. After this, the day was my own; for I consider the Americans, when not excited (which they too often are) are a very good-tempered people ... The affair ended with many of them shaking hands with me and our taking a drink at the bar ... The landlord said to me afterwards, "I reckon you got out of that uncommon well, captain." '[20]

He reached Burlington in time for Christmas, watching pretty girls festoon the church with garlands of evergreens. At the Christmas Day service, he reflected, 'Last Sunday, I was meditating over the blackened walls of the church at St Eustache and the roasted corpses lying within its precincts; now I am in another church ... in the company with some of the prettiest creatures in creation. As the copy-book says, *variety is charming*!'[21]

That was only the beginning. Many Americans – including politicians – had seen the French-Canadians' uprising as an extension of their own revolutionary war and so grieved at its failure. 'It is probable that the British soldiers may put down the present movement,' declared the New York *Morning Herald* in the early stages of the rebellion, 'but others will arise sooner or later and blood will be spilled until the Canadians gain their point and ultimately become independent.'[22] It later reported the arrest of hundreds of *patriotes* and the 'most unmerciful war'[23] being waged against them. They admitted to 'gunpowder barrels smuggled across the frontier into Lower Canada' from the United States and when a rebel leader escaped to New York, he was hailed as 'the Champion and Martyr of Liberty.'[24]

They were outraged by the cutting-out of their steamer, accusing the British of piracy and murder and, early in January 1838, the same newspaper proclaimed that the United States was 'in a state of half-madness, calling out for war' and invoking 'the enduring principle of the revolution of 1776.'[25] Marryat had learned a lesson and kept quiet when he reached New York but when he arrived at Philadelphia and resumed his stay with the old family friend Samuel Breck, he felt he could relax. This was a mistake particularly when, as his host noted, 'the captain, accustomed to act the cock of the party, plied the bottle as a true son of Neptune, though not to intoxication.'[26] In the climate of hostility to the British, Breck was acutely sensitive to any criticism of the city and the nation by his guest. He observed that such visitors were, 'if English, a parcel of offensive smellfunguses, too prejudiced to see clearly, too supercilious to acknowledge the good they see and too disgustingly insolent in telling us what they do not like.'[27] Aware that his welcome had evaporated, Marryat left Philadelphia for Washington.

Here, he had two principal aims: to continue his research into American politics and economics; and to urge the abolition of publishing piracy, from which his books were still suffering. In the first, he was successful, meeting Martin Van Buren, the eighth President of the United States, whom he considered 'a very gentleman-like, intelligent man.'[28] In the second, he was unsuccessful. However, the war fever brought about by the French-Canadian rebellion and the *Caroline* affair seemed to have cooled and his reception was friendly.

Here, as in Philadelphia, he also interested himself in the state of black Americans. Like most Europeans of his time he doubted whether those of African descent could ever equal their own achievements. But he added, 'I do not mean to say that there *never* will be great men among the African race' and 'in Philadelphia, the free coloured people are a very respectable class ... and show great intelligence and keenness ... They are both numerous and wealthy. The most extravagant funeral I saw in Philadelphia was that of a black: the coaches were very numerous, as well as the pedestrians, who were all well dressed and behaving with the utmost decorum.' Yet, he reported, 'In the United States, a negro, from his colour, and, I believe, his colour alone, is a degraded being. Is not this extraordinary, in a land which professes universal liberty, equality and the rights of man? In England, this is not the case. In private society no one objects to sit in company with a man of colour, provided he has the necessary education and respectability.'[29]

In April, he was back in Upper Canada, which he thought 'the finest portion of North America,'[30] because he was arranging to sell the lease of the land he had bought there to a friend of his family, who was planning to emigrate. On the 23rd, he was in Toronto and invited to a St George's Day dinner and to propose a suitable toast. Comfortable in the company of Canadian loyalists, he rose, raised his glass and proposed, 'To Captain Drew and his brave comrades, who cut out the *Caroline*.'[31] The toast was drunk and the convivial dinner continued.

Soon afterwards he set out for Detroit and, once over the frontier, realised that the toast to his old shipmate had reignited hostility to the British and that he himself was now an object of hatred. At Lewiston, on the American side of the lake, he saw a poster headed, 'MORE INSOLENCE!!!'[32] reporting his toast and commanding, 'Persons in this village, having any novels of this author, will please to hand them in at the Lewiston Hotel this day before four o'clock, p.m., for the purpose of having a *novel* spectacle made of them this evening.'[33] Writing to his mother, he told her, 'They have burnt me in effigy, dancing round the fire and tossing in *Peter Simple, Jacob* and *Japhet* and all the rest of them, one after another. There is no knowing to what honours a man may come; it is not everybody who is burnt in effigy; I shall be tarred and feathered yet before I get out of the country.'[34] To a friend, he wrote, 'They have made a bonfire of my works ... I understand that tar and feathers await me in Buffalo. The feathers ought to be paid me as I have been pluck'd all my life; but to the tar I have no objection to that, it being in the way of my profession.'[35]

The demonisation of Marryat spread quickly through American newspapers. He was no longer seen as the famous visiting author, the gallant naval officer and the jolly raconteur but as the supercilious, arrogant, lisping Englishman. In Detroit a jeering mob gathered beneath his windows and he was glad to escape by departing on an expedition into the West. By way of the Great Lakes, he entered the Wisconsin Territory to stay at United States Army forts and continue his study of the Indians. It was hazardous at times and he narrowly escaped drowning in the Wisconsin river but now he met the soldiers, trackers and fur-traders on the frontier and the Sioux Indians, whom he described as 'the most perfect gentlemen in America'.[36] But he aroused the antagonism of the Indian agent at Fort Snelling when, on meeting the Sioux and speaking through an interpreter, he 'announced himself as an Englishman ... spoke of their great nation' and told them 'that their great British fathers had not forgotten them.'[37] The agent thereupon told him that 'his exploration of the country closed at Fort Snelling.'[38]

This concluded his research into American Indians but did not prevent him from writing his survey. He estimated that there there were three hundred and thirty thousand Indians in the West and that more than sixty thousand of these were warriors, who could 'certainly sweep away the whole white population west of the Mississippi'[39] and so would necessitate defensive garrisons of up to thirteen thousand troops. He also aired the theory that they were descended from the 'lost tribes' of Israel, although he did not speculate as to how they had reached America.

So Marryat abandoned plans to travel further west and headed for St Louis, where he arrived on 3 July. There, he found himself again the focus of anti-British bile when he saw his own effigy swinging from a gallows in the Independence Day parade. Bravely, he attended the theatre and went out to dine but found the heat as stifling as in Calcutta and, after a few days, was relieved to leave by steamer on the 'wild and filthy waters, boiling and eddying' of the Mississippi, 'a vile sewer',[40] heading for Louisville and Cincinnati. Still he was surrounded by hatred, inflamed by the press; 'The newspapers abuse me but that is all and that is nothing in America',[41] he mused.

It was in Cincinnati that he found an opportunity to state his own case. He was as pleasantly surprised to find 'a beautiful, well-built, clean city' and he was gratified that, despite his persecution, a dinner had been arranged in his honour. Introduced by the chairman as 'The Wizard of the Sea', and sensing a sympathetic audience, he took the opportunity to defend in his speech what Americans saw as his notorious toast to Captain Drew. He pointed out that on St George's Day he had paid tribute to 'the last naval achievement, which had occurred but a short distance from where we stood. It was not for me to enter into the doubtful question how far we were justified in taking the vessel out of an American port. Sailors have nothing to do with such questions – they obey *orders* ... It is the ignorance of the truth, so studiously circulated, which has caused this excitement ... The facts were: the *Caroline* was *chartered* by the rebels, *manned* and *armed* by the rebels, *fired first* upon our boat and was *defended* by the rebels to the best of their ability as the loss on the British side so plainly testifies.'

He reminded his audience that, on Independence Day, he, as a British officer, had been obliged to drink American toasts to the victors of Bunker Hill and New Orleans, which, he recognised were 'of as much importance in their results to America as were those of Trafalgar and Waterloo to the English.' But he himself had been 'paraded in effigy round the town of St Louis with a halter around my neck merely because I had paid a deserved compliment to the gallantry of one of my own country and profession.' A long, eloquent speech concluded with his assertion that he had 'too much confidence in the Americans not to feel assured that the tide would soon turn and honour and justice eventually gain the day ... and, feeling that I am before a conscientious jury, I now ask of you your verdict – Guilty, or Not Guilty?' The response was, he said, 'a universal and deafening shout of "Not Guilty!" ' Immediately taking advantage of this, he proposed another toast: 'The Ladies of Cincinnati!'[42]

His triumph was assured when one of the audience, a Captain Joseph Pierce, rose to say that twenty-four years earlier, he had been a member of the crew of an American privateer, captured off Newfoundland by the British frigate *Newcastle*. For the forty days he had spent as prisoner, Captain Lord George Stuart had treated him with 'indignity, harshness and severity.' However, he continued, 'Our guest at that time was junior lieutenant of the *Newcastle*, then about twenty years of age ...' The ship's company had been forbidden to speak to the prisoners, who were kept 'huddled together between the guns of the main deck.' But Marryat, 'and he alone', had broken the rules and 'meliorated in a degree' their lot. 'Lieutenant Marryat was the first man belonging to the frigate who spoke to him. He was the man that took him by the hand as he went over that ship's side, on his way to prison, and said, "Pierce, be of good cheer". From that time to the present time, he had never met him. He was proud to take him by the hand at this time ...' Thereupon, he proposed a toast to, 'Health and long life to Captain Frederick Marryat, the man who, under the dictates of humanity, dared to break through the rules of a tyrant ...'[43]

Leaving Cincinnati in a glow of goodwill, Marryat plunged back into unpopularity. Arriving at Lexington in Kentucky, he was accused by a newspaper of insulting his host and even the latter's denial of the story failed to lessen the hostility. Returning to Louisville in mid-September, he, for the first time, became embroiled in a sexual scandal. There he met a Mrs Collyer, the flirtatious wife of a phrenologist, a couple who were staying at the same hotel. The husband's jealousy was so aroused that he announced that he would be away for the night, then furtively returned to their room and hid under the bed. At one o'clock next morning, his patience was rewarded by the arrival of his wife and the captain in night attire. At this the phrenologist emerged from hiding, shouting, 'Fire!', 'Rape!', 'Treason!'[44] and attacked Marryat, while the wife collapsed, weeping, on the bed. When the hotel manager and most of the other guests crowded into the room, Marryat protested that he had heard Mrs Collyer was adept at the treatment of sprained joints and he had been seeking her ministrations for this. The story appeared in the local newspaper and litigation seemed certain. Then, surprisingly, the wronged husband wrote to the newspaper that he himself had been under the influence of drink that night and had misunderstood Marryat's intentions. Few believed him and a theory circulated that he had withdrawn his charges in order to avoid a duel.

Before leaving Louisville, Marryat tried again to clear his name and recover his popularity. Underlying the specific objections to his behaviour over the past year was the Americans' suspicion that he was planning to write a critical, mocking book about them and to this was now added a spate of anonymous letters. So he wrote a verbose letter to the *Louisville Journal*, declaring his innocence of social espionage. 'It appears to me,' he wrote, 'that I am considered to be travelling through this country as a spy ... availing myself of American hospitality and in grateful return holding up to ridicule the domestic manners and customs of those who have kindly admitted me into their circles.' He denied this, continuing, 'I did not come three thousand, five hundred miles by water and since peregrinate about fifteen thousand more ... to ascertain whether the American people ate their dinner with two- or three-pronged, or silver forks, or took up green peas with their knives ... whether the children sat down in high chairs, had silver mugs to splutter in, or china ones with their names in gold letters ...'[45] So it continued at great length, perhaps laying him open to the charge that he protested too much.

There was to be another visit to Montreal before the end of the year and there he learned that, although the rebellion seemed to be over, the insurgents still held Navy Island in the Niagara river. He had heard that the rebels had been firing their American artillery at the Canadian shore, where the British had had to mount guns and mortars of the Royal Artillery and it had needed a 24-pounder to silence the battery on the island. Having missed the cutting out of the *Caroline* and half-expecting war with the United States – a Canadian volunteer in that action was being charged with murder by the Americans – he was avid for service afloat, even so far from the sea, and offered his services. He was told that other naval officers on half-pay had done likewise and his services were unlikely to be required, so continued his travels south to New York. Yet he still dreamed of naval glory, writing to his mother that he might be making another journey to Niagara: 'They will have great difficulty at Navy Island, should they attack it ... I shall therefore wait to see what takes place; if they are beat back at Navy Island' and if he was summoned, 'I will go.'[46]

Then, on second thoughts, he realised that if he did manage to return to Canada in mid-winter, he would be stranded there by snow and ice until May, so decided to return home, telling his mother, 'If I am appointed to the Lakes, from my knowledge of the country I had rather be at home to communicate my ideas to the Government' and he asked her to forward to a naval friend in London 'the enclosed plan of Navy Island, as it will be interesting to the Admiralty.'[47]

He had received a worrying letter from Edward Howard*, who, he noted, 'writes me in very bad spirits. He says that I am much injured by remaining away from England and my popularity is on the wane.' Although affecting disdain for writing – 'I am rather tired of it' – and, claiming that he would 'like to disengage myself from the fraternity of authors and be known in future only in my profession as a good officer and seaman',[48] he knew it was time to go home. In January 1839, he returned across the Atlantic.

---

* Howard was to die suddenly at the end of 1841.

CHAPTER ELEVEN

An Affair between Me and the Public

On his return to Europe, Marryat immediately visited his family, now living in Paris. Kate was established there with their four daughters – Blanche, Augusta, Emily and Florence – while their two surviving sons, Frederick and Frank, were following their father into the Navy. There were two diametrically opposing outcomes of this visit: Kate became pregnant and the couple decided to live apart; she in Paris and he in London. A deed of separation was agreed because of 'differences and disputes' that had arisen and 'from incompatibility of temper, an absolute separation from bed, board and cohabitation hath, by mutual agreement, actually taken place ...'[1] He was to pay his wife an annual allowance of £500.

Marryat returned to London and his Duke Street lodgings, which he furnished with souvenirs of his two years in America: 'prairie curiosities – bear, buffalo and opossum skins; bowie-knives ... and odds and ends of all sorts. Now the bowie-knives were harmless enough but the skins with which his rooms were literally hung, the chairs covered and the floors carpeted were very much to the contrary. They had never been properly dressed and, in plain English, they were *tenanted* and strongly required a visit to the furrier.

'Many literary ladies and others of note and distinction honoured his rooms with their presence, admired the pictures, stroked the panther, went into ecstasies over the great black bear with real silver claws ... and fell in love with the blue fox; but, somehow or other, after the inspection, they all felt – how can their feelings be expressed? – *irritated*. In fact, each successive visitor was glad to drive home again and change his, or her clothes.'[2]

Soon afterwards, Marryat decided to move to his mother's house at Wimbledon. There would be no need for the heavy, expensive furniture from Duke Street, so, in a characteristic burst of generosity, he had it carted to the little house of an impoverished artist he knew, where only the chairs could be manhandled through the front door; the furs were sent to a furrier in Oxford Street for fumigation and storage. At his new abode, too, he displayed his souvenirs until 'there was scarcely a room in Wimbledon House that was not decorated with some of the spoils which Captain Marryat had collected on his travels ... a Burmese shrine with silver idols, rifled from a pagoda; the carved tusks of a sacred elephant; opossum skins from Canada, embroidered with porcupine quills and coloured beads; toys in tortoiseshell and ivory, with precious stones and curious shells, were scattered everywhere, recalling memories of the Rangoon war, America, India and the celestial Empire.'[3]

In his own apartments there, overlooking the park, he prepared his American diaries for publication on lined foolscap in 'a little old black leather blotting book' on a table 'covered with an African lion's skin.'[4] Despite his earlier misgivings, he plunged into the literary life again, complaining, 'what with printers, engravers, stationers and publishers, I have been much overworked. I have written and read till my eyes have been no bigger than a mole's and my sight about as perfect.'[5] As well as *A Diary in America*, he had written a novel, while on his travels – *The Phantom Ship*, based on the legend of 'The Flying Dutchman' – and that was also about to be published; and another novel, *Poor Jack*, about a Channel pilot, was being illustrated by Clarkson Stanfield.

Still restless, Marryat moved to a little house in the Gothick taste, Gothic Lodge, nearby and close to Southside House where Nelson and the Hamiltons had once passed evenings at cards. He also visited his property in Norfolk in December, enjoying the shooting – 'as soon as the widgeon are sent up I shall send some down to you,' he wrote to a friend. 'I will not forget the oysters'[6] – and spending Christmas with a fellow-member of the Garrick Club, Sir Jacob Astley, at his mansion, Melton Constable Hall: 'The servants had a ball and we went down to it and joined them. What with punch, pushing and pretty housemaids, it was good fun.'[7]

He broke the return journey in Norwich, which he described with as much gusto as New York. While waiting until 'Phaebus unyokes his anything but fiery coursers, the Ipswich mail will put its horses to and then I am off to London.'[8] It was market day, bright and frosty, and he visited 'Mr Wombwell's menagerie of wild beasts ... No want of pretty girls staring at the paintings outside, which invariably have the merit of portraying things larger than life in all cases, except in dwarfs, who are the only exception to the rule. I was rather amused at a painting outside an exhibition, on which was written, "The Largest Travelling Alligator in All Europe". Now, although the painting represents him thirty feet long, still he may not be more than five inches and yet the assertion be correct. I did not go into see him as the price was only a penny and what sized alligator could you expect to see for a penny?'[9]

Back in London, he began to savour metropolitan life again. The social set that attracted Marryat was bohemian and this, in its higher ranges, revolved round the literary salon presided over by Lady Blessington, the authoress; now past fifty but still attractive and amusing, her scandalous life had excluded her from polite society. To this she had responded by creating her own circle of 'the best male society';[10] here, Marryat was welcome, she finding him 'full of talent, originality and humour.'[11] Kate Marryat, hearing of her estranged husband's success with the notorious hostess, wrote him a stiffly reproving letter, to which he replied, 'Do not think that because I visit Lady Blessington and others that I prefer their company. I do not, but I must mix in the world as it is, employed as I am.'[12] To be closer to such friends, he moved again, first to lodgings at 120 Piccadilly, then taking a relatively modest, narrow-fronted, five-storey house, 3 Spanish Place off Manchester Square in the fashionable residential district of

Marylebone. It was delightful to again be talking, drinking and smoking with in such convivial company. Amongst many were Theodore Hook with his jokes and conjuring tricks; the eccentric, bibulous George Cruikshank; the charming and hospitable Clarkson Stanfield; the elegant, good-looking historical novelist Harrison Ainsworth, who had just published *The Tower of London* to wide acclaim; the painter Edwin Landseer, famous for his paintings of royalty and animals; and the writer Sir Edward Bulwer-Lytton, whose evocation of Ancient Rome in *The Last Days of Pompeii* had caused a sensation. This was probably the happiest of all his London homes, for, as was recorded, 'It was here, in the tiniest of houses, furnished according to his taste, a very gem in point of its adornments – rich in pictures and *objets d'art*, clothed in velvet and decorated with hot-house flowers – he received visitors and made the little rooms brilliant with their conversation and their wit.'[13]

His guests shared a mutual friend, whom Marryat did not know, a man who was now more discussed than any in London: Charles Dickens. Since his *Pickwick Papers* had enthralled the passengers on the ship to New York, Dickens had become even more famous with the publication of two novels, *Oliver Twist* in 1833 and, in the following year, *Nicholas Nickleby*, and he was being taken up by fashionable bohemia. Even in Lady Blessington's sumptuous salon at Gore House in Kensington, to which he had recently been introduced, the young writer could prompt such praise as that of the writer Leigh Hunt: 'What a face to meet in a drawing-room! It has the life and soul of fifty human beings!'[14] Another writer, Anthony Trollope, said, 'he warmed the social atmosphere wherever he appeared with that summer glow, which seemed to attend him ... His laugh was brimful of enjoyment.'[15]

Then, in January 1841, Clarkson Stanfield wrote to Dickens, 'I have before told you that my friend Captain Marryat is very anxious to have "what all covet", the pleasure of your acquaintance and, if therefore you have no objection to meet him, will you come and take a beef steak with me on Wednesday 27 ... I will ask Maclise* and Jerdan† to meet you ...'[16] By return of post, Dickens replied, 'I shall be delighted to join you and to know Marryat';[17] he brushed aside a potentially unpleasant confrontation, a year before, when Longman, Marryat's publisher, had advertised *Poor Jack* as of more worth than 'those shoals of trash, which we owe to *Pickwick* and *Nicholas Nickleby*', then clumsily claimed that they had referred to other, unworthy books, which had tried to imitate Dickens's success.

When they met, Charles Dickens was aged twenty-seven – twelve years younger than Marryat – but married and living with his wife, also named Kate, and their small children; two daughters and a son, the birth of a second being imminent – in a grand, stucco-fronted house, 1 Devonshire Terrace, having recently moved from a modest house in Holborn. As expected, he had a remarkable presence but quite unlike any his new acquaintance had formerly known. There was something of the actor about him in looks, manner and dress. He was not handsome like Marryat whose 'firm, decisive mouth and massive, thoughtful forehead ... the humorous light that twinkled in his deep-set grey eyes, which bright as diamonds, positively flashed out their fun.'[18] Dickens's face was also clean-shaven but attractively mobile, his 'magnificently lustrous eyes' cast 'perpetually discursive glances' and 'wavy locks of hair' swagged his forehead and temples. He laughed easily, entertained with genial mockery and sharp mimicry and, beneath it all, boiled his creativity. The two men took to each other at once. They shared a recognition of the absurd and could present it entertainingly, sometimes mixed with pathos and even tragedy. But while Marryat re-created the world that he himself had experienced in his books, Dickens's imagination erupted with cavalcades of characters and panoramas of widely varied scenery. Dickens did not see Marryat as a rival but recognised his skill in presenting the world of the sea and seamen, which he himself could only try to imagine. Thanking Marryat for sending him his latest novel, Dickens wrote, 'I

---

* Daniel Maclise, the painter.
† William Jerdan, editor of the *Literary Gazette*.

have been chuckling, and grinning, and clenching my fists and becoming warlike for three whole days past.'[19]

While Marryat was enthralled by Dickens's pyrotechnic displays in conversation, Dickens was amused by the contrasts in Marryat and friendship quickly ripened. The latter was by no means entertaining all the time and could be moody: 'Captain Marryat could be charming, especially with young people,' it was said, 'though his manners were brusque and, at first, somewhat alarmed them.'[20] When a mutual friend, Henry Vizetelly, the engraver, first met him, he found 'nothing of the jovial "salt" about him ... On the contrary, his manners were grave and he had a rather peremptory way of speaking, which his friends, though never in his hearing, for that would have been dangerous, were in the habit of terming his "quarterdeck style".'[21] There was his formidable physical presence – broad shoulders, deep chest – and a hint of lurking violence. In contrast, there was his lisp, which none dared to mock; but it was Dickens who, writing to a friend about a religious fresco he had seen, quipped, 'I can make out a Virgin with a mildewed Glory round her head and ... what Marryat would call the arthe of a cherub.'[22]

But the captain would be transformed when there were children about; his own were in Paris and he loved being invited to parties for the young at Devonshire Terrace. Dickens's friend, John Forster, remarked: 'Captain Marryat ... had a frantic delight in dancing ... especially with children, of whom and whose enjoyments he was so fond as it became so thoroughly a good-hearted man to be ... He was among the first in Dickens's liking.'[23] The Dickens children taught him to dance the polka, prompting Charles Dickens himself to be so amused at the thought of it that one night he 'jumped out of bed and practised it in the dark of a cold floor.'[24] Marryat was always remembered when a children's party was being planned at Devonshire Terrace, Dickens once writing that to celebrate a son's birthday, 'I am going to let off a magic lantern and other strong engines. I have asked some children of a larger growth (nearly all of whom you know) to come and make merry. If you are in town, and will join us as early as half-past seven or so, you will give us *very great* pleasure.'[25]

Both men delighted in the company of children and at their parties, were equally popular, 'that excellent Dickens playing the conjuror for one whole hour ... after supper, when we were all madder than ever with the pulling of crackers, the drinking of champagne and the making of speeches, a universal country dance was proposed;'[26] and that was when Marryat would take the lead. In quieter moments, too, Marryat was attractive to children and one was to remember, 'His knowledge of nature was most extensive and he might often be seen surrounded by an audience of delighted little ones, listening with open eyes and mouths to his descriptions of the deep, or the natural history of the creation.'[27]

Marryat and Dickens had another common interest. The latter had hankered after a visit to America ever since Marryat's *Diary* had been published and, as the two men talked, became so enthralled that he, too, was planning to cross the Atlantic. In preparation, he was reading all travel books and an American journalist interviewing him at Devonshire Terrace found his study piled with 'Marryat's, Trollope's, Fidler's, Hall's and other travels and descriptions of America' and 'highly-coloured maps of the United States.'[28] Marryat's *Diary in America* had, as might be expected, aroused angry reaction across the Atlantic and this seemed likely to rebound on Dickens, since it was widely known that the two were friends. He asked advice on his route and means of transport and Marryat responded by urging him to support his campaign against American piracy of British books. Dickens decided to stay a shorter time than his friend's two years and write a shorter, more commercial book than his massive survey.

Charles and Kate Dickens sailed for Boston on 4 January 1842, on the newly-built *Britannia*, the first ship of the new Cunard Line powered by both sail and steam. Sixteen days later, having weathered an appalling winter storm, they reached Halifax, arriving at Boston on the 22nd to begin their tour. This was to be based upon Marryat's but was to last a quarter of the time, excluding his more westerly excursions and his forays into the Indian reservations; he, too, tried and failed to establish the rule of authors' copyright. He was home again in June.

Dickens was welcomed on 9 July with a boisterous whitebait dinner at Greenwich,* at which Marryat presided. Others present included Clarkson Stanfield, George Cruikshank, Harrison Ainsworth, Daniel Maclise, Richard Barham, the clergyman and the author of *The Ingoldsby Legends*, and Dickens's confidant, the lawyer and biographer John Forster. Cruikshank and Barham sang ballads and the guest's health was drunk with, as the poet and journalist Thomas Hood reported, 'a delectable clatter which drew from him a good, warm-hearted speech, in which he hinted the great advantage of going to America for the pleasure of coming back again.'[29] At the end, Dickens offered the well-wined Cruikshank† a lift back into London and reported that he 'came home in my phaeton, on his head – to the great delight of the loose Midnight Loungers in Regent Street. He was last seen taking gin with a waterman.'[30]

Writing furiously, Dickens was able to see his *American Notes* published in October of that year. Obviously based upon Marryat's *Diary*, it was equally amusing but more urbane and concise, omitting the serious surveys of politics, economics, transport and the condition of the Indians. It was an immediate success; far more so than Marryat's, although that had given more general insight into American life. Predictably, too, it caused fury in the United States, which had greeted Dickens as a popular celebrity, once the large, pirated editions had been published there.

Dickens had written the *Notes* with a light touch, keeping his general opinions to the end. He had been careful to begin these with some flattery, describing the Americans as being 'by nature, frank, brave, cordial, hospitable and affectionate. Cultivation and refinement seem but to enhance their warmth of heart and ardent enthusiasm'; he found 'an educated American one of the most endearing and generous of friends.'[31] Then followed the criticisms. He was appalled by slavery in the South – he had briefly visited Virginia – and said so. But it was more personal

---

* Probably at the Trafalgar Tavern, or the Ship Inn.
† George Cruikshank (1792–1878) was to become teetotal and a zealous campaigner for temperance.

criticisms that particularly struck home. 'One great blemish in the popular mind of America,' he wrote, 'is Universal Distrust.' Addressing the Americans directly, he continued, 'It has rendered you so fickle, and so given to change, that ... you no sooner set up an idol firmly, than you are sure to pull it down ... directly you reward a benefactor, or a public servant, you distrust him, merely because he *is* rewarded ... Any man, who attains a high place among you, from the President downwards, may date his downfall from that moment.'[32]

He criticised 'the love of "smart" dealing, which gilds over many a swindle and gross breach of trust', quoting a conversation with an American about a prosperous and popular public figure: 'He is a public nuisance, is he not?' Dickens had asked. 'Yes, sir.' 'A convicted liar?' 'Yes, sir.' 'And he is utterly dishonourable, debased and profligate?' 'Yes, sir.' 'In the name of wonder, then, what is his merit?' 'Well, sir, he is a smart man.'[33]

American opinion was outraged, so, like Marryat, the honoured guest was instantly transformed into an ungrateful villain. An American newspaper described Dickens as a 'flash reporter' from 'the stews of London' and 'a low-bred scullion unexpectedly advanced from the kitchen to the parlour'[34] and that was only the beginning. The two men now had something more in common but it was clear that Dickens had overtaken his friend both as a novelist and as a writer of travel books.

Marryat was generous-hearted, particularly towards a friend, but he was aware of a new crisis in his life. Partly it was literary: he had used his store of seafaring experience and needed to explore new avenues in fiction; he had written about his travels on the Continent and in America, but Dickens – now off for a tour in Italy – now commanded that readership. He also tried and failed to make a success of magazine journalism and publishing, while Dickens seemed to be looking forward to such an enterprise.*

Yet, financially, he had been a success and it was estimated that the initial payments for each of his novels had been between £1,100 and £1,600 and his half-dozen most popular novels had

---

* His *Households Words* began publication in 1850.

together earned something like £20,000*. Marryat had enjoyed spending his money more than investing it and now he heard that the investments in West Indian plantations, which he had inherited from his father and were the mainstay of his income, had slumped, due to a depression in the sugar trade. He was also bitter over lack of recognition for his other achievements, particularly his code of signals, which was in global use. Writing to Lady Blessington, he complained that while it was used in both merchant ships and warships, his signals had now been adopted by 'all the English colonies and dependencies to the government, to communicate with vessels ... For this service, I have never received any remuneration whatever from our own government.'[35] Nor was it only the lack of financial reward: Lord Palmerston, the Foreign Secretary, had forbidden him to wear the insignia of the *Légion d'Honeur*. 'As for my literary reputations, it is an affair between me and the public; but I think you must acknowledge that I have claims ... I see the Whigs giving away baronetcies for literary services ... and, Clay, my opponent at Tower Hamlets, for contesting elections ... Now that I have decided claims upon the country, [they] should not throw me away like a sucked orange; if they do – why, virtue must be its own reward.'[36]

It was time to reconsider his prospects. Since his return from America, Marryat had published four books: *Olla Podrida*, a collection of his travel journalism and essays; more naval fiction in *Percival Keene*, the story of a boy's seafaring adventures and eventual acquisition of a fortune, a title and a beautiful bride; and another story of virtue rewarded, this time with a rural setting, in *Joseph Rushbrook, or The Poacher*. There was also another novel written for a new readership, that of children. *Masterman Ready* was the name of a resourceful old seaman, who is shipwrecked on a remote island, together with an English family. Their adventures are essentially a reworking of the successful *Swiss Family Robinson* with realism and detail derived from the

---

* The equivalent at the beginning of the twenty-first century being in excess of £1,000,000.

author's own experience; it was told with a freshness and original touches and was a success. In January 1843, he sent a copy to Charles Dickens for his son and the latter responded by inviting Marryat to another children's party – 'We old boys and girls will muster in sufficient strength to defend ourselves ...' – and added that his five-year-old son was 'not (being of very tender years) a fast-goer in the reading way, yet; and is consequently not in the possession of *Masterman Ready*. But I will undertake for his being very proud of the book as your gift, when he is much older. And if he be not delighted with its contents, he is no son of mine ...'[37] Dickens had not yet written for children, so, for Marryat, this might be another way forward.

Yet it was Dickens who had displaced Marryat as the most successful British novelist. Both *Oliver Twist* and *Nicholas Nickleby* had shown his brilliance in commanding stories, characters and scenes and steering his readers from comedy to tragedy and back again. Marryat delighted in his friend's company yet there was an underlying simmer of resentment which came to light when he drew attention to the nature of the violence in *Oliver Twist*. Priding himself on gentlemanliness, he would have recognised that Dickens had sprung from the *petit bourgeoisie* and sometimes lacked taste. In a poem called *Oh! We're Getting Very Vulgar*, which he never published, one of the four verses ran,

> *Our authors once were gentlemen in all they said or wrote,*
> *And Byron, Moore or Campbell, we all were proud to quote;*
> *But now, with Sykes to murder Nancy, in we must go.*
> *Oh! we're getting very vulgar and most exceeding low.*[38]

But he was feeling stale. 'Are you not tired of writing?' he asked Lady Blessington. 'I am, most completely and, could I give it up, I would tomorrow.'[39] He would stay with friends in the country for the shooting but even that failed to stimulate him, telling his confidante, 'I have just returned from Norfolk, where I was wet through every day and, to escape the cold, filled myself with tobacco smoke and gin ... I am miserably out of tune and feel terribly ill-natured. I feel as if I could wring the neck of a cock-robin, who is staring in at my window.'[40]

Yet the bleak East Anglian countryside attracted him. As a writer, he was feeling a failure, if unnecessarily so. Although still only just past the age of fifty, the Admiralty had implied that he could expect no more commands. He kept any amorous affairs to himself, although there was talk of two women, a 'Mrs B' and a 'Mrs S' of Liverpool. Of the latter, his daughter Florence would say that he continued to regard her with 'the highest sentiments of friendship and esteem'[41] but, whatever their relationship, it did not blossom; he had already written to her, 'A little repose after your gay life in London will be of service to you ... You are at Liverpool with your husband and children ... I in my dungeon, unpitied and alone.'[42]

He hatched wild schemes to escape, of 'starting at once for Austria, buying a chateau in Hungary, or camping out in the desert for three years, by which means a great fortune would be realised'[43] but each evaporated on further consideration. He missed the company of his eight surviving children. Both boys were now in the Navy; Blanche, the eldest girl had recently married and was living in Bruges; the other five, Charlotte, Augusta, Emily, Florence and Caroline, who had been conceived in Paris, were still living there with their mother. So, at the back of Marryat's mind there began to form – like the plot of a new novel – a plan that could combine all the positive elements of his life.

CHAPTER TWELVE

It was a Stage

Captain Marryat's fashionable friends were surprised when he disappeared from London in the early summer of 1843. He was no longer to be seen at Lady Blessington's soirées, or Charles Dickens's children's parties, gossiping with Harrison Ainsworth, or drinking with George Cruikshank. He was still remembered as the handsome, witty man about town, the war hero and the famous novelist. Only his intimates realised the depth of his malaise: his disappointment in his own literary achievement, lack of recognition by the Admiralty and the King, his failed marriage and the realisation that he had spent the fortunes inherited from his father and his uncle and was now running through his own literary earnings, high as these had been; and, as he put it, 'Since the total wreck of West India property, I shall have little to leave my children but a good name.'[1]

Captain Marryat had escaped to his remote house in Norfolk. He did not present his withdrawal from London as a retreat; indeed, he tried to rationalise it. 'Most sailors, when they retire from the service, turn to agriculture', he mused, 'and, generally speaking they make very good farmers. There appears something very natural in this. When Adam was created a man in full vigour, he naturally took to the labours of the field. And what is a sailor – who, although he has run all over the world, has never lived in it – but a sort of Adam?'[2] Carried along by the allegory, he claimed that 'the greatest pleasure of man ... consists in imitating the deity in his creative power' and so the farmer 'changes the face of nature; he raises woods where nothing higher than the thistle waved to the breeze, he levels forests and turns the site of them into verdure and fertility.'[3]

He felt at home on the Norfolk coast. Not only was nearby Blakeney a small port for the coastal trade but so were Wells and Burnham Overy Staithe to the west and, farther in each direction, King's Lynn and Great Yarmouth. There was a strong naval tradition, too: when Nelson had been recalled to sea from Burnham Thorpe, he had recruited many Norfolkmen to take to sea with him; much closer to Langham, three earlier admirals – Myngs, Narborough and Shovell – had lived. From his own land, Marryat could look north to a sea flecked with sails.

He had occasionally revisited Langham, since he had stopped living there nearly a decade earlier, and been dismayed by what he found. Most of his tenants had shown neither the ability nor the intention of maintaining his property in good order. Now, he discovered, the tenant of the largest farm and the Manor Cottage itself had 'taken all he could out of the land without putting anything in it' and filled the drawing-room of the empty house 'with rows of beds, which he let out to tramps at twopence a night.'[4] He was now able to eject the tenant farmer and the tramps and decided to live there himself. The renovation and furnishing of the house would be expensive, but he had sold the copyright of his signals code and would receive a royalty; the need for money gave new vigour to his plans for writing more fiction.

The idea of becoming a hospitable squire became appealing and he wrote to his sister-in-law, 'Suppose you wait till I have been down to Langham and put things to rights. I have no curtains but I have four spare beds to offer you; and, if you bring down your cook, you might contrive to exist. I can promise you plenty of game, plenty of sea breezes but no bathing; you must go to Cromer for that. By the by, what a nice plan it would be to put the nurse and children at Cromer, while you stayed part of the time with me. You can go nearly the whole way by steam.'[5] The railway was snaking out from London into East Anglia and in 1840, had reached Norwich, via Cambridge; the rest of the journey to Langham would be by coach to Holt and thence by hired chaise. Now he would be able to invite Dickens and his set for convivial stays in the country to mix tobacco smoke and steaming punchbowls with those bracing sea breezes; the idea was immensely appealing to his generosity.

During the summer, Marryat was joined by his five unmarried daughters – Charlotte, Augusta, Emily, Florence, and Caroline – who had left their mother in Paris and together they prepared the Manor Cottage for guests. The outside walls were colour-washed pale pink, the thatch trimmed and roses trained up the front as high as the eaves, while stone vases of flowers were set along the terrace above the lawn. Indoors, the former tramps' dormitory was restored to its glory as the drawing-room, deco-rated with John Audubons's coloured engravings from his *Birds of America*, its trellised pillars reflected in mirrors set into the folding doors so as to remind the Marryats of the Café des Milles Colonnes in Paris. The long, narrow dining-room with French windows overlooking the lawn, was hung with Clarkson Stan-field's original illustrations for *Poor Jack* and the bedrooms were furnished with a touch of metropolitan opulence; his own, uphol-stered in blue and called 'the Blue Room'. One visitor noted 'what capital pictures were there, what first-rate bronzes and marbles and what a splendid library.'[6] There were sixteen clocks in the house and, like his former patron, the Duke of Sussex, he tried to ensure that they all struck the hour simultaneously.

Before he could begin to arrange house-parties, he himself was receiving invitations from the Norfolk aristocracy and gentry, who were delighted by his return. The gaiety of the Marryats was infectious: just before his daughters arrived, he had been staying with Lord Townshend at Raynham Hall, where, he said, 'that polka is certainly an epidemic'; once they had arrived at Langham, it was, he laughed, 'polka upstairs and downstairs, in the dining-room before and after dinner ... They have com-menced it in the kitchen and one or two of the maids are pretty expert. We have established a Sunday school and, as they go two and two, I fully expect that they will polka to church and back again. Emily declares that it was the polka that David danced before the ark.'[7]

When John Forster wrote, asking him to a farewell party for the actor William Macready on his departure for an American tour, he declined because it coincided with 'an invitation from one of the *nobs* of this county to dine with him.' When he had been watching cricket with the Earl of Leicester at Holkham Hall, he added, several of the guests 'were asked *expressly to meet me*.'[8] He concluded by suggesting a gathering of his and Dickens's friends at Langham in September.

He also wrote to Stanfield, urging 'that we may not be disappointed in our intended party down here in September and I think you had better at once make arrangements ... I believe we have only mentioned Landseer, Maclise, Dickens, Forster and yourself. Are there any more you would wish to add to the list? as I can find room for one, if not two,' as I only expect Blanche and my boy Frank, who has just arrived from the Mediterranean in the *Vanguard*. The harvest is so late that we do not expect to begin this ten days and therefore the corn will not be off the ground until about the 10th of September. I mention this as those who are fond of shooting will not have any until the harvest is in. But I suspect that shooting is not the great desideratum with you and those that accompany you. You come for fresh air, amusement, fun and a hearty welcome, all of which I will try hard to procure for you.'[9]

Dickens had been planning to accompany Macready to Liverpool for further jollifications before sailing. Hearing of this, Marryat advised against it because *American Notes* had made Dickens as unpopular as himself in the United States; his presence with Macready might be reported in American newspapers and inhibit the actor's welcome in New York. 'As soon as I heard what you had said, I resolved, of course, to keep away,' Dickens replied, 'and did so.'[10] Of Marryat's invitation to a house-party at Langham in September, he countered with the proposal that they should gather in the third week of October 'for the pleasures of Langham', that he would notify Forster and Maclise and that 'we will send you a threatening letter as the time approaches.'[11]

Marryat began planning festivities for his house-party. There would be game for the table in October and he looked up his recipe for a bouillabaisse made from haddock, a cod's head, eggs, onion and parsley. He also remembered the ingredients for one of his favourite cocktails, 'Moonbeams'[12] consisting of two glasses of Madeira, a small glass of brandy and four glasses of water, sweetened, then topped with brown toast, sprinkled with grated lemon peel and nutmeg and left to blend and cool.

But there was no further word from his intended guests and, on 9 October, he wrote to Forster, 'As you appear to be the locomotive that can put this first-class train in motion and as this is the second week in October, I write to you to ascertain whether the honourable parties are still of the same mind and intend to honour me with a visit. I am sorry that by putting it off they have lost so much fine weather – but there is still a little sunshine left. Dickens said he would come in the third week in October, others the second – so how is it to be? I know not ... If it has become really inconvenient for their engagements, I should be sorry that they come down and consider it a bore ... I do not consider that, although I asked them as a party, therefore a party it must remain. Let those come who like and those who do not, put it off till another time ...'[13]

None of them came, but his son Frank did so and, Marryat laughed, 'like all midshipmen, he turns the house upside down and very much disturbs the economy and well regulating of a family. However, midshipmen do not remain long on shore, so at present I submit to it, although he ought always to be followed by a housemaid with a broom to sweep after him and a carpenter to repair the damages.'[14] He delighted in his two sons, both midshipmen. He thought Frank 'very much like Frederick in his humour and mischief but considerably steadier, still not over-steady';[15] the boy had his father's bounce, snub nose and talent as a caricaturist. His elder brother, Frederick, who was still at sea, was a 'fine, wild, generous fellow'[16] and his high spirits – with an occasional touch of cruelty – were mischievous: once, when escorting a blind, retired admiral, continually telling him that he was being saluted so that 'the old admiral was never allowed to rest quiet two minutes without raising his hand to his hat.'[17]

He also delighted in his girls, at first refusing to hire a governess for them and teaching them himself, beginning with

Italian lessons; he could also speak French and German. 'My young ladies have already obtained a reputation since their arrival', he was writing in November, 'not for female accomplishments, or beauty, but for being *true game*, as people call it – Emily for mounting a pony never mounted before ... and Augusta ... [when] rat-catching ... actually seized with her hands an enormous rat, whose bite would have crushed the bones of any finger she had. All the people present were astonished, not only at her boldness, but at her escape from being bitten, which was marvellous.'[18]

Marryat took to country life with characteristic enthusiasm. He rode about his estate on a tubby little Hanoverian piebald pony named Dumpling; devoted to its master, it would allow him to fire his shot-gun from the saddle without shying but was likely to give anyone else a deliberately uncomfortable ride. When shooting, Marryat would wear a monocular glass suspended in front of his right eye from the rim of his 'shocking bad hat.'[19] When out of doors, the once-smart naval officer and man-about-town 'cared nothing ... for his dress, or personal appearance,' noted his daughter Florence, 'and, with the exception of his linen, the garments, which he usually wore, were scarcely worth the consideration of the poorest in the village.'[20] In the house, however, he was 'a scrupulously clean man and very neat in the arrangement of his drawers and wardrobe. Packing, or, as he termed it, "stowing away" was his forte; and he could manage to get a larger quantity into a smaller space than anyone, except a sailor, like himself ... If a person's character may be read upon his toilet table, a stranger would have pronounced Captain Marryat to be a dandy.'[21] He also grew his hair – now greying – to shoulder length.

Marryat breakfasted at eight, then did not eat again until dining twelve hours later. Each morning he would strap on gaiters and ride round his land, watching, or directing whatever work was in hand. He was usually followed by his dogs, including Zinny, 'a large, black-and-tan spaniel of the King Charles breed ... who never dared trespass beyond his master's boots but from that lowly position languished and cringed and rolled over, a deprecating mass of stupidity and floss silk.' There was also Juno, 'a tiny, black Italian greyhound, all spring and activity, with slender limbs and almost hairless skin, who would leap upon the author's table and indulge in a wild scamper over his papers and, when rebuked for her forwardness, creep under his coat and lie there blissfully contented'; when her master took snuff it discomforted Juno, 'into whose eyes it was sure to fall whenever she tried to bury her nose in the folds of his waistcoat.'[22]

'Captain Marryat tried very hard to be a regular farmer,' Florence remembered, 'but ... he was a farmer in theory only and not in practice', yet his neighbours loved him as his 'talent and cordiality went hand in hand to win him golden opinions, if his skill in farming was not entitled to honest admiration.' He continually concocted grand schemes, planning to produce guano, flood a large, low-lying meadow on the road to Binham as a wildfowl decoy and even reclaim the salt-marshes at Cley and, as he forecast, 'be a millionaire in no time.'[23] Mounting Dumpling, he 'rode about from dyke to ditch and from ditch to dyke, standing patiently for hours while he watched the men drain the Fox Covert, or exorcise the will-o'-the-wisp from the Decoy Meadow.'[24]

Not surprisingly, he excelled as an employer and landlord. 'He built model cottages and instituted model pigsties', continued Florence, 'but both cottagers and pigs proved averse to anything like a progressive movement.'[25] He had sympathy for the lot of his farm workers, realising that while they worked daily with his livestock, they and their families rarely ate meat themselves and that this was the principal cause of poaching. As Florence noted, 'he raised a great tumult by his attempts to balk his brother magistrates in their vengeance against the poacher; indeed, he appointed the most active local poacher, William Barnes, to be his gamekeeper.'[26]

Determined to reward his workers, he wrote to a god-child, 'All the men who work on the farm were invited to a Christmas dinner in the kitchen and they sat down two and twenty at the table in the servants' hall and were waited upon by our own servants. They had two large pieces of roast beef and a boiled leg of pork; four dishes of Norfolk dumplings; two large meat pies; two geese, eight ducks and eight pigeon; and, after that, they had four large plum puddings. These poor men work hard all the year round and never get anything to eat but bread for themselves and their wives and children; and they are thankful if, by hard labour, they can find bread to live upon ... Don't you think they ate very heartily? Indeed they did and, as they had plenty of strong beer to drink, they made very merry and enjoyed their Christmas Day.'[27]

Marryat was finding agriculture fascinating but bewildering, imagining new schemes but having to rely on the older farm hands for their implementation. What he could do with ease was to write and he continued to do so. Since *Masterman Ready*, he had had more novels for children in mind. He wanted to make use of the material he had accumulated in America and was inspired by a visit to Langham by a young Frenchman named Lasalle, who had travelled farther west into Indian territory than had Marryat and now entertained the Norfolk villagers, as Florence put it, by 'performing war dances and lassoing horses on the farm of the Manor for their edification and amusement.'[28] Although the French had, in fact, for long travelled more widely than the British in North America, Marryat found something bizarre, and even comical, about a Frenchman amongst Indians and settlers and was inspired to write, soon after he settled at Langham, a novel based on Lasalle's travels called *The Adventures of Monsieur Violet in California, Sonora and Western Texas*. This he followed by another, designed specifically for children, called *The Settlers in Canada*, which was published in 1844; then an African adventure, conjured up in his imagination, *The Mission, or Scenes in Africa*, about the search for survivors of a shipwreck and, as he said, 'full of lions and rhinoceroses and all manner of adventures, interspersed with a little common sense here and there.'[29]

He enjoyed writing at the Manor Cottage, spreading his papers on the dining-room table, from which he could look through the tall windows to the flowers on the terrace and the lawn and the trees beyond. He also constructed a rectangular dais of flints on the lawn in front of the house so that, seated there, he could look north to the horizon of the North Sea and south across his land and the shallow valley of the Stiffkey river to the wooded ridge beyond.

Away from the distractions of London, he could give his imagination free rein and, having exhausted his stock of personal reminiscence, again thought of writing historical novels. The next he wrote was another seafaring story, *The Privateeersman*, set in the eighteenth century and this was followed by another of what he called his 'juveniles', set a century before that. This was *The Children of the New Forest*, a story of the Civil War and the adventures of the orphaned children of a royalist cavalier. Inspired by his own children's enjoyment of the countryside and his own pleasure in their lives, the story flowed as easily as it had when writing *Peter Simple* a dozen years before; it was also the sort of story that he could tell as well as Charles Dickens. So, when he was asked to write a history of the Great War, a biography of the American naval hero, Paul Jones, or of Lord Collingwood, he refused, replying to the hopeful publisher, 'With respect to your inquiry as to my reasons for not writing *Collingwood*, one is that I have lately taken to a different style of writing, that is, for young people. My former productions, like all novels, have had their day and, for the present at least, will sell no more; but it is not so with the *juveniles* ...'[30]

The literary world of London seemed infinitely distant; none of his literary friends ventured into Norfolk, but they did write and urged him to visit them. Stanfield wrote to him, 'Charles Dickens is about to leave England with his family for one whole year to visit foreign parts, previous to which we are to bestow on the said Charles Dickens a complimentary dinner to be eaten at Greenwich. Now, Forster, Maclise and myself ... would be very glad indeed if you could and *would* make one amongst us on the occasion. I wish you would! I think really a run up to town would do you good.'[31] Marryat did not go. That autumn, Harrison Ainsworth wrote, 'I hope your agricultural pursuits will prosper. It must be quite a new life to you. When you come to town at Christmas, I hope you will bear in mind that you will find a hearty welcome here.'[32] He did not go at Christmas but he did begin to make arrangements for a London jaunt, engaging a governess to stay with his daughters; both boys were away at sea, Frank having joined the ship bound for the East Indies.

So, in February 1845, before Dickens departed, Marryat re-visited London for several days of wining and dining. The principal reason was to meet 'Mrs S', his friend from Liverpool, but she did not keep the rendezvous; even so, he enjoyed himself. 'Yesterday went to a get-up at Dickens's', he told her in a letter, 'very pleasant indeed – lots of fun – Wilson and Parry sang; children then had a ball and supper and made speeches and sung convivial songs; afterwards, ball and capital supper; everyone there: Talfourd, Macready, Cruikshank, Landor, Stanfield, Forster and a hundred more.' He ended his letter with one of the puns that were being bandied about by London wits: "What was Joan of Arc made of?" "She was Maid of Orleans." Is that new?'[33]

Marryat returned to Norfolk in the disappointing knowledge that his jolly London friends were unlikely to visit him there. 'If you manage it, come down and stay here – you shall do as you please and so will I,' he wrote to Forster. 'The weather is beautiful and the country is really, without exaggeration, one *mass of violets*';[34] but still they did not come. So Marryat continued to construct a new environment and this included a new friend.

About two miles to the north at the village of Morston, close to Blakeney on the edge of the salt marshes stood a row of Coast-guard cottages and, facing the coastal road a handsome little house, newly-built of pale Holkham brick, for the senior officer of the Excise service, a retired lieutenant of the Royal Navy on half-pay. This was Lieutenant George Thomas, a contemporary of Marryat's, a cheerful, ruddy-cheeked man with a fringe of beard around his chin. Their naval careers had been equally dramatic; not only had Thomas fought in many boarding and cutting-out expeditions, but he had served under celebrated captains – including Sir Edward Pellew, now Lord Exmouth – and had been wounded in the War of 1812 and been present at the burning of Washington and the Battle of New Orleans. In 1815, he had retired with a pension earned by his most recent wound but, two years later, was at sea again under the command of Marryat's mentor, Lord Cochrane, serving in the navies of Chile, Brazil and Greece in their wars of independence. In 1834, he had come ashore and been given command of the Coastguard at Morston.

To find a naval officer with a career akin to his own was rewarding enough, but for the new friend also to have fought under Cochrane's command forged a bond. So almost daily Marryat would ride Dumpling down the long, straight lane to Morston, or Thomas would ride up to Langham, and the two men would sit in the garden, or round the fire, where, said a friend, they 'would talk over the service as it had been in their day and the degeneracy of the service as it was [now]',[35] while Thomas's little daughter, Annie, would play with the Marryat girls like a sister. The half-pay lieutenant became as valued, and more steady, a friend as any of the notables in London.

So the salons, dining-rooms and smoking-rooms of St James's and Kensington gradually faded and, in 1844, he was replying to another invitation from a metropolitan hostess, 'Country life and country pursuits agree with me and I can there cultivate the virtues of temperance and sobriety much better than when dining out in London and being compelled to drink against my will. Many thanks for your kind invitation, but all your baits to be as a gourmet, added to the wish to see you ... cannot take me away from my farm.'[36]

The farming was enjoyable but not profitable, regularly losing more than £1,000 a year, which was about the size of the advance payment on each of his novels. He was still working his way through his third fortune. His lack of commercial instinct was demonstrated by his favourite project, the decoy, for which he had flooded a hundred acres of his best grazing land. It was a success but when it began to produce five thousand birds a year for the London market, Marryat ordered it to be drained; this despite him telling a friend, 'There is a large capital invested in a farm ... a farmer is as much a man of business as a merchant.'[37]

In 1845, Charles Dickens was back in London and persuading his friends to join him in amateur theatricals. Again Forster wrote to Marryat, sending him a play-bill, 'Look at this bill enclosed; it is all Dickens's doing. I am a lamb at the slaughter. *But will you come up?* Stanny, and all of us, are in it. Tell me and you shall have the card of invitation by return of post. Many are coming from far greater distances than Langham. *Do come ...* Now, be a gentleman, a trump – a first-rater and come "special" for the play. Tickets are at a premium, I can tell you.'[38] Marryat did not go because he had established his own self-contained world in Norfolk, writing that August, 'My boy Frederick is with me, just come home from Hong Kong – a very queer, eccentric fellow, as idle as he is talented. My young ones are all well. I expect my mother down ... and am preparing to receive the old lady with all the honour due to her age and grey hairs. *Addio*, or, as Fred says, *Chin chin*, which is the Chinese salutation.'[39]

One old friend did, however, come to see him.* On his long, slow journey from London he wondered whether he would find changes in Marryat, whom he had not seen for years. That had been at Spanish Place, where it had been 'an incessant round of dining out and giving dinners. At his table you met all the celebrities of the day.'[40] Before that, he remembered him on the Continent, 'always living *en prince*' and at Sussex House, where he had 'kept up a round of incessant gaiety and ... splendid extravagance'; there Marryat and his friend, Captain Chamier, had entertained with 'various tricks of sleight-of-hand' and Theodore Hook 'was wont to bewilder the company with his ventriloquisms ... Marryat then lived in the atmosphere of a court as well as in the odour of literature.'[41]

Now his friend was seeking him deep in rural Norfolk. Leaving the coach at The Feathers inn at Holt, he found the only

---

* His account of the visit, published in the *Cornhill Magazine* of July 1867, was unsigned and the writer has never been identified, except that he must have known Marryat for about fifteen years and was to survive him for at least twenty. He may well have been Captain Frederick Chamier (1796–1870) himself.

means of reaching Langham was by hiring a chaise and in this he set out into the night. After half an hour of jolting along country roads, they turned into a gravel drive and saw the lights of a house among the trees. A moment later, the front door was flung open and there was Captain Marryat. 'Why, is it you? Why didn't you give me notice that I might have sent for you?' he began. 'It was the same voice as of old', thought the visitor, 'deep-chested, cordial and cheery.'[42] In the hall, he looked hard at his host: 'His face was clean-shaved and his hair so long that it reached almost to his shoulders, curling in light, loose locks like those of a woman. It was slightly grey. He was dressed in ... a short velveteen shooting-jacket and coloured trousers.'

'What can make you live down here?' he asked.

'I have had enough of the world,' replied his host. 'I like this sort of life: besides, look at all my girls and boys. I want to retrench.'[43]

Supper was brought and, after much talk, the visitor asked, 'What time do you get up in the morning?' 'About five at this time of year.' 'About – about *what*? Are you mad? Do you expect me to get up at that hour?' Marryat then explained that he woke early but, so as not to disturb the servants by unbarring the front door, dressed and jumped out of his bedroom window on the ground floor. He added, 'We breakfast at eight.'

The guest woke long before breakfast-time next morning and looked out of his window at the early sunlight on the trees, throwing long shadows across the lawn. Beyond, the garden was divided from the farmland by a ha-ha and the young, green barley, which 'looked almost as pretty as if the whole had been grass.' Everywhere there seemed to be animals: 'A dozen or more young calves feeding about the lawn; two or three ponies and a donkey under a clump of larches in one direction, a long-legged colt and his mama ... coops with young fowls stood upon the gravel walk in front of the dining-room doorstep.'[44]

As he watched he heard a familiar laugh and, he said, 'along the garden walk I saw Captain Marryat coming with several of his family. Two or three dogs capered round and about; a jackdaw sat on the shoulder of one of the girls; and, as they neared the lawn, they were joined by a flock of pigeons, which wheeled round and round their heads, settling for a moment, sometimes on the shoulder of one, sometimes on the hat of another, or coming six in a row upon any arm that was held out to them.' Thereupon the calves 'ran headlong at their master, catching his coat-tails [and] sucking his fingers ... The ponies advanced and sniffed at his hands and face and one of them knocked his hat over his eyes ... I turned from the window, feeling that, at this rate, I should never be dressed.'[45]

After breakfast, Marryat showed his guest round the farm, the latter finding that 'ploughed fields and manure-heaps and agricultural machines ... to my vitiated tastes ... seemed dull work. Marryat stood about, directing and ordering; sometimes listening to a long Norfolk speech, which seemed to me in an unknown tongue; then walking off to the stack-yard, where a grand battue of rats was going on and eagerly calling out "loo-loo-loo" to the dogs with the rest. Then, as a climax, he marched me off to the decoy lake ... The decoy man, a rough-looking fellow in a fur cap, was a reclaimed poacher and he looked entirely his original character. Marryat always held that reformed blackguards made the most honest servants. He had a very unmagistrate-like leniency for poaching and, having convicted this man, Barnes, ... placed him as his gamekeeper and decoy man; and I know he never had reason to repent his trust in him.'[46]

Marryat was at work on another book for children and his own occupied much of his time. 'He threw himself like a child into his children's pleasures: one morning helping to make a kite, the next listening to doggerel verses, or, in the evening, joining with them in acting charades. He would leave off in the middle of writing his book to ... enter into the fanciful papering of a boudoir with all the enthusiasm of a girl. When one of the girls came to him wailing that she had torn her dress and that their governess would be furious, he took hold of the dress, tearing the hole six times as large as at first and laughingly answering, "There, say I did it." ' When he boasted that he himself had baked some little fruit tarts for dinner, a daughter asked him whether he had washed his hands first. 'Lor' bless my you, dear, I declare I forgot all about it,' he confessed. 'Then you shall eat them all yourself,' she scolded. 'You have never washed your hands since you pulled about those dead rats this morning; you know you haven't.'[47] The old friend summed up, 'It always struck me that Marryat was like an elder brother, rather than a father, to his own children.'[48]

Remembering his host as having been 'an epicure of the first degree', he was surprised when he said, 'I say, we have nothing in the world for dinner. You go down to the lake and see if you can get anything and I will take my gun.' So, for dinner that evening they ate a huge eel and a rabbit. 'It was a Robinson Crusoe sort of life,'[49] the guest decided. Between meals, Marryat would write at the dining-room table and was following *The Children of the New Forest* with *The Little Savage*, the adventures of a small boy shipwrecked on an uninhabited island. Then, after dinner, 'when the dining-room table was pushed on one side and we all played blind-man's buff ... he laughed and shouted as gleefully as any of the younger ones, holding one of the children in front of him: she delighted to be, as she thought, in such a safe position, and then suddenly awakened to a sense of danger by the practical joke of being jumped forward into the very arms of the blind-man, while her treacherous parent escaped; or dancing impromptu fancy dances with ... the juveniles.'[50]

Occasionally, when alone with his friend, and lounging on his lion-skin sofa, he would talk about the old days and old friends, particularly Stanfield, Ainsworth, Bulwer-Lytton and 'Charlie Dickens'.[51] Once, in a reverie, 'his deep-set eyes fixed straight forward and his mind evidently at work', he jumped to his feet, commanding, 'Silence!' Then he laughed, 'I thought Bulwer was in the room. I was talking to him. I forgot myself.'[52] He still corresponded with them occasionally and Stanfield sent his son to stay at Langham; otherwise, the literary lions of Lady Blessington's salon had receded into the past as surely as the frigate captains. When asked how he passed his time otherwise, so far from the excitement of

London, he replied, 'Oh, nothing in particular. But, you see, this is such a lovely time of year. It is sufficient amusement for me to walk along the lanes and watch the green buds coming out in the quickset hedges.'[53]

The pastoral bliss was not to last. The demons of profligacy and restlessness still lurked. Farming might be enjoyable but it was losing him money and he again looked to his old profession for support. Visiting London in the summer of 1847, he called at the Admiralty to ask about the possibility of a new command because, at fifty-five, he was not too old; failing that, he sought an annual pension of, he suggested, £150 and reminded them of his services in the Great War and Burma. With so many retired officers seeking employment, or pensions, he was coolly but politely brushed aside. He exploded with frustration and anger and this was followed by a recurrence of his internal haemorrhages necessitating a return to Norfolk for recuperation. This proved so slow that he returned to London for further medical examinations. While there, in December, he wrote to the First Lord of the Admiralty, Lord Auckland, telling him that 'your lordship's reception was so mortifying that, from excitement and annoyance, after I left you I ruptured a blood vessel ...'[54] He then outlined his grievance, which was that his claims to a new appointment, or a pension, had been overlooked in favour of others. Lord Auckland replied that he had had no intention of hurting Marryat's feelings, telling him 'I know the record of your services to stand handsomely on our books'[55] and that he would propose him as the recipient of a pension, which had become available since the death of an old admiral. Marryat replied gratefully and it seemed that his future was secure.

His health, however, did not improve and his doctor advised him to rest on the south coast and he took lodgings at Hastings in the elegant new Wellington Square. It was while there that he received shattering news. His son, Frederick, had been lost at sea. Aged twenty-eight, tall, dark-haired and handsome he had reminded his father of himself as an impetuous young officer. On 20 December that year, the steam frigate *Avenger*, of which he was second lieutenant, had struck a reef in a Mediterranean storm and all but four of her company of some two hundred and seventy had been drowned. One of the survivors wrote to Marryat that, 'The last that was seen of your fine son was on deck, upraiding in his jocular manner, some people who were frightened, when a sea swept over the ship and took him with it.'[56]

His father never recovered from the shock. He moved to Brighton but his condition continued to deteriorate. There, he narrowly missed Charles and Kate Dickens, the former writing to say that he was delighted to hear that Marryat had recovered: 'I assure you, my dear fellow, I was heartily rejoiced and drank your health at dinner with all the honours.'[57] Dickens had been misinformed and, after a month, Marryat returned to London for more medical advice. After the final consultation, he returned to his lodgings to meet some of his family and, in reply to their questions, said 'with an undisturbed and half-smiling countenance, "They say that in six months I shall be numbered with my forefathers." '*[58]

There was now no question of him completing the first novel he had written about a woman, *Mademoiselle Virginie* – later re-titled *Valerie* – the story of an aristocratic French refugee, who comes to England and works as a governess before finding love and happiness – and his son Frank undertook to finish it for him. But there was satisfaction in knowing that Frank's own illustrated book about his last voyage, *Borneo and the Indian Archipelago* was soon to be published.

At the Manor Cottage, a mattress-bed was made up for him on the floor of the drawing-room, so that, cared for by his daughters and his housekeeper, he could see his garden, birds and animals in the garden and 'the mimic sky and birds and flowers'[60] painted on the walls and ceiling. His favourite flowers were pinks and moss roses and bunches of these were brought to his room

---

* Contemporaries attributed Marryat's recurrent illnesses to 'the bursting of blood vessels', with which his daughter, Florence, agreed, adding that these 'not gaining time to heal, resulted in ulceration, which eventually destroyed the coats of the stomach.'[59] Oliver Warner, in his biography of 1953, suggested 'long-seated kidney trouble ... complicated by an organic disease.' A recent theory is that, as a young man, Marryat had suffered from, but overcame tuberculosis and then developed internal cancer.

each morning. In the belief that solid food brought about haemorrhages, he only took lemonade and he soon began to lose weight, becoming 'as gentle as a little child' and his mind wandered. Then, said Florence, 'he would dictate whole pages of what he fancied literature.' Sometimes he was in pain and then 'in the dreamy condition produced by constant doses of morphia, he held stirring, imaginary conversations with Dickens, or Bulwer, or some of his old shipmates.'[61]

Religion began to occupy his mind and one morning early in August, one of his daughters was reading him the prayers for Good Friday. He then dictated a long testament of belief, beginning, 'What a wonderful thing God is!'[62] After speaking of his faith, he added, 'I make these remarks as, some day or other, they will be curious to the reader. 'Tis a lovely day and Augusta has just brought me three pinks and three roses and the bouquet is charming. I have opened the window and the air is delightful. It is now exactly nine o'clock in the morning and I am lying on a bed in a place called Langham, two miles from the sea on the coast of Norfolk. As those who read this will probably hear how strangely life has been preserved in me for many days, I shall ask myself before them how I feel.'

'To use the common sense of the word, I am happy. I have no sensation of hunger whatsoever, or of thirst; my taste is not impaired; my intellect, notwithstanding the narcotics, is this morning, I think, very pure; but the great question is, "How do I feel, if I may use the term, as an isolated Christian towards God?' I feel that I love Him ... After years of casual and, latterly, months of intense, thought I feel convinced that Christianity is true and ... that the basis of Christianity is love ... It is now half-past nine o'clock." '

He then said, 'World, adieu!'[63]

At dawn on 9 August 1848, his housekeeper was sitting beside him and thought him asleep. She said afterwards that she had 'heard him murmur a sentence of the Lord's Prayer; as he finished it, he gave a short sigh, a shiver passed through his frame and he was gone.'[64]

Epilogue

The death of Captain Marryat at the age of fifty-six did not create a stir and his obituaries were brief; there was nothing like the upsurge of grief and mourning that was to attend the death of Charles Dickens twenty-two years later. Partly, this was because critics had taken to dismissing him as a writer for children, forgetting his great, earlier novels of the sea. It was also due to preoccupation with the news of the revolutions of independence, or republicanism, throughout Europe, which, that year, marked the beginning of the end of the old world in which Marryat had lived.

His body was carried by his farm workers to the churchyard of St Andrew in Langham and a guard of honour was mounted by Lieutenant Thomas's bluejackets from Morston. He was buried to the south-west of the church, where a handsome tomb was built, a marble tablet being set in the wall of the chancel within.

Frank Marryat, his only surviving son, took over the running of the estate, but soon left for California, taking William Barnes, the poacher-turned-gamekeeper, with him to join the gold-mining stampede. Leaving Barnes in America, he returned and wrote two books, *Gold Quartz Mining in California* in 1852 and *Mountains and Molehills* two years later. He married Alice Turner but died in London of tuberculosis in 1855. Barnes eventually returned to Langham and displayed gold nuggets to the wondering drinkers in The Bluebell inn.

Of the girls, both Charlotte and Augusta wrote books for children; the former marrying Lynal Thomas, had children and died in 1888; the latter dying, unmarried, in 1898. Emily married Dr H E Norris, whose brother married Caroline, both had children, and they died in 1888 and 1930 respectively. Florence married

Major-General Ross Church and, on his death, Colonel Francis Lean, dying in 1899. Florence herself had become a writer of novels and books about spiritualism. Marryat had asked that his papers be destroyed and that no memoirs of him should be written. Perhaps sensing that there were areas of his life that he wanted to remain private, Florence decided to write his biography but only to do so with a discretion of which she thought he would approve; this was published in 1872 as *The Life and Letters of Captain Marryat*. His mother outlived both her sons and her two grandsons.

Marryat's successor as a great maritime novelist, Joseph Conrad, wrote of him, 'To this writer of the sea, the sea was not an element. It was a stage, where was displayed an exhibition of valour and of such achievement as the world had never seen before ... His novels, like amphibious creatures, live on the sea and frequent the shore ... They live; there is a truth in them, the truth of their time; ... His adventures are enthralling; the rapidity of his action fascinates ... His greatness is undeniable.'[1]

The most potent epitaph was spoken by his younger daughter, Caroline, when well past ninety, after the world war that had been given the name of Marryat's Great War and shortly before her death in 1930, when the fashionable writers were Evelyn Waugh and Noel Coward. When she was asked, 'Mrs Norris, do you remember Langham?' At once the old face changed, said her questioner, 'and the expression was that of a high-spirited girl. She spoke, in a few broken words, of the animals, the happiness of that house of her childhood.' Then she said, 'You don't remember my father – he was a *man*.'[2]

Reference Notes

Abbreviations: NMM = National Maritime Museum; NRO = Norfolk Record Office; PRO = Public Record Office

Chapter One

1. Lloyd, *Captain Marryat*, p2.
2. Marryat, Florence, *Life and Letters*, Vol 1, p9.
3. Ibid, p12.
4. Ibid, p13.
5. Lloyd, *Captain Marryat*, p18.
6. *Frank Mildmay*, 1834, p11.
7. Ibid.

Chapter Two

1. Lloyd, *Captain Marryat*, p13.
2. *Mildmay*, p13.
3. Ibid, pp15–6.
4. Ibid.
5. Ibid, p18.
6. Ibid.
7. Ibid.
8. Ibid, p19.
9. Ibid, p18.
10. Robinson, *British Tar*, p311.
11. *Mildmay*, p18.
12. Lloyd, *Captain Marryat*, p31.
13. Ibid, p32.
14. Ibid.
15. Ibid, p33.
16. Warner, *Captain Marryat*, p26.
17. *Mr Midshipman Easy*, Chap 10.
18. NMM, MS 52/003/7; MRY/6.
19. Marryat, Florence, *Life and Letters*, Vol 1, p19.
20. Ibid, pp231–7.
21. Ibid, pp232–4.
22. Ibid, p19.
23. Dundonald (Lord Cochrane), *Autobiography*, Introduction, 1995.
24. Ibid.
25. Lloyd, *Captain Marryat*, p47.

26. *Mildmay*, p49.
27. *The King's Own*, Chap 20.
28. Ibid.
29. Lloyd, *Captain Marryat*, p48.
30. Pocock, Tom, *Remember Nelson* (London 1977), p118.
31. Lloyd, *Captain Marryat*, p54.
32. Dundonald, *Autobiography*, Vol 1, p235.
33. Ibid, pp235–6.
34. Ibid, p235.
35. Ibid, p236.
36. Warner, *Captain Marryat*, p30.
37. Marryat, Florence, *Life and Letters*, Vol 1, p28.
38. NMM, 52/003/7; MRY/6.
39. Marryat, Florence, *Life and Letters*, Vol 1, pp59–60.
40. Lloyd, *Captain Marryat*, p60.
41. Ibid.
42. Marryat, Florence, *Life and Letters*, Vol 1, pp34–5.
43. Ibid, pp35–6.
44. Lloyd, *Captain Marryat*, p 48.
45. Warner, *Captain Marryat*, p31.
46. Marshall, *Royal Naval Biography*, Vol 3.
47. Lloyd, *Captain Marryat*, pp76–7.
48. Lloyd, *Captain Marryat*, p78.
49. Ibid.
50. Ibid, p79.
51. Ibid, p83.
52. Ibid, p85.

Chapter Three

1. Dundonald, *Autobiography*, Vol 1, Chap 19, p338.
2. Ibid, p342.
3. Ibid.
4. Ibid, p343.
5. Ibid, p345.
6. Ibid, pp346–7.
7. Ibid.
8. Ibid, p349.
9. Ibid, p356.
10. Ibid, p357.
11. Ibid, pp355–6.
12. Ibid, pp353–56.
13. Ibid, p359.
14. Ibid, p362.
15. Lloyd, *Captain Marryat*, p15.
16. Dundonald, *Autobiography*, Vol 1, Chap 19, p351.
17. Lloyd, *Captain Marryat*, p93.
18. Dundonald, *Autobiography*, Vol 1, Chap 20, pp360–1.
19. Ibid, p369.
20. Ibid, p368.
21. Lloyd, *Captain Marryat*, p21.
22. *Mildmay*, Chap 11, p129.

23. Ibid, p130.
24. Ibid, pp130–1.
25. Dundonald, *Autobiography*, Chap 21, pp376–7.
26. Ibid, p380.
27. Ibid, p279.
28. *Naval Chronicle*, Vol 21, pp403–7.
29. Ibid, p380.
30. Ibid.
31. Ibid, pp381–4.
32. Ibid, pp382–3.
33. Ibid, p384.
34. Ibid, p386.
35. *Mildmay*, Chap 11, p133.
36. Dundonald, *Autobiography*, Vol 1, Chap 21, p389.
37. Ibid, p394.
38. Ibid, p395.
39. Ibid.
40. Ibid, p396.
41. Ibid, p397.
42. Marryat, Florence, *Life and Letters*, Vol 2, pp121–2.

Chapter Four

1. *Mildmay*, Chap 11.
2. Lloyd, *Captain Marryat*, p118.
3. *Mildmay*, Chap 11.
4. Lloyd, *Captain Marryat*, p117.
5. Webley MSS, The Mariners' Museum, Newport News, Virginia, USA.
6. Lloyd, *Captain Marryat*, pp139–140.
7. Ibid, p141.
8. *Mildmay*, Chap 14.
9. Lloyd, *Captain Marryat*, p142.
10. *Mildmay*, Chap 14.
11. Ibid.
12. Ibid.
13. Ibid.
14. Ibid.
15. Lloyd, *Captain Marryat*, p148.
16. *Mildmay*, Chap 16.
17. Ibid.
18. Ibid.
19. Lloyd, *Captain Marryat*, p162.
20. Marryat, Florence, *Life and Letters*, Vol 1, pp74–5.
21. Lloyd, *Captain Marryat*, pp153–4.
22. *Mildmay*, Chap 23.
23. Ibid.
24. Ibid.

Chapter Five

1. *Gentleman's Magazine*, 19 June, 1816.
2. Lloyd, *Captain Marryat*, p173.

3. Ibid, p178.
4. Ibid, p179.
5. Ibid, p174.
6. Marryat, Florence, *Life and Letters*, Vol 1, pp81–2.
7. Lloyd, *Captain Marryat*, p176.
8. Ibid, p191.
9. Crawford, Captain Abraham, *Reminiscences of a Naval Officer* (London 1851), Chap 3.
10. Lloyd, *Captain Marryat*, p193.
11. *Peter Simple*, Chap 53.
12. Ibid, Chap 54.
13. *Manning Pamphlets, 1693–1873*. Navy Records Society, Appendix 3, p347.

Chapter Six

1. Marryat, Florence, *Life and Letters*, Vol 1, p103.
2. Lloyd, *Captain Marryat*, p213.
3. *Olla Podrida*, Chap 25.
4. Ibid.
5. Ibid.
6. Ibid.
7. Ibid.
8. Ibid, Chap 24.
9. Ibid.
10. Ibid, Chap 25.
11. PRO, Adm 1/1297. A.1076.
12. Warner, *Captain Marryat*, p69.
13. *Olla Podrida*, Chap 23.
14. Ibid.
15. Lloyd, *Captain Marryat*, p222.
16. Ibid, p224.
17. Ibid.
18. *Olla Podrida*, Chap 26.
19. Ibid.
20. Ibid.
21. Ibid.
22. Ibid.
23. Ibid, Chap 27.
24. Ibid.
25. Ibid, Chap 26.
26. Ibid.
27. Ibid.
28. *Olla Podrida*, Chap 27.
29. Ibid.
30. Lloyd, *Captain Marryat*, p234.

Chapter Seven

1. Marryat, Florence, *Life and Letters*, Vol 1, p127.
2. Warner, *Captain Marryat*, p76.
3. Ibid, p151.
4. Ibid, p80.

5. *Newton Forster*, Chap 1.
6. Lloyd, *Captain Marryat*, p241.
7. PRO, Adm 1/2204.
8. Albemarle, Lord, *Fifty Years of My Life* (London 1876).
9. PRO, Adm 1/2205/49.
10. Ibid.
11. Ibid.
12. Ibid.
13. Ibid.
14. Warner, *Captain Marryat*, p152.
15. Marryat, Florence, *Life and Letters*, Vol 1, pp160–1.
16. New York Public Library Archives, Lloyd, *Captain Marryat*, p248.
17. Ibid.
18. Ibid.
19. NRO, MC/30.
20. Marryat, Florence, *Life and Letters*, Vol 1, p153.
21. Ibid.
22. *American Diary*, Pt 2, Vol 2, p151.
23. Marryat, Florence, *Life and Letters*, Vol 1, p161.
24. *Olla Podrida*, Chap 1.
25. *Peter Simple*, Chap 12.
26. Ibid, Chap 14.

Chapter Eight

1. Warner, *Captain Marryat*, pp98–9.
2. Ibid, p100.
3. NRO, MS/4687.
4. Warner, *Captain Marryat*, p101.
5. NMM, MRY/11–12, Scrapbook, p28.
6. Ibid.
7. Marryat, Florence, *Life and Letters*, Vol 1, p204.
8. Ibid, p201.
9. NMM, MRY/11–12, Scrapbook, p28.
10. Ibid.
11. Ibid.
12. Sadleir, Michael, Introduction to *Peter Simple* (London 1929), pxxix.
13. Warner, *Captain Marryat*, p101.
14. NRO, MS/4687.
15. Warner, *Captain Marryat*, p99.
16. Marryat, Florence, *Life and Letters*, Vol 1, p156.
17. Ibid, Vol 1, p158.
18. Ibid, p155.
19. Warner, *Captain Marryat*, p137.
20. Dorling, p198.
21. *The Pirate*, Chap 4.
22. Dorling, *Men o'War*, p198.
23. Warner, *Captain Marryat*, p94.
24. Lloyd, *Captain Marryat*, p258.
25. Ibid, pp258–9.
26. NMM, MRY/11–12, Scrapbook, p30.
27. Lloyd, *Captain Marryat*, p259.

28. Ibid.
29. NMM, MRY/11–12, Scrapbook, p30.
30. *Sunday Herald*; Lloyd, *Captain Marryat*, p260.
31. NMM, MRY/11–12, Scrapbook, p30.
32. New York Public Library Archives, 8/3/1834.
33. *Olla Podrida*, Chap 3.
34. Ibid.
35. Ibid, pp20–1.
36. Ibid, Chap 6.
37. Ibid.
38. Gautier, *Marryat*, p106.
39. Marryat, Florence, *Life and Letters*, Vol 2, pp222–3.
40. Ibid.
41. NRO, MS/4687.
42. Warner, *Captain Marryat*, pp105–6.
43. Ibid, p104.
44. Forster, *Life of Dickens*, 1873; Warner, *Captain Marryat*, pp108–9.
45. Marryat, Florence, *Life and Letters*, Vol 1, p254.
46. Ibid, p258.
47. Ibid, p259.
48. *Olla Podrida*, Chap 41.

Chapter Nine

1. *Diary in America*, Vol Pt 1, Vol 1.
2. Ibid.
3. Ibid.
4. Ibid, Chap 21.
5. Ibid.
6. Ibid, Pt 2, Vol 2, p136.
7. Ibid, Pt 1, Chap 3.
8. Ibid, Chap 2.
9. Ibid, Chap 3.
10. Ibid, p247.
11. Ibid, pp248–9.
12. Ibid, Chap 2.
13. Hone, Philip, *Diary* (New York 1881), Vol 1, p260.
14. *Diary in America*, Pt 2, Vol 1, p99.
15. Ibid, p177.
16. Ibid, p149.
17. Ibid, pp117–124.
18. Ibid, p26.
19. Ibid, p267.
20. Warner, *Captain Marryat*, p118.
21. *Diary in America*, Pt 1, Chap 5.
22. Ibid, Chap 7.
23. Ibid.
24. Marryat, Florence, *Life and Letters*, Vol 2, pp9–17.
25. Ibid, p1.
26. *Diary in America*, Pt 1, Chap 68.
27. Ibid.
28. Ibid, Chap 4.

29. Ibid, Chap 5.
30. Ibid, Chap 8.
31. Ibid, Chap 9.
32. Ibid.
33. Ibid, Chap 9.
34. Ibid, Pt 2, Vol 2, p1.
35. Ibid, p4.
36. Ibid, pp146–7.
37. Ibid, pp9–10.
38. Ibid, Pt 1, p147.
39. Ibid, Pt 2, Vol 2, p17.
40. Ibid.
41. Ibid, Pt1, p255.
42. Ibid, Pt 2, Vol 2, p120.
43. Ibid, p126.
44. Ibid, p148.
45. Ibid, Vol 1, p9.
46. Ibid, p11.
47. Ibid, p10.
48. Ibid, p17.
49. Ibid, Pt 1, Chap 12.
50. Zanger (ed), *Diary*, p14.
51. *Diary in America*, Pt 1, p154.
52. Ibid, Pt 2, Chap 13.
53. Ibid.
54. Marryat, Florence, *Life and Letters*, Vol 2, p24.
55. Schoolcraft, Henry R, *Personal Memoirs* (Philadelphia 1851), p562.
56. *Diary in America*, Pt 1, Chap 14.
57. Davenport, *Life and Recollections*.
58. *Diary in America*, Pt 1, Chap 16.
59. Ibid, Pt 2, Vol 3, pp65–6.
60. Marryat, Florence, *Life and Letters*, Vol 2, p25.
61. Zanger, *Diary*, p16.

Chapter Ten

1. *Diary in America*, Pt 1, Chap 19.
2. Harvard College Library, Marryat to Charles A Davies, 11 December 1837.
3. *Diary in America*, Pt 1, Chap 19.
4. Jenkins, Kathleen, *Montreal, Island City of the St Lawrence* (Montreal 1966), pp116 and 299, fn 64.
5. Ibid.
6. Ibid.
7. Ibid.
8. Ibid.
9. Marryat, Florence, *Life and Letters*, Vol 2, p65.
10. *Diary in America*, Pt 1, Chap 19.
11. Marryat, Florence, *Life and Letters*, Vol 2, pp65–6.
12. Ibid.
13. Ibid.
14. Ibid.
15. Marryat, Florence, *Life and Letters*, Vol 2, p66.

16. Bryce, George, *A Short History of the Canadian People* (London 1887) pp380–397.
17. *Diary in America*, Pt 1, Chap 20.
18. Ibid.
19. Ibid.
20. Ibid.
21. Ibid.
22. *New York Morning Herald*, 30 November, 1837.
23. Ibid, 19 November, 1837.
24. Ibid.
25. Ibid, 4 January, 1838.
26. Breck, Samuel, *Recollections* (Philadelphia 1877), p114; Gautier, *Marryat*, p119 fn.
27. Breck, p293.
28. *Diary in America*, Pt 1, Chap 22.
29. Ibid, Chap 21.
30. Ibid, Chap 23.
31. Marryat, Florence, *Life and Letters*, Vol 2, p30.
32. Ibid, p37.
33. Ibid, pp37–8.
34. Ibid.
35. *New York Morning Herald*, 2 June, 1838.
36. Zanger, *Diary*, p20.
37. Minnesota Historical Collections, V1/240.
38. Ibid.
39. *Diary in America*, Pt 2, Vol 3, p205.
40. *Diary in America*, Pt 1, Chap 31.
41. Marryat, Florence, *Life and Letters*, Vol 2, p37.
42. Ibid, pp40–51.
43. Ibid, pp52–3.
44. *Lexington Intelligencer*, 2 October, 1838.
45. Marryat, Florence, *Life and Letters*, Vol 2, pp55–64.
46. Ibid, pp68–71.
47. Ibid.
48. Ibid, pp71–2.

Chapter Eleven

1. Gautier, *Diary*, pp128–9 fn.
2. Marryat, Florence, *Life and Letters*, Vol 2, pp79–80.
3. Ibid, p85–6.
4. Ibid, p87.
5. Ibid, p89.
6. Ibid, p95.
7. Ibid, p97.
8. Ibid, p92.
9. Ibid, pp93–4.
10. Lytton Papers MS.
11. Blessington, Lady, *The Idler in France* (London 1841) Vol 2, p85.
12. Warner, *Captain Marryat*, p136.
13. Marryat, Florence, *Life and Letters*, Vol 2, p115.
14. Pope-Hennessy, *Dickens*, p94.

15. Ibid, p111.
16. *Dickens Letters*, Vol 2, p191 fn.
17. Ibid.
18. Marryat, Florence, *Life and Letters*, Vol 2, p120.
19. *Dickens Letters*, Vol 3, pp342–3.
20. Marryat, Florence, *Life and Letters*, Vol 2, pp122–3.
21. Vizetelly, Henry, *Memoirs* (London 1893) Vol 1, p165.
22. *Dickens Letters*, Vol 3, p420.
23. Ley, J W T (ed), John Forster's *Dickens* (London 1928), p529.
24. Ibid.
25. *Dickens Letters*, Vol 3, p420.
26. Priestley, J B, *Charles Dickens* (London 1961) Vol 1, p54.
27. Marryat, Florence, *Life and Letters*, Vol 2, p123.
28. Johnson, Edgar, *Charles Dickens* (London 1952) Vol 1, p360.
29. Hood, Thomas, *Letters* (Toronto 1973) p486.
30. *Dickens Letters*, Vol 3, p264.
31. Dickens, Charles, *American Notes* (London 1842) Chap 18.
32. Ibid.
33. Ibid.
34. Johnson, Edgar. *Charles Dickens* (London 1952) Vol 1, p442.
35. Madden, *Blessington*, Vol 3, pp223–4.
36. Ibid.
37. *Dickens Letters*, Vol 3, p420.
38. Morrison, Alfred (ed), *Blessington Papers* (London 1895) pp178–9.
39. Ibid.
40. Marryat, Florence, *Life and Letters*, Vol 2, p74.
41. Ibid, p76.
42. Ibid, p122.
43. Ibid.

Chapter Twelve

1. Hannay, *Life*, p152.
2. Marryat, Florence, *Life and Letters*, Vol 2, p127.
3. Ibid, p128.
4. Ibid, p129.
5. Ibid, pp124–5.
6. *Cornhill Magazine*, July 1867, p155.
7. Marryat, Florence, *Life and Letters*, Vol 2, pp167–8.
8. Ibid, pp139–40.
9. Ibid, pp141–
10. *Dickens Letters*, Vol 3, p556.
11. Ibid.
12. NMM, Davis MSS, Dickens-Watson correspondence.
13. Marryat, Florence, *Life and Letters*, Vol 2, pp147–8.
14. Ibid, p150.
15. Ibid.
16. Ibid.
17. Ibid, p154.
18. Ibid, p152.
19. Ibid, p135.
20. Ibid.

21. Ibid, pp135–6.
22. Ibid, pp132–7.
23. Ibid, p225.
24. Ibid, pp132–3.
25. Ibid, p132.
26. Ibid, p137.
27. Ibid, p229.
28. Ibid, p141.
29. Ibid, p176.
30. Ibid, p196.
31. Ibid, pp169–170.
32. Ibid, p179.
33. Ibid, pp186–7.
34. Ibid, pp196–7.
35. *Cornhill Magazine*, July 1867, p160.
36. Marryat, Florence, *Life and Letters*, Vol 2, p159.
37. Ibid.
38. Ibid, opp206–7.
39. Ibid, p210.
40. *Cornhill Magazine*, July 1867, p150.
41. Ibid.
42. Ibid.
43. Ibid, p152.
44. Ibid.
45. Ibid, p153.
46. Ibid, p154.
47. Ibid, p157.
48. Ibid, p156.
49. Ibid, p160.
50. Ibid, pp160–1.
51. Ibid.
52. Ibid.
53. Ibid, p161.
54. Marryat, Florence, *Life and Letters*, Vol 2, p265.
55. Ibid, p269.
56. Ibid, p279.
57. Ibid, pp283–4.
58. Ibid.
59. Ibid, p264.
60. Ibid, p287.
61. Ibid.
62. Ibid, p298.
63. Ibid, pp299–300.
64. Ibid, p289.

Epilogue

1. Conrad, *Life and Letters*, pp53–4.
2. Meyerstein, E H W M, *Letters* (London 1959), p145.

Bibliography

Barham, R H Dalton, *The Life and Remains of Theodore Edward Hook* (London 1853)

Biron, Charles, *Pious Opinions* (London 1923)

Conrad, Joseph, *Notes on Life and Letters* (London 1924)

Davenport, Major E M, *Life and Recollections* (London 1869)

Denison, Lt-Col George T, *Soldiering in Canada* (London 1900)

Dorling, Captain Taprell ('Taffrail'), *Men o'War* (London 1929)

Dundonald, Earl of (Cochrane, Lord), *The Autobiography of a Seaman* (London 1861)

Ellis, S M, *William Harrison Ainsworth and His Friends* (2 vols, London 1911)

Forster, John, *The Life of Charles Dickens* (London 1872–4)

Gautier, Maurice-Paul, *Captain Frederick Marryat: L'Homme et L'Oeuvre* (Paris 1973)

Hannay, David, *The Life of Frederick Marryat* (London 1889)

Johnson, Paul, *The Birth of the Modern: World Society, 1815–1830* (London 1991)

Ley, J W T, *The Dickens Circle* (London 1918)

Lloyd Christopher, *Captain Marryat and the Old Navy* (London 1939)

Madden, R R, *The Literary Life and Letters of the Countess Blessington* (3 vols, London 1918)

Marryat, Florence, *The Life and Letters of Captain Marryat* (2 vols, London 1872)

Marshall, J, *Royal Naval Biography* (London 1830)

Merwe, Pieter van der, *The Spectacular Career of Clarkson Stanfield 1793–1867* (Tyne and Wear 1979)

Meyerstein, E H W, 'Captain Marryat and the *Ariadne*', *The Mariner's Mirror* (July 1935)

O'Byrne, W O, *A Naval Biographical Dictionary* (London 1849)

Patten, Robert L, *George Cruikshank's Life, Times and Art* (2 vols, London 1992)

Pope-Hennessy, Una, *Charles Dickens* (London 1945)

Robinson, C N, *The British Tar in Fact and Fiction* (London 1909)

Sadleir, Michael, *Blessington-D'Orsay: a Masquerade* (London 1933)

Smith, G C M, *The Life of John Colbourne, Field Marshal Lord Seaton* (London 1903)

Storey, Graham; Tillotson, Kathleen; Burgis, Nina (eds), *The Letters of Charles Dickens* (London 1965)

Van Damme, Ellen and Horner, Douglas E, *Aspects of Langham: A Norfolk Village* (Langham 1987)

Warner, Oliver, *Captain Marryat: a Rediscovery* (London 1953)

William, James, *The Naval History of Great Britain* (London 1826)

Woolf, Virginia, *The Captain's Death Bed and Other Essays* (London 1950)

Zanger, Jules (ed), *Diary in America; Captain Frederick Marryat* (London 1960)

Books by Captain Marryat

A Code of Signals for the Use of Vessels Employed in the Merchant Service (1817)
Suggestions for the Abolition of the Present System of Impressment in the Naval Service
  (Pamphlet, 1822)
The Naval Officer; or Scenes and Adventures in the Life of Frank Mildmay (1829)
The King's Own (1830)
Newton Forster, or the Merchant Service (1832)
Peter Simple (1834)
Jacob Faithful (1834)
The Pacha of Many Tales (1835)
The Pirate, and The Three Cutters (1836)
Japhet in Search of a Father (1836)
Mr. Midshipman Easy (1839)
The Diary of a Blasé, or Diary on the Continent (1836)
Snarley Yow (1837)
The Phantom Ship (1839)
A Diary in America (1839)
Poor Jack (1840)
Olla Podrida (1840)
Masterman Ready (1842)
Joseph Rushbrook, or The Poacher (1842)
Percival Keene (1842)
Narrative of the Travels and Adventures of Monsieur Violet in California, Sonora
  and Western Texas (1843)
The Settlers in Canada (1844)
The Mission, or Scenes in Africa (1846)
The Privateersman: One Hundred Years Ago (1846)
The Children of the New Forest (1847)
The Little Savage (1849)
Valerie (1849)

Index